Dionysius I of Syracuse
and Greek Tyranny

Dionysius I of Syracuse and Greek Tyranny

L.J. Sanders

CROOM HELM
London•New York•Sydney

© 1987 L.J. Sanders

Croom Helm Ltd, Provident House,
Burrell Row, Beckenham, Kent BR3 1AT

Croom Helm Australia, 44-50 Waterloo Road,
North Ryde, 2113, New South Wales

Published in the USA by
Croom Helm
in association with Methuen, Inc.
29 West 35th Street
New York, NY 10001

British Library Cataloguing-in-Publication Data

Sanders, L.J.
    Dionysius I of Syracuse and Greek tyranny.
    1. Dionysius *I, of Syracuse*   2. Syracuse
    (Ancient city   3. Greece — History —
    Spartan and Theban Suptemacies, 404-362 B.C.
    I. Title
    938′.06   DG55.S9
    ISBN 0-7099-5403-4

Library of Congress Cataloging-in-Publication Data

Sanders, L.J., 1942–
    Dionysius I of Syracuse and Greek tyranny.

    Bibliography: p.
    1. Dionysius I, ca. 430-367 B.C. 2. Syracuse (Sicily) —
History — Historiography. 3. Syracuse (Sicily) — Kings and
rulers — Biography. I. Title.
DG55.S9S26   1987   937′.8′0072   87-3605
ISBN 0-7099-5403-4

Typeset in 10pt Baskerville Roman
by Leaper & Gard Ltd, Bristol, England
**Printed and bound in Great Britain
by Billing & Sons Limited, Worcester.**

Contents

To my Mother and to the
memory of my Father

Preface

Dionysius I of Syracuse, though arguably the most significant personage in Greek history from Pericles to Philip of Macedon, has, to say the least, been accorded a somewhat cool reception by modern scholars. This phenomenon results from two facts. In the first place, much of the data available to them happens to consist of the remnants of a vast body of anecdotal material distinctly hostile to that tyrant, culled chiefly from the account of Dionysius' arch foe and chief detractor, Timaeus of Tauromenium, found in such sources as Cicero, Athenaeus and Plutarch (to name the most prominent). Even more significant is the fact that modern accounts are based largely upon what their authors conceive to be negative data regarding the tyrant, found in the relevant sections of Diodorus of Agyrium's *Bibliotheke*, our sole continuous and substantial surviving account of Dionysius' reign, whose hostile material, they maintain, derived from Timaeus.

The purpose of this study is to question the premises upon which the hostile evaluations of modern historians regarding Dionysius are based, specifically

(a) to delineate the untrustworthy basis of the hostile anecdotal and Timaean traditions;
(b) to propose that, apart from Timaeus, the bulk of the ancient historiographical testimony regarding Dionysius I was a positive one;
(c) to suggest that the positive tone enshrined in these works is more in accord with historical reality than that found in the hostile tradition;
(d) finally to demonstrate that Diodorus' account is not in fact essentially reflective of Timaeus' negative testimony but rather constitutes a much more positive assessment of Dionysius than most modern historians and source critics have been willing to admit — a depiction, in fact, probably largely deriving from Philistus' favourable account.

To achieve the above purposes, three subjects are examined in this monograph: the pre-Diodorus non-historiographical tradition; the pre-Diodorus historiographical tradition; and the Diodorean narrative itself. Some of the ideas encountered herein have appeared in previous studies, albeit in more succinct and somewhat premature form, viz. in *Scripta Classica Israelica* V (1979-80) 64-84; *Historia* XXX. 4 (1981) 394-411; and *Kokalos* XXV (1979) 207-219. Of the many colleagues and former teachers who have facilitated my research work and reduced the number of errors which this work would have otherwise contained, I should like to single out Professor J.A.S. Evans who initially supervised the doctoral thesis from which the present *oeuvre* is derived. I should also like to express my deep gratitude to Professor Lionel Pearson for, notwithstanding the radically different approaches and conclusions which characterise our respective research on Dionysius and the Western Greek historiographic tradition, graciously granting me the privilege of previewing the chapter on the Dionysii from his forthcoming *Greek Historians of the West: Timaeus and his Predecessors*. Finally, debts of gratitude are owed the Social Sciences and Humanities Council of Canada for providing me with a leave Fellowship to pursue my research; to Mrs Margaret Blevins for tackling with such fortitude and infinite patience an often scarcely legible handwritten text; and to Dr Donald M. Watt, copy editor for Croom Helm, for drawing my attention to numerous errata which would otherwise have remained undetected.

Abbreviations

In the notes to the chapters, the following abbreviations for the journals have been used:

AA:	Antike und Abendland
AAP:	Atti dell'Accademia di Scienze e Lettere e Arti di Palermo
AC:	Antiquité Classique
AClass:	Acta Classica
AHR:	American Historical Review
AJPh:	American Journal of Philology
APSR:	American Political Science Review
AR:	Antioch Review
ASNP:	Annali della Scuola Normale Superiore di Pisa
ASS:	Archivio Storico Siciliano
BASP:	Bulletin of the American Society of Papyrologists
BRL:	Bulletin of the John Rylands Library
BSC:	Bollettino Storico Catanese
CHJ:	Cambridge Historical Journal
CJ:	Classical Journal
CNV:	Classical News and Views
CPhil:	Classical Philology
CQ:	Classical Quarterly
CR:	Classical Review
CS:	Critica Storica
CW:	Classical Weekly
EHR:	English Historical Review
G and R:	Greece and Rome
GRBS:	Greek, Roman and Byzantine Studies
HSPhil:	Harvard Studies in Classical Philology
HT:	History and Theory
HZ:	Historische Zeitschrift
JHS:	Journal of Hellenic Studies
JRS:	Journal of Roman Studies
LS:	Leipzige Studien
MAL:	Memorie della Classe di Scienze Morali e Storiche dell'Accademia dei Lincei
MDAI:	Mitteilungen des Deutschen Archäologischen Instituts (Rom. Abt.)

NJCP:	Neue Jahrbücher für classische Philologie
PACA:	Proceedings of the African Classical Association
PBA:	Proceedings of the British Academy
PCA:	Proceedings of the Classical Association
PP:	La Parola del Passato
PSI:	Papiri greci et latini (publicazioni della Società Italiana)
PSQ:	Political Science Quarterly
RAL:	Rendiconti della Classe di Scienze Morali, Storiche e Filologiche dell'Accademia dei Lincei
RBPH:	Revue Belge de Philologie et d'Histoire
REG:	Revue des Etudes Grecques
RFIC:	Rivista di Filologia e di Istruzione Classica
RIL:	Rendiconti dell'Istituto Lombardo
RSAnt:	Rivista Storia dell'Antichita
RSIN:	Rivista Storica Italiana Napoli
RhM:	Rheinisches Museum
SKAWB:	Sitzungsberichte der Königlischen Academie der Wissenschaften zu Berlin
SIFC:	Studi Italiani di Filologia Classica
TAPhA:	Transactions of the American Philological Association
WJA:	Würzburger Jahrbücher für die Altertumswissenschaft
YClS:	Yale Classical Studies

1

The Origins of the Hostile Tradition

I

The hostile tradition concerning Dionysius I which reached fruition with the testimony of Timaeus of Tauromenium in the third century BC, we shall demonstrate in this chapter, had its origins in the fourth century BC and during the tyrant's own lifetime, and initially constituted a response on the part of the tyrant's enemies, particularly concentrated at Athens, to Dionysius' manipulation of the cultural media for propagandist purposes. Consequently, in order to determine the validity of the material constituting the hostile tradition, the latter must initially be considered within the context of Dionysius' cultural aims.

The tyrant was certainly a man of no mean intellectual accomplishment. Well educated from youth, he was by profession a scribe (Cic. *Tusc.* V. 22. 63; Dem. XX. 161; Diod. Sic. XIII. 96. 4; XIV. 66. 5; Polyaen. V. 22) and his debut in politics reveals that he was possessed of considerable rhetorical powers (Diod. Sic. XIII. 91. 3). Whatever worth can be attributed anecdotes regarding the tyrant's use of the writing-desk of Aeschylus to gain inspiration or his purchase and dedication of the harp, pen and writing-tablets of Euripides in the temple of the Muses (Lucian *Adv. Indoct.* 15; *Vit. Eurip.* p. 9), at the very least, they testify to later tradition's acceptance of substantial aesthetic and poetic aspirations on the part of the tyrant.[1] Musical and medical pursuits are certainly attributed to Dionysius (Cic. *Tusc.* V. 22. 63; Aelian *VH* XI. 11). Among his acquaintances are to be included the philosopher-historian Aristippus of Cyrene (Diog. Laert. II, 73, 83) who might well have acted as tutor for the young Dionysius II,[2] the historian Philistus (F. Jacoby, *Die Fragmente der griechischen Historiker* (Leiden

1

1955), vol. 3b, no. 556. T. 1a, 17b, 3, 4, 5c), Plato (Plut. *Dion* IV. 4; Diod. Sic. XV. 7. 1; Nep. *Dion* II. 2; Diog. Laert. III. 18; *Epist.* VII. 327 a-b), the tragedian Antiphon (Philostrat. *Vit. Soph.* I. 15), the mime-composer Xenarchus, the son of Sophron (Photius and Suda *s.v.* 'Ρηγίνους'), the dithyrambic poet Philoxenus of Cythera (Diod. Sic. XV. 6. 2ff; Athen. I. 6e; Suda *s.v.* 'Φιλόξενος'; Lucian *Adv. Indoct.* 15; Paus. I. 2. 3; Cic. *Ad Attic.* IV. 6. 2; Ammian. XV. 5. 37; Plut. *De Tran. An.* 471e-f; Plut. *De Alex Fort.* II. 334c; Aelian *VH* XII. 44); Isocrates (*Nic.* 23; *Archid.* 45; *Ep.* I; cf. Diod. Sic. XIV. 8. 5; Aelian *VH* IV. 8), Aeschines the Socratic (Diog. Laert. II. 63) and possibly Lysias (Pseudo-Lys. VI. 6-7), the historian Xenophon,[3] the tragedian Carcinus[4] (Suda *s.v.* 'Καρκίνος'; cf. Diod. Sic. V. 5. 1), Isocrates' pupil Eunomus,[5] the orator Andocides (Pseudo-Lys. VI. 6), the Sicilian rhetorician Aristoteles (Diog. Laert. V. 35) and the historian Hermias of Methymna.[6]

But far from being content simply to befriend men of learning, Dionysius himself undertook the composition of tragedy and per-haps — if we accept the Suda's testimony (Jacoby, *FGH*, vol. 3b, no. 557) — of comedy and history as well. We certainly know that he wrote an *Adonis, Alcmene, Leda, Limos*, a *Ransom of Hector*, possibly a *Medea* and we have one reference to a play in which Dionysius attacked Plato (Tzetzes *Chil.* V. 182-185).[7]

Given Dionysius' broad, cultural relationships and interests, we should not be surprised to note how Dionysius kept fully abreast of contemporary political theorising about one-man rule and sought to depict his regime as one of justice and moderation, of *nomos* as opposed to *physis*, so that it might be rendered com-patible with the ideals of contemporary theorists. Hence he named his daughters Dikaiosyne, Sophrosyne and Arete (Plut. *De Alex. Fort.* V. 338c), possibly under the inspiration of Aristippus who also had a daughter named Arete (Diog. Laert. II. 72, 86). In his tragedies — which a reference to the death of Doris, Dionysius' Locrian wife (F. 9./Lucian *Adv. Indoct.* 15), in a play whose title is unknown, suggests contained allusions to con-temporary events — Dionysius stated that 'tyranny is naturally the mother of injustice' (F. 4) and referred to the 'gazing eye of justice, regarding all equally' (F. 5). The recognition of the imper-manence of despotic power is further suggested by two fragments from the *Alcmene* and *Leda* where we read that 'anxiety is for every man', 'that only the gods are completely happy' (F. 2) and that 'no mortals can ever judge themselves happy until they have seen their happy end' and that 'the dead man alone is secure and happy' (F. 3) — sentiments certainly not unique to Greek tragedy but significant within the context of Dionysius' theoretical aims with respect to his tyranny. Finally, when Dionysius writes that 'tyranny is naturally the mother of injustice' and we read that the tyrant told his mother that he could harm the city's laws but not those of nature (Plut. *Solon* XX. 4; *Reg. Apophth. Dionys. Mai.* VI, p. 175), we are aware that we are dealing with a man well-versed in contemporary political vocabulary regarding the respective claims of *nomos* and *physis*, and it is clear that it was Dionysius' aim to depict his rule as one of law and morality as opposed to one based on *physis*. It is furthermore highly probable that the culminating point of the *Alcmene* was the birth of the son of Zeus and Alcmene, Heracles, the benefactor of mankind, upon whom Dionysius might have attempted to model himself. Finally, given, as we shall demonstrate below, the significance of the appeal of Aeschylus to Dionysius, and Apollo's reproaching of Achilles for the hero's lack of justice in *Iliad* XXIV. 39-40, the theme of the establishment of justice and harmony in true Aeschylean fashion might well have permeated Dionysius' *Ransom of Hector*.[8]

Poetry accordingly served as an instrument of propaganda for the tyrant. This is further suggested by the fact that Dionysius is said to have written a play in which he attacked Plato. Moreover, other literati were employed as instruments of propaganda: Xenarchus who attacked the tyrant's Rhegine opponents, probably before the capture of Rhegium in 387 BC (Diod. Sic. XIV. 111 ff);[9] Aristippus, whose *On the Daughter of Dionysius* (Diog. Laert. II. 84) might have portrayed positively, as an exemplar of the virtue which Dionysius depicted in his plays, Arete who was probably named after the philosopher's own daughter (Diog. Laert. II. 72, 86); and possibly the Sicilian rhetorician Aristoteles, whose reply to Isocrates' *Panegyricus* (Diog. Laert. V. 35) might well have contained a response to the Athenian orator's criticism of Dionysius (*Paneg.* 126; 169);[10] the historian Hermias, who might have been Dionysius' court historian;[11] and the historian Philistus, who justified Dionysius' rule — though admittedly after his exile in 384 BC — as far as we can tell in a thoroughly Thucydidean and Machiavellian manner rather than in the ethical mould preferred by Dionysius (Jacoby, *FGH*, vol. III b. no. 556. T. 17a, b, 21, 24, 16b, 15c).

When we proceed to determine for whom such propaganda was initially intended, we inevitably associate it with the Sicilian community who we surmise was encouraged to subscribe to the view of Dionysius' regime as an enlightened one, established in accord with the dictates of *nomos* rather than *physis*. Certainly the connection of Adonis with Persephone is likely to have given Dionysius' *Adonis* a Sicilian flavour.[12] Further, since we are cognisant of the monarchic antecedents of Dionysius' ideology which one encounters in the works of all three Athenian dramatists,[13] of the intimate ties which linked Aeschylus and Euripides and their works to Sicily, of Dionysius' supposed acquisition of Aeschylean and Euripidean *memorabilia* (Lucian *Adv. Indoct.* 15; *Vit. Eurip.* p. 9), of the likelihood that Dionysius' *Alcmene* was influenced somewhat by the plays of that name written by Aeschylus and Euripides, and of a possible Aeschylean theme in the *Ransom of Hector* as well as of the prevalence of a possible Aeschylean style in the works of Dionysius' court poets, Antiphon and Carcinus,[14] it would appear that Dionysius fully appreciated the great popularity enjoyed by the two dramatic poets in Sicily — a popularity, moreover, which he proceeded to utilise advantageously for propagandist purposes. At the same time, we may deduce from Dionysius' consistently frustrated attempts to achieve theatrical success in the Greek world and from his dramatic and colourful intervention during the Olympics of 388 BC (Diod. Sic. XIV. 109; Lys. XXXIII) that Dionysius' cultural propagandist policies were aimed at an audience whose location was not prescribed by Sicilian boundaries. That such propaganda was, moreover, directed particularly at Athens is suggested by the ultimate triumph at the Lenaean games of the tyrant's last play, the *Ransom of Hector* which, with its Aeschylean theme of reconciliation, is not inappropriately dated to the 370s — a period indeed which we shall see witnessed the growth of a political *rapprochement* between Dionysius and Athens. The considerable body of support, moreover, which accrued to the pro-Dionysius faction at Athens is suggested both by the very vigour of Lysias' assault on Dionysius at the Olympics of 388 BC (Lys. XXXIII; Diod. Sic. XIV. 109. 1; cf. XV. 7. 1) and by the equally marked hostility of an unknown play by Polyzelus (F. 11/Schol. Aristoph. *Plut.* 550) attacking the Syracusan-Athenian *entente* of Dionysius' last years, and of Ephippus' play, the *Geryon* (F. 18a), directed towards Athens' attempts in the early 370s to make alliances with Macedon and Syracuse and raise revolts among the Lycians against Persia.[15] The precise political aims of the pro-Dionysius faction are clearly revealed in its attempt in 393 BC, at the height of Dionysius' entente with Sparta, two years after Dionysius' settlement of the Messenians at Tyndaris to win over the despot with an honorary decree (G. Dittenberger, *Sylloge Inscriptionum Graecarum*, 3rd edn (1915-24) vol. 1. 128/M.N. Tod, *A selection of Greek historical inscriptions* (2 vols. Oxford, 1946-48) vol. 2, no. 108), the purpose of which according to Lysias (XIX. 20) was to isolate Sparta by the creation of an alliance between Athens, Cyprus and Syracuse, Dionysius in the process agreeing not to send warships which he had already prepared to dispatch to the Lacedaemonians.

Given Dionysius' monarchical position and the nature of the monarchical propaganda which Dionysius attempted to disseminate, we should not be surprised to note that the pro-Dionysius faction at Athens, courted by Dionysius, was characterised by distinct leanings towards despotism. Thus one of its central figures, Isocrates, who indeed sent a letter to Dionysius after Leuctra, calling upon the tyrant to save Greece,[16] throughout his career afforded democracy merely a second place to Panhellenic union, hegemony and monarchy. Hence as Momigliano showed long ago,[17] even in the *Panegyricus*, Isocrates' appreciation of Athens and its league stems above all from his admiration for Timotheus whom he eulogised in the later *Antidosis* of 353 BC (101-41). Nor should we be surprised to note how, with the dissolution of Isocrates' dream for Athenian hegemony, the orator turned towards monarchic individuals, Thebe and Tisiphonus, the children of Jason of Pherae, Dionysius I of Syracuse and Archidamus of Sparta. Isocrates' aim of educating monarchs was most perfectly realised in the Cypriot tracts, *Evagoras*, *Nicocles* and *To Nicocles*, and in the latter two works, we note significantly anti-democratic sentiments, relating to the folly of the lot system and rule of the wise by the foolish (*To Nic.* 17-18; *Nic.* 14, 17-18). In the *Areopagiticus*, he carried these ideas to their logical conclusion by openly advocating the extension of the powers of the Areopagus and the replacement of lot by election. Ultimately, Isocrates turned towards Philip of Macedon, whom he invited to lead Greece as a new Agamemnon,[18] and to his old hero Timotheus, whose great quality was his refusal to bend to the multitude. Thus clearly in Isocrates Dionysius possessed a convinced monarchist.

The same applies to Plato who visited Dionysius in 388 BC (Plato *Epist.* VII. 324a-b; Xen. *Hell.* V. 1; Plut. *Dion* V. 3; Diog. Laert. III. 19). Though the various accounts of the visit are confusing and contradictory and, as we shall suggest, its cause might be associated with political factors, Dionysius' interest in contemporary political theory and above all in monarchical speculation leads us to agree with Diodorus (XV. 7. 1) and Nepos (*Dion* II. 2) that a direct invitation from the tyrant brought the philosopher to Dionysius' court rather than interest in Pythagoreans (Philodemus) or geographical curiosity (Diog. Laert. III. 18) or simple fate (Plut. *Dion* IV. 1).[19] Plato, for his part, as the seventh *Letter* reveals, was drawn to Syracuse as a result of his dissatisfaction with developments at Athens: the oligarchic revolution, the restored democracy, the execution of Socrates (324c-326e). Plato could now effect his philosophical ideas in a philosophical environment, working perhaps with Dionysius himself or more likely with Dion, a younger person more prone to accepting the philosophic influence.

But what did philosophy entail in concrete political terms? Obviously anti-democratic sentiments of an oligarchic or aristocratic or indeed monarchic type. Hence in the *Republic*, the kings ruled the majority because the *demos* was incapable of grasping at the truth. A young philosophic tyrant was required. To Plato it was contradictory to speak of the φιλόσοφον πλῆθος. The man who flattered the crowd was against philosophy. Lot was to be despised because it did not result in true equality. In the *Laws*, Plato's attitude was essentially the same.

On a practical level, Plato was led to attempt to influence, at a later stage, Dionysius II and Hermias of Atarneus. Plato's primary concern was to work through a monarch. His final projects in the eighth *Letter* concern the creation of a triumvirate from Dionysius' own family. And lest one argue that Plato's attraction to Dion arose from Dion's sympathy for Plato's philosophical ideas rather than from the absolutist sympathies which Dion entertained, to counter this theory we note that Dion had achieved fortune and renown in the service of Dionysius and throughout the so-called 'liberation' was opposed to and opposed by the majority party — the democrats under Heracleides. Finally it must be stressed that Plato was very much attracted towards the Thirty Tyrants and that it was their failure, and not their initial coup, that disillusioned Plato.[20]

Finally Xenophon, whom we have seen, might have been in touch with Dionysius, certainly in the *Hieron* for purposes as we have seen that can only be guessed at, not only centred his political ideology around monarchy but also placed this within a Sicilian context. Like Isocrates and Plato, he did not consider democracy as true equality. Hence already in the *Agesilaus* and *Lacedaemonian Constitution*, kingship was emphasised to the detriment of other political institutions and, even in the *Anabasis*, the view was distinctly upheld that the removal of the ideal man was accompanied by the collapse of the institutions of the state. We are consequently not surprised to discover the historian in the *Agesilaus* and *Cyropaedia*, assuming a reactionary stance and looking back to tribal kingship. After his old admiration for Sparta, as manifested in the *Agesilaus*, was shattered by Sparta's collapse, his realisation that Spartan rule had been tyrannical led him to hope for the tyrant's conversion to monarchy. Thus the *Hieron*, probably dating from 360-353 BC, marked the final step in Xenophon's acceptance of monarchy.[21]

But not only do we perceive that Dionysius appealed to elements at Athens who were distinctly anti-democratic.[22] The monarchical position of this faction's most notable representatives in its ethical thrust corresponded closely to that entertained by Dionysius in his tragedies. To Isocrates, Philip must show goodwill to the Greeks like Heracles (*To Philip* 109-116) — a hero who the evidence of Dionysius' *Alcmene* suggests might have been particularly dear to Dionysius. In the *Helen* (18-21), the Athens of Theseus is eulogised and Theseus is considered a wise ruler of the progeny of Poseidon. In the *To Nicocles* (5-6, 17), Isocrates stresses the importance of justice for a ruler.[23] Emphasis is thus laid upon higher moral standards, and practical politics are combined with ethical-philosophical concepts and the ideal of justice.[24]

Plato's ideal ruler must also possess knowledge of *dikaiosyne* and *sophrosyne* (*Rep.* 501a-c).[25] For this reason in the *Gorgias* (471), Plato condemns Archelaus of Macedon for murdering his uncle Alcetas, for not seeing to the education of his brother and for throwing the latter into a well.[26]

Xenophon's political idealism is similarly based upon ethical considerations. The historian felt that, because not all men were virtuous and disciplined, the only hope lay with the ideal ruler. Agesilaus possesses nobility, zeal and courage and Cyrus has virtue, is of noble ancestors and is descended from the gods. He is contrasted with Artaxerxes who does not possess Persian *arete* and philhellenism (*Ages.* VII. 1; *Cyrop.* VII. 5. 84; VII. 2. 14; VIII. 1. 37; IV. 1. 24; VII. 2. 24; I. 6. 1; II. 1. 1; IV. 1. 24; VIII. 8. 12. 15).

Dionysius seems to have deliberately attempted to emphasise his royal position and pose as peer of the Great King, and in doing so, he indicated the extent to which he understood the character of contemporary political theorising. The cumulative evidence of Baton of Sinope (Jacoby 268. F. 4), Theopompus (115. F. 187), Duris (76, F. 14) and Diodorus (XIV. 44. 8) indicates that Dionysius had a four-horse grey chariot, diadem and purple or dappled or tragic actor's cloak in Eastern fashion.[27] Also noteworthy is Pseudo-Lysias' (VI. 6) including Dionysius with βασιλέας πολλοῦς, Scipio Africanus the Elder referring to Dionysius and Agathocles as Kings (Polyb. XV. 35. 6) and, above all, the Syracusan-Athenian treaty of 367 BC (Tod, *Greek historical inscriptions*, vol. 2, 136. 11. 10-11) being clearly concluded between Athens, Dionysius and Dionysius' descendants — a clear indication of the hereditary quality of Dionysius' monarchy which the tyrant sought to emphasise on an international level. Two further references to the regal as opposed to the tyrannical aspect of Dionysius' rule occur in Diogenes Laertius (II. 66) and Diodorus (XV. 74. 5); the former referring to Aristippus of Cyrene rather contemptuously as a 'royal dog'; the latter noting that Dionysius was buried by the royal gates — πρὸς ταῖς βασίλισι καλουμέναις πύλαις. Finally, acquaintance — albeit superficial — with *proskynesis* and hence anticipation of Hellenistic ruler-cult is suggested by Pseudo-Aristotle's reference (*Oecon.* II. 11. 15) to Demeter's appearance on one occasion before the tyrant and by an admittedly late reference in Dio Chrysostom (*Or.* XXXVII. 21) to statues of the tyrant depicting him with god-like attributes.[28]

Dionysius' emulation of Persian monarchy can be explained by a consideration of the importance with which Persia was viewed by Isocrates, Plato and Xenophon.[29] Whereas in Isocrates and Xenophon we encounter an emphasis upon the splendour of Persian monarchy, in Xenophon again and in Plato, the ethical standards were the decisive factors. Thus in the *To Nicocles* (32), Isocrates recommends sumptuous dress and in Xenophon's *Cyropaedia* (VII. 1. 40) we are told that Cyrus considered it necessary to cast a spell over his subjects, since Median dress could conceal defects. To Plato in the *Laws*, Cyrus and Darius illustrate Persian nobility. Their gift of freedom results in Persian progress. Luxury and effeminacy, on the contrary, ruin Cambyses and Xerxes (*Laws* III. 694c. 4-6). In the Seventh *Letter* (332a-b), we read that the laws and character of Darius I have been responsible for the subsequent preservation of the Empire. Finally, in the *Gorgias* (470e), Plato discusses the happiness of the King of Persia and its dependence upon justice. Similarly, as we have seen, in Xenophon, Cyrus' nobility earns praise.

Accordingly, it is evident that the Persian monarchy appeared prominently in political theorising of the early fourth century BC. Dionysius' emulation of Persia and emphasis upon his royal position revealed again the tyrant's awareness of the precise nature of contemporary political thinking, and his assumption of Persian-type dress was perhaps based upon the recommendation of Isocrates and Xenophon. It is significant that both Lysias (*Or.* XXXIII; cf. Diod. Sic. XIV. 109. 4; XV. 23. 4) and the historian Ephorus (70. F. 211) identified the Dionysii with the Great King, although it must be admitted that these references are based essentially upon the political identification of Syracuse and Persia.[30]

II

Dionysius' propaganda policies failed in the face of a counter-propaganda which ridiculed the tyrant's poetical attempts, portrayed his relations with his literati in a poor light and negated the very sentiments concerning the just nature of Dionysius' hegemony which the tyrant had attempted to disseminate. The source of this reassessment, we maintain, was Athenian, deriving from a faction, probably centred around the orator Lysias, hostile to the pro-Dionysius monarchically-inclined clique which favoured closer ties with the tyrant's regime. To this element, Dionysius' very association with Persia in an ideological and political sense and the distinctly anti-democratic, aristocratic and above all monarchic viewpoint of the tyrant's supporters must have been obviously anathema. More important, however, we suggest that the failure of an abortive attempt on Athens' and Dionysius' part in the late 390s and early 380s to cement an alliance created circumstances which favoured the aspirations of the forces rallied against the tyrant's interest, who were, as a result, able to discredit the aims of the pro-Dionysius clique in the city, create turmoil within Syracuse itself and in the process negate the propagandist sentiments of the tyrant.

To comprehend these developments of the late 390s and the early 380s, we do well to remember that three factors threatened the designs of the pro-Dionysius faction at Athens, seeking the establishment of an *entente* between Athens and Dionysius. First, there was the obvious fact — adequately documented — that traditionally Syracuse was an ally of Sparta — a policy dating back to the period of Athenian involvement in Sicily in the mid-fifth century BC (Diod. Sic. XIII. 85. 3; 87. 4-5; 88. 7; 93. 1-4; 96. 1; XIV. 10. 2-4; 62. 1; 63. 4; 78. 5; Xen. *Hell.* III. 4. 1). Secondly, the hostility of Syracuse and Carthage proved a barrier to peace between Syracuse and Athens, since Athens and Carthage were *de facto* allies because of mutual opposition to the Dorian Siceliot bloc under Syracuse. In 407 BC in fact, an alliance between Athens and Carthage had been cemented (IG I². 47./*SEG* X. 136).[31] Finally, Dionysius' political association with Persia, Sparta's traditional supporter, further threatened the establishment of an *entente* between Syracuse and Athens.

Thus a peaceful accord between Athens and Dionysius was dependent upon two considerations. First, the maintenance of an amicable relationship with Carthage alone rendered possible a solid *entente* between Dionysius and Athens, Carthage's ally. Secondly — indeed this was the more important factor — a change in the balance of power in Greece, including the collapse of Sparta, the growth of unity between Sparta and Athens and the consequent possibility of Persian-Athenian co-operation, was necessary. Such developments actually took place in the 370s, when Dionysius was at peace with Carthage and Sparta's collapse at Leuctra led to a *rapprochement* between Athens and Sparta and consequently between Athens and Dionysius — moves facilitating in turn a Persian-Athenian *entente*.[32]

More important, for our purposes, we note an earlier attempt to create an alliance between Dionysius and Athens; for it was from the reaction to the failure to conclude such an *entente* that the hostile tradition appears to have emerged. Indeed the revival of Athenian power following the defeat of Sparta at Cnidus in 394 BC and the uneasy peace between Syracuse and Carthage following the Punic defeat of 396 BC, created circumstances which favoured a *rapprochement* between Athens and Syracuse. Hence we find the philo-Syracusan party at Athens in 393 BC, honouring Dionysius together with his brothers Leptines and Thearidas and his brother-in-law Polyxenus with a decree, the aim of which seems to have been the creation of a triple alliance, involving Athens, Syracuse and Cyprus and the abrogation of the Syracusan-Spartan *entente* (*Syllog.* I², 128/Tod, *Greek historical inscriptions*, vol. 2, p. 108; cf. Lys. XIX. 19; Plut. *Dion* V. 3; Diog. Laert. III. 19).[33]

The negotiations between Dionysius and Athens were threatened by two developments. First in 392 BC Carthage and Dionysius renewed hostilities (Diod. Sic. XIV. 95. 1). In view of Carthage's close political ties with Athens, this development clearly imperilled the creation of an effective *entente* between Athens and Syracuse — though the peace which followed is likely to have favoured an immediate resumption of peace negotiations. More serious was the appearance at Syracuse in 388 BC of the Spartan Pollis, attempting to gain an alliance between Syracuse, Persia and Sparta and thus restoring the former *entente*. These moves were to culminate in the Peace of Antalcidas. The inevitable consequence of these projects which drew Syracuse close to Sparta and indeed to Persia and took the form of concrete naval aid to Sparta, brought by Dionysius' brother-in-law, Polyxenus, was the disruption of the peace moves between Syracuse and Athens which had begun in 393 BC (Xen. *Hell.* V. 1. 26, 28; Plut. *Dion* V. 3; Diog. Laert. III. 19).

What is particularly noteworthy for our purposes is that the first evidence regarding Dionysius' serious cultural and literary interests and relationship with the literati at his court is dated to this period during which Dionysius and Athens decided to court one another politically. Thus Plato's visit is dated to 388 BC (Plut. *Dion* V. 3; Plato *Ep.* VII. 324a-b; Diog. Laert. III. 19); the *Cyclops* of Philoxenus which allegedly satirised politics at Dionysius' court to 389 BC (Aristoph. *Plut.* 290) and the details in Diodorus XV. 7. 2 regarding Dionysius' relations with his literati to 386 BC. Lysias' attack upon Dionysius at the Olympic games, dated by Diodorus both to 388 and 386 BC (Diod. Sic., XIV. 109. 1; XV. 7. 2) obviously took place in 388 BC since 386 was not an Olympiad.[34] Therefore Dionysius' attempt to court the Greek states in a cultural-political sense, especially Athens, judging by Lysias' opposition to that state's policies *vis-à-vis* Dionysius, is to be dated to 389-388 BC or thereabouts. Finally, Dionysius' heavy propagandist activity with respect to the nomenclature bestowed upon his daughters is significantly also dated to the latter part of the 390s.[35]

The placement of all this data chronologically within the context of what appears to be the first occasion upon which Dionysius and Athens began moving towards a political accord and Diodorus' misleading statement to the effect that all Dionysius' literary and cultural interests were to be dated to the last twenty years of the tyrant's reign and hence began in 387 BC do not seem accidental in view of the Athenian national origins of Plato and Lysias and the Athenian connection of Philoxenus, suggested as we shall see by the popularity at Athens of the Cyclops' dance from Philoxenus' *Cyclops*-poem as reproduced by Aristophanes in the second *Plutus*. Indeed we are presented with the possibility that the growing likelihood of the establishment of a concordat between Dionysius and Athens encouraged Dionysius to play a wider cultural as well as political role in the affairs of the Greek mainland than was possible within the context of the tyrant's opposition to Athens and support of the notoriously philistine Sparta. In the process, the tyrant was able to draw closer to the literati who were obviously largely centred at Athens, the cultural centre of mainland Greece, and invite this element to his court with the dual purpose of satisfying his own and his city's aesthetic aspirations and perhaps more important of utilising these literati as instruments of imperial propaganda, particularly within Sicily and at Athens. Moreover, while we have suggested a willingness on Plato's part to meet the tyrant to attempt to effect concretely his political ideals, the broader issue of Dionysius' entente with Athens must also have favoured the meeting between philosopher and tyrant.

It is further not inappropriate in view of the existence within Athens of a strong pro-Dionysius clique and of the visit of the literati to Dionysius' court at the time of the attempted *rapprochement* between Dionysius and Athens that the first evidence which we possess of Athenian hostility to Dionysius and his supporters dates to these very years which witnessed the failure of the attempted peace initiative — the result probably of the fact that the credibility of the policies of the pro-Dionysius faction was quite clearly seriously questioned by the moves inaugurated by Persia and Sparta culminating in the King's Peace, meriting, in fact, vigorous opposition from its opponents. Thus in the second *Plutus* of 388 BC of Aristophanes — a work which we shall see reproduced hostile sentiments towards Dionysius encountered in the *Cyclops*-poem of Dionysius' court-poet, Philoxenus of Cythera — *Penia* lamented the fact that the Athenians were so stupid that they could not distinguish between Thrasybulus and Dionysius (*Plut.* 550). In the following years, Aristophanes appears to have continued his assault upon Dionysius in his last two non-extant plays which were staged by his poet-son, Ararus. Thus underlying the chief theme of the *Kokalos* of 387 BC, dealing with the familiar myth of the escape of Daedalus from Minos and hospitable reception at the court of King Kokalos of Sicily, there very probably resided the theme of

Plato's visit to Dionysius of one year previously, Dionysius within this context being equated with Kokalos and Plato with Daedalus.[36] Given the less than harmonious character of the meeting between philosopher and tyrant which our sources testify to and the negative stance adopted by Aristophanes towards Dionysius in the *Plutus*, it is tempting to conclude that Dionysius was exposed to ridicule in the *Kokalos* and that Aristophanes' interpretation of the event might well have influenced the hostile anecdotal tradition concerning the philosopher's visit to Dionysius in 388 BC which subsequently developed. Aristophanes' last play, the *Aiolosikon* of 388 BC, moreover, again concerned with a Sicilian theme, more specifically with the Aeolian migration westwards, very likely equated the mystical western ruler Aeolus with Dionysius — an equation which probably rested both upon positive and negative factual evidence.[37] However, given the anti-Dionysius tone of his two previous plays, we suspect that the negative depiction ultimately assumed preeminence and that a glaring contrast was effected between the image which prevailed of the just and pious king of Sicilian tradition — sentiments calling to mind Dionysius' propaganda — who was noted for his colonisation of Lipara — an action which, of course, could be easily identified with Dionysius' own colonisation ventures — and the more brutal manifestation of despotism, revealed by the sack of Metapontum and the murder of Autolyte, the stepmother of Aeolus — again testimony easily equatable with Dionysius' sacking of hostile cities, particularly in Southern Italy and a tradition probably originating at this period, subsequently recorded by Plutarch (*De Alex. Fort.* II. 5. p. 338b), describing the tyrant's murder of his mother. It would thus appear that the *Aiolosikon* directly assaulted Dionysius' propagandist message in a manner resembling, as we shall see, Philoxenus' *Cyclops* and posed a question not unlike that which later confronted Plutarch, puzzled by the contrast manifested between Dionysius' brutal actions and the tyrant's noble aims (*De Alex. Fort.* II. 5, p. 338c).

The most direct assault upon Dionysius was that launched by Lysias at the Olympics of 388 BC to counter Dionysius' attempt on that occasion to court popularity for himself and his regime from the Greek states whose representatives were assembled at Olympia.[38] Lysias' condemnation of Dionysius as an associate of the Great King, Artaxerxes II, was particularly appropriate, given the nature of the political activity leading to the King's Peace. The

seriousness of Lysias' attack and indeed of the Athenian opposition to the policies of the pro-Dionysius' clique is suggested
both by the fact that Dionysius' Olympic tent was assaulted by
the mob (Diod. Sic. XIV. 109. 1) and by Dionysius of Halicarnassus' comment that Lysias' aim was to drive Dionysius from
his kingdom and free Sicily (Lys. XXIX. ff). If Speech VI of Lysias
was written by the orator or emanated from the orator's coterie, a
marked change of heart towards Dionysius obviously manifested
itself in this element.

We also note that the poet Cinesias whose poetry had already
significantly been parodied by Dionysius' opponent Aristophanes
in the *Aves* (1372 ff) and who had been generally ridiculed by both
Aristophanes (*Lysistr.* 860; *Ran.* 1437; *Eccles.* 330) and by another
opponent of Dionysius', Lysias (XXI. 20; F. 73) was attacked by
the poet Strattis in a play entitled *Cinesias*. Since a Cinesias proposed the decree honouring Dionysius in 393 BC (Tod, *Greek
historical inscriptions*, vol. 2, p. 108) and since Cinesias on other
occasions had earned the ire of opponents of Dionysius, we may
agree with Webster amongst others that political dissatisfaction
with the pro-Dionysius element at Athens, which almost certainly
included Isocrates, underlay the attack upon Cinesias.[39]

To what extent counter-moves from Dionysius' Athenian supporters manifested themselves can scarcely be determined,
though undoubtedly appealing is Sordi's suggestion that
Xenophon's *Hieron*, especially Chapter XI with its advice to the
tyrant to embellish the city's reputation by competing with other
dynasts and even superiors, to take risks and outbid friends with
kindness, combined with the assurance that none will be jealous
of the tyrant's happiness, might well have constituted a reaction
to Lysias' onslaught. The advice to cultivate friends, moreover
(*Hieron* XI. 14-15) assumes particular relevance within the context
of Dionysius' conflict with his friends (Diod. Sic. XV. 7).[40]

Further in line with our suggestion that the visit of the literati
to Dionysius' court was largely spawned by the development of
an amicable relationship between Dionysius and Athens, and
that opposition to Dionysius at Athens stems directly from the
failure to implement positively these policies of amity, we should
expect to discern some manifestation of friction between
Dionysius and the literati present at the Syracusan court. It is
consequently highly pertinent to note that the rift between
Dionysius and Plato, reflected in the narrative of Dionysius'
enslavement of Plato is not only dated significantly to 388 BC but

is also associated with the renewal of the Sparta-Persia-Syracuse *entente* which we have seen nullified the peace negotiations. Thus Plutarch (*Dion* V) and Diogenes Laertius (III. 19) distinctly mention that Plato was sold to the Spartan Pollis who came to arrange this triple alliance. This association of Plato with the Spartan envoy who sought to render ineffective the negotiations between Dionysius and Athens consequently provokes the possibility that the dispute between philosopher and tyrant might well have been caused, to a considerable extent, by the deteriorating relations between Syracuse and Athens rather than simply by Dionysius' anger following a negative intellectual encounter between tyrant and philosopher as Plutarch (*Dion* V. 1-2), Diogenes Laertius (III. 18) and Diodorus (XV. 7. 1-2) maintain.[41]

Perhaps the most significant evidence for Dionysius' crisis with the literati at his court during these critical years in which Dionysius' and Athens' attempts to forge an alliance met with failure is furnished by the testimony concerning the career of the dithyrambic poet, Philoxenus of Cythera, more specifically by that relating to his chief work, the *Cyclops* of 388 BC which, with its central theme of Polyphemus' love for the Nereid Galatea who is employed by Odysseus to deceive the Cyclops, was regarded already by Phaenias of Eresus (Athen. I. 6e) in the late 4th century BC as an allegorical interpretation of Dionysius' negative encounter with Philoxenus resulting in Philoxenus' incarceration in Syracuse's quarries,[42] Dionysius in the poem being equated with Polyphemus, the cave of the Cyclops with the prison into which Philoxenus was thrown and Philoxenus himself with Odysseus.[43] Evidence, moreover, for the close identification of Philoxenus' assault on Dionysius with the Athenian-Syracusan political scene is furnished by the reproduction of the Cyclops-theme in the *Plutus* of Aristophanes, a play which we have observed openly criticised the peace-moves of the late 390s and early 380s and was performed a year after the production of the *Cyclops* in 388 BC.

Though various traditions are given concerning Philoxenus' breach with Dionysius,[44] it is clear that the *Cyclops* reflected and further emphasised contentious issues which had arisen between Dionysius and Philoxenus. While one tradition saw the incorporation of Galatea into the myth as an attack upon the tyrant whose mistress, Galatea, Philoxenus was supposed to have seduced (Athen. I. 6e; Schol. Aristoph. *Plut.* 290), the other account saw Philoxenus' disgrace as due to criticism of the tyrant's verses (Diod. Sic. XV. 6; Lucian *Adv. Indoct.* 15; Ammian. XV. 5. 37; Plut. *De Alex. Fort.* II. 334c).[45] The poet's mockery of the tyrant's poetical aspirations were clearly repeated in the *Cyclops*, since a novel feature of the poem was Polyphemus' solo, sung to the accompaniment of a lyre, which was so popular that Aristophanes parodied it in the *Plutus*.[46] In view of the equation of Dionysius and Polyphemus apparent in the poem, obviously Philoxenus initiated a very real assault upon the tyrant's poetic achievements.

Undoubtedly, the attack upon the tyrant's poor verses was at root political and stemmed from the opposition of the tyrant's enemies at Athens. In the first place, we should remember that the *Cyclops* was produced at a time of Dionysius' break with the literati — a period which witnessed a worsening of Syracusan-Athenian relations. Secondly, as we have seen, reproduction of the *Cyclops*-motif in the *Plutus* occurred in a play which attacked the policies of the pro-Dionysius-Athenian faction. It is further apparent from the fact that full appreciation of Dionysius' literary achievements in the Greek world came only at the end of his life with the victory of the *Ransom of Hector*, an event which we have argued is to be placed within the context of the peace-moves between Athens and Dionysius of the years after Leuctra, that Dionysius' victory at the Lenaean games was as much a political as a literary one. Finally Diodorus explicitly states that Lysias' attack upon the tyrant at the Olympic games of 388 BC was motivated by political considerations (Diod. Sic. XIV. 109. 1).

The effectiveness of Philoxenus' depiction of Dionysius as a Cyclops is apparent when this portrait is considered within the context of Euripides' satyr-play of the same name. In Euripides' *Cyclops*, the theme of which is Odysseus' freeing of the satyrs, including their father, Silenus, from the Cyclops, the Cyclops is portrayed as the epitome of *physis* who has contempt for *nomos* and has only faith in his own brute strength. Lesky indeed compares him to Callicles and Thrasymachus who in Plato's *Gorgias* and *Republic* defend the equation of right and might.[47] Now, we have seen that Dionysius was deeply interested in the *nomos-physis* question and that the evidence suggests that he tried to turn his tyranny into a 'good' or 'just' monarchy. The testimony of the nomenclature of Dionysius' daughters, the fragments from the tyrant's tragedies and Plutarch's consternation at the contradiction between the evidence of the tragedies and the facts which he received regarding Dionysius' actions certainly indicate this. It would therefore appear that utilisation by Philoxenus of the *Cyclops*-motif enabled the poet to depict Dionysius as an epitome of brute strength and thereby directly contradict the sentiments expressed in the dramas. The full effectiveness of Philoxenus' employment of a Euripidean theme to attack Dionysius may be measured by our emphasising the marked attraction which Euripides' poetry exerted upon Dionysius and by our noting as well the immense popularity that Athenian dramatist's work assumed for Greek Sicily as a whole.

A further novel feature of the *Cyclops* of Philoxenus, was the introduction into the myth of the person of Galatea who was loved and sought after by Polyphemus (i.e. Dionysius) in an uncouth way.[48] One result of the introduction of this motif was to underline the brutality of the tyrant and support the Euripidean depiction of Dionysius as an epitome of *physis* rather than of *nomos*. More significant is the fact that one tradition claimed that Galatea was the name of the tyrant's mistress and that for seducing her, Philoxenus was sent to the quarries.[49] There is little doubt that Philoxenus by his actions towards Galatea and by his reproduction and popularisation of details of the scandal in the poem is likely to have encouraged gossip-mongering about the tyrant, highly disadvantageous to Dionysius' popularity not unlike that which affected Pericles in the face of gossip surrounding the person of Aspasia or Elpinice, Cimon's sister. More significant, we should note that Dionysius' empire was governed by Dionysius in conjunction with members of a new oligarchy who were united to the tyrant by marriage alliances.[50] Obviously any unauthorised interference with such politically inspired unions posed a direct threat to the tyrant's control. We know indeed that Philistus was exiled according to Plutarch (*Dion* XI. 3) for unwisely allying himself in marriage with Leptines' daughter. This was obviously because the dynastic basis of the Empire, based as it was upon this delicate network of family alliances, was endangered. No less serious, we suggest, was sexual involvement with a tyrant's mistress, privy presumably to confidential information of a political and governmental nature and certainly likely on the basis of parallel examples of the importance assumed by other despots' mistresses, both from antiquity and from subsequent epochs, to have exerted an importance at the very least equal to that of Dionysius' wives. Philoxenus' liaison with Galatea must accordingly have posed a threat not unlike

Philistus' *faux pas* which, particularly in view of its popularisation in a poem and placed within the context of Philistus' indiscretion of the same period, renders Dionysius' harsh actions against the poet quite understandable and justifiable.

Accordingly Philoxenus' indiscretions *vis-à-vis* Galatea and attack upon Dionysius' poetical aspirations and popularisation of these themes in the *Cyclops* poem would have appeared to have represented far more than an attack upon the tyrant's literary attempts or his relations with a mistress. On the one hand, Dionysius' cultural propagandist policies and his representation of his rule as just in the eyes of the Siceliots was attacked and Dionysius was equated with the short-sighted Cyclops who epitomised *physis* and had contempt for *nomos*. On the other hand, while Philoxenus' popularisation of his liaison with Galatea subjected the tyrant to gossip-mongering extremely detrimental to the image of his regime which the tyrant was attempting to disseminate, the liaison itself within the context of events surrounding Philistus' secret marriage to Leptines' daughter, appeared in Dionysius' eyes to threaten the whole network of dynastic alliances upon which the tyrant's maintenance of power depended. When we consider, moreover, these events in conjunction with Plato's rift with Dionysius, the attack upon Cinesias launched by the anti-Dionysius faction at Athens under Strattis, the onslaught of Lysias upon the tyrant at the Olympic games of 388 BC, the production of the second *Plutus* of Aristophanes of the same year, which reproduced the *Cyclops*' ridicule of Dionysius' poetical aspirations and attacked the policies of the pro-Dionysius faction at Athens, and the Athenian poet's subsequent attacks upon Dionysius in the *Kokalos* and *Aiolosikon*, it is apparent that Philoxenus' opposition to Dionysius and the appearance of the *Cyclops* constituted the most vigorous and damaging element amongst the anti-Dionysian forces stemming from Athens which decisively negated the propaganda projects of Dionysius and the philo-Syracusan element at Athens. Indeed so significant was the attack upon the tyrant launched by the *Cyclops* that in the following year its data hostile to Dionysius were utilised by Aristophanes in the second *Plutus*.

The seriousness of the situation is revealed by the fact that Dionysius, whose major aim had been the creation of the 'just' monarchy, particularly in the eyes of and with the support of the literati, felt obliged to undertake drastic action against the literati at his court. Philoxenus was incarcerated (Diod. Sic. XV. 6), probably before the appearance of the *Cyclops*. Hence the reference to Philoxenus' prison in the poem. Certainly the narrative concerning Dionysius' enslavement of Plato reflects some type of hostile confrontation between tyrant and philosopher. Moreover, despite variations in the various *testimonia* regarding motivation for the visit and Plato's fate which might initially suggest its late composition in the Hellenistic period, the essential underlying historical validity of the narrative is suggested both by Aristophanes' *Kokalos* of 388 BC which seems to have dealt with the theme of Plato's confrontation with Dionysius to which Dionysius' own play on the subject might well have been a response and by the association of the anecdote with the precise historical context of Pollis' visit (Plut. *Dion* V. 3; Diog. Laert. III. 19) and the war between Athens and Aegina (Plut. *Dion* V. 3). Another individual who may have suffered in the purge was the tragedian Antiphon[51] who, according to one tradition, was put to death by the tyrant (Arist. *Rhet.* II. 6. 1385a; Philostrat. *Vit. Soph.* I. 15. 3; Plut. *Vit. X. Orat.* p. 833). As will be seen, Antiphon seems to have recommended tyrannicide and the harsh treatment meted out to him is comprehensible not only within the context of Antiphon's recommendation itself but even more so in view of the overall attack launched upon Dionysius' propaganda policies, dynastic basis of power and schemes *vis-à-vis* Athens. Though, as we shall see, Philistus' exile possesses much more complex causation than that underlying the fate of the other literati at Dionysius' court, the expulsion of so staunch an adherent of the tyranny as Philistus is only fully comprehensible within the context of a major crisis between Dionysius and the literati, in which the actions of Philoxenus of Cythera and the appearance of the latter's poem, the *Cyclops*, obviously played a major role.

Opposition to Dionysius from the extreme democratic element at Athens opposed to the establishment of close ties between Athens and Syracuse continued, even at the end of Dionysius' reign when such relations were, in fact, cemented. Hence the appearance of an unknown play by Polyzelus and Ephippus' *Geryon* attacking the tyrant. Above all, Athenian literary figures, particularly the comic poets, developed the motifs found in Philoxenus' *Cyclops* by concentrating their attention either upon the literary failing of Dionysius or upon the tyrannical nature of the government. Antiphon seems to have followed Philoxenus in attacking Dionysius' literary accomplishments (Plut. *Vit. X. Orat.* p. 833; Phil. *Vit. Soph.* I. 15. 3; Arist. *Rhet.* II. 6, 1385a) and

Eubulus wrote a comedy mocking the tyrant's poetical endeavours. More precise reproduction and amplification of Philoxenus' anti-Dionysius viewpoint seems to have characterised, on the one hand, Antiphanes' *Cyclops* with its Cyclops-recitation, as Folcke suggests, possibly directed at Galatea and, on the other, Alexis' *Galatea*, though in fairness it should be noted that a direct link between the latter play and Dionysius' mistress of that name is not firmly established. Finally in the *Homoioi* of Ephippus an individual expresses the hope that his worse enemies will be forced to learn the dramas of Dionysius.[52] As a result, the general tradition about Dionysius' poetry is unfavourable with emphasis being placed upon the viewpoint that underlying Dionysius' literary activity is pure unadulterated vanity and willing subjection to flattery. The plays themselves, moreover, were condemned as farfetched, being characterised by weak scansion and unusual expressions. What should, of course, be emphasised is that though we have no positive evidence with which to refute the verdict of antiquity, its source as delineated above should never be gainsaid. Moreover, the tradition which maintained that Dionysius constantly attained a second or third prize (Tzetz. *Chil.* V. 180) and the popularity of scene-depictions from Dionysius' dramas, the *Adonis, Leda* and *Alcmene*, on South Italian vases of the second part of the fourth century BC do render somewhat suspect the universal negative assessment of subsequent generations.[53]

We have seen that the *Cyclops* also assaulted the political ideology espoused by Dionysius and portrayed the tyrant as an epitome of unrestrained brutality and *physis*. This tradition was also developed and elaborated on and probably characterised both Antiphanes' *Cyclops* and Alexis' *Galatea*, both comedies very likely closely linked thematically with Philoxenus' *Cyclops*. We even find Isocrates in 380 BC (*Paneg.* 126; 169) turning temporarily against Dionysius and speaking about ravaged Italy and enslaved Sicily — a stance subsequently abandoned and only briefly resuscitated after the tyrant's death in the *To Philip* (65) of 346 BC[54] — to which the counter-attack of the Sicilian rhetorician Aristoteles, at the instigation of Dionysius, was directed (Diog. Laert. V. 35). Antiphon seems to have criticised Dionysius' tyrannical position and recommended tyrannicide by asserting that the best bronze in the world was that from which the statues of Harmodius and Aristogeiton were made (Philostr. *Vit. Soph.* I. 15; Plut. *Vit. X. Orat.* p. 833). In Eubulus' *Dionysius*, dated by

Webster to the 370s, though by Edmonds and Folcke to 367 BC, Dionysius emerges as the typical tyrant, depending upon traitors like Procles of Naxos (F. 28/Phot. *Bibl.* 190. p. 150) who does not listen to criticism (F. 25/Athen. 260c), is as 'dumb as a thrush' (F. 29/Phot. Sud. Cram. A. p. 396. 33) and only accords freedom to jesters and flatterers (cf. Diod. Sic. XIV. 109. 6) — an assessment, we add, whose validity is particularly negated by testimony attributed not to a supporter but to an arch-foe of the tyrant, Lysias (Lys. VI. 6-7). In Strattis' *Atalanta*, moreover, the word 'Dionysius-beard-conflagration' is coined. A similar term, found in an earlier play of Strattis, *Zopyros Perikaiomenos*, where a man is told to be brave and singe himself like a moustache (probably an allusion to Dionysius' alleged fear of a barber) derives, as suggested by Webster, from the *Heracles Perikaiomenos* of Spintharos which provided a blueprint for the later hostile anecdotes about the suspicious Dionysius, fearing the razor and having either himself or his barber or his daughters singe his beard. Finally, following Folcke, we observe how Polyzelus' evidence (F. 11/ Schol. Aristoph. *Plut.* 550) suggests that Timaeus' later attack upon Dionysius' luxurious lifestyle (566, F. 111/Polyb. XII. 24. 3) was largely derived from evidence originally embedded in Polyzelus or another Middle-Comic writer.[55]

Platonic hostility towards Dionysius' regime is certainly evident in the narrative of Plato's enslavement by the tyrant, which is, of course, also reflective of a less than positive meeting between the two men in the course of Plato's visit in 388 BC, occasioned, we have suggested, by the deteriorating political relations of Syracuse and Athens. Its likely ultimate source, Aristophanes' *Kokalos*, might well have provoked Dionysius' own alleged drama about his relationship with Plato which might have sought to set the proverbial record straight, certainly from Dionysius' own point of view. More specific criticism of Dionysius' regime which justified in Plato's view its reform is found in *Epistle* VII where Dionysius' rule constitutes a despotism, involves the enslavement of the Western Greeks, is based upon mistrust, military might and the support of lackeys and needs to be replaced by the rule of law (327d, 331e, 332c, 334c). The latter picture is essentially reproduced and amplified in Plato's portrait of tyranny in the eighth book of the *Republic* (VIII. 565 ff), where tyranny is characterised as a 'bitter servile servitude' and 'fire of enslavement' (569b). Clearly this estimation of tyranny was occasioned by Plato's experiences with the elder Dionysius — a fact gleaned both from the importance of the Dionysii within the context of Plato's political experiences and from a comparison between Plato's description of the establishment of tyranny and Diodorus' account of Dionysius' seizure of power (Diod. Sic. XIII. 91. 3 ff).[56] The degree to which scepticism must dictate our stance towards this depiction of Dionysius' regime which we emphasise must be associated with the crisis of 386 BC and is probably based upon the hostile Athenian tradition, based upon Philoxenus' *Cyclops* and popularised by Aristophanes in the *Plutus* (290) is indicated clearly by the impossibility of reconciling Plato's references to despotism and enslavement with the philosopher's own bent for despotism and despotic individuals. Certainly Plato's notorious despotic inclinations which we have argued to a large extent drew the philosopher to Dionysius' court in the first place render such references highly suspect.

That indeed Plato did not consider Dionysius' regime in such an unfavourable light is suggested by his criticism in the seventh *Letter* of the Syracusan regime for the fact that men over-indulge themselves in drink and sex — the βίος ευδαίμων (326b-327b). Now a contradiction does seem to exist (unless one appeals to the Neronian experience), for one cannot have it both ways. Either the Syracusans were subject to a 'bitter servile servitude' or they lived hedonistic lives. It is also pertinent to note that the reference to a state of perpetual *stasis* which Plato sees as a result of this hedonism is highly suspect since by 388 BC Dionysius' hegemony had been well established. Such conflict only re-emerges with the accession to the throne of the younger Dionysius.

But we must then ask, whence derives this portrait of western hedonism and what was its significance to Plato? I believe that fragment 134 of Theopompus' *Philippica* provides a hint, since this fragment, which derives from Theopompus' important excursus on Sicilian history, condemns Dionysius I for promoting luxury and debauchery — precisely the vices delineated in *Epistle* VII. Certainly if we remember, as von Fritz has shown[57] that Theopompus, as well as sharing Plato's sentiments concerning Dionysius, also like the philosopher, displayed distinctly anti-democratic sentiments (No. 115. F. 88-9, 288, 22, 20, 333, 295, 259); that his opposition to democracy seems, on the basis of fragment 62 which recounts Theopompus' disapproval of Byzantines frequenting taverns after the introduction of democracy, to have strong moralistic colourings; and that the criticism of Dionysius is not based on despotic but on moral grounds — we should not be wrong in concluding that Plato's view of Dionysius' subjects leading hedonistic lives like that of Theopompus represents Plato's inherent distaste for democracy which his initial encounter with Dionysius aroused. In other words, we claim that Plato like Theopompus initially felt that the weakness of Dionysius' regime lay in its being too democratic or liberal and that the view of the despotic Dionysius stems from the period of the crisis with the literati and the onslaught of the comic poets.

Plato's original anti-democratic bias also left its mark upon the description of the rise of tyranny in the *Republic* (VIII. 565 ff) which we have seen clearly reflected Plato's ultimate views on the rise of Dionysius I and to some extent is based upon the hostile Athenian testimony current at the time. The text narrates how orators champion the people against the supposed designs of the rich. Allegations of an attack upon the life of the tyrant follow and a bodyguard is granted. The tyrant, ruling through mercenaries, burdens the citizens with taxation, confiscates temples and stirs up wars to make the presence of a strong leader essential. Undoubtedly much of this detail corresponds to the description found in Diodorus' text: the ruse to obtain the bodyguard, the enrolment of foreign mercenaries, the deliberate attack upon the rich, the ignorance of the masses, war as a security for the tyrant's position (Diod. Sic. XIII. 91. 3 ff).[58] However, in two respects, it differs considerably and it is clear that Plato took only what suited him, and could be utilised to confirm his own viewpoint, from Diodorus' source (as we shall argue Philistus), or more likely from oral tradition, and by his very selectivity considerably distorted the realities of the situation. First, it is clear that Diodorus' view of the patriotic Dionysius (Diod. Sic. XIV. 41-4) and the popular and democratic basis of Dionysius' rule (XIV. 45. 2; 61. 3, 96. 2, 7. 5, 9. 4; 65. 2-3) is ignored. Secondly no hint is provided regarding the facts that Dionysius' hegemony was based upon the support of a new aristocracy and that men of wealth like Philistus aided in the establishment of the tyranny. Both omissions can be explained within the context of Plato's anti-democratic bias — though we have seen that the first view can be attributed to some extent to Plato's deliberate utilisation of Athenian popular opinion which was deeply influenced by Philoxenus' *Cyclops*. Thus we note that Plato's contempt for the *demos* would have led him to depict the Syracusan *demos* as sheep who, oblivious of Dionysius' scheming, were to find that their champion's rule was in fact ultimately based upon the support of mercenaries and slaves. This picture which significantly accords closely with that provided by the Syracusan knight Theodorus (Diod. Sic. XIV. 65-9) clashes clearly with that presented by Diodorus' narrative, originating, we suggest below, from Philistus, concerning the popular basis to Dionysius' rule and obviously stems from Plato's inherent distaste for the *demos*.

Plato's omission of reference to the tyranny's oligarchic character can similarly be explained. As a man of convinced oligarchic sympathies who despised popular government, Plato would be loath to concede any oligarchic association to the *demos* at the time of the establishment of Dionysius' despotate. Moreover, again in order to emphasise the demagogic nature of Dionysius' hegemony, any mention of the despot's oligarchic support had to be totally curtailed.

The result was the creation of the classic portrait of the demogogic tyrant who deceives the ignorant populace, found originally in the testimony of Plato and adopted by Aristotle (*Pol.* 1305a, 27). This viewpoint, we must emphasise, derived partly from Plato's absorption of current hostile Athenian comic data, stemming ultimately from Philoxenus' *Cyclops* but more so from Plato's contempt for democratic government which led the philosopher to omit mention of the really solid popular basis to Dionysius' hegemony and to ignore the clear fact that Dionysius' hegemony depended upon aristocratic support as well.

And lest we hesitate to condemn Plato for falsifying historical data, we note the testimony of the eighth *Letter* (353 ff) which refers to the appointment of two *strategoi autokratores* during the crisis of 405 BC which culminated in Dionysius' seizure of power: Dionysius and Hipparinus, the father of Dion. Now according to Diodorus (XIII. 94-5-95. 1), only one *strategos autokrator* was chosen, namely Dionysius. Diodorus' testimony is clearly accurate since the relationship between Dionysius and Hipparinus took place well after 405 BC, in fact in 398 BC, when the tyrant married Aristomache, Hipparinus' daughter together with the Locrian Doris (Diod. Sic. XIV. 44. 4) — an event only possible after the death of Dionysius' first wife, Hermocrates' daughter (Diod. Sic. XIII. 96. 3).[59] The first official mention of Hipparinus occurs on the Athenian inscription of 393 BC, honouring Dionysius (Tod, *Greek historical inscriptions,* vol. 2, no. 108).

The reason for Plato's falsification of evidence is easy to determine. In 367 BC, upon Dionysius I's death, Dion in vain championed his sister Aristomache's sons, Hipparinus the younger and Nisaeus, the elder Hipparinus' grandsons, against the claim of succession of Dionysius II, the son of Doris, Dionysius I's Locrian wife, who actually prevailed (Plut. *Dion* VI. 2; Nepos *Dion* II. 4). Plato, moreover, proposed a similar plan in the eighth *Letter* (355e-356b), after Dion's death, whereby the Syracusans were to be ruled by three priest-kings — the son of the elder Dionysius, on the one hand, and the grandson of Hipparinus and the son of Dion, on the other. In both cases, Dion and Plato were pressing the claims of the family of the elder Hipparinus, and to add to the validity of these projects, probably Plato falsely claimed that Hipparinus was appointed *strategos autokrator* together with Dionysius in 405 BC.[60]

We further observe that when Diodorus notes the marriage of Dionysius to Aristomache, he does not mention the name of Aristomache's father. He merely refers to her as τῶν πολιτικῶν τὴν ἐπισημοτάτην (Diod. Sic. XIV. 44. 8). Diodorus or his source, ultimately as we shall demonstrate, Philistus, presumably having no particular interest in supporting Dion's intrigues nor indeed having a Platonic axe to grind, had no reason to mention Hipparinus. By contrast, the degree to which Aristotle accepted the Platonic assessment of Dionysius is seen by his erroneous association of Hipparinus and Dionysius as *strategoi autokratores* during the crisis which led to Dionysius' elevation (*Polit.* 1306a; cf. Plut. *Dion* III. 2).

III

The stereotyped hostile viewpoint of Dionysius I had become well established at Athens by the middle of the fourth century, at which point the story about the dream of the priestess forecasting Dionysius' future destructive role which ultimately found its way into Timaeus' history, as we shall see in a somewhat transformed state, seems to have been already circulating (Aesch. *On the Embassy* II. 10; Heracleid. Pontic. ap. Tertull. *De Anim.* 46). Speusippus denounced Dionysius as godless and wicked in a polemic against Isocrates (*Ad. Phil.* 10 ff). Demosthenes, attacking Aeschines, according to the latter, likened his opponent to Dionysius, and Aeschines took offence at this comparison (*On the Embassy* II. 10).[61] Finally as we have seen, to Aristotle, Dionysius had become the demagogic tyrant (*Polit.* 1305a, 27).

By the beginning of the third century, a considerable amount of material hostile to Dionysius had accumulated, particularly associated with Athenian comedy and the philosophic opposition. The anecdotes which concentrated upon Dionysius' suspicion and hostility towards his family and friends, were clearly derived from the comic theatre.[62] The demogogic viewpoint of the tyrant, dealing with the suppression of liberty at Syracuse, though based, as we shall see, to a considerable extent upon the type of evidence which a favourable source like Philistus is even likely to have accepted, ignored the oligarchic and popular basis of Dionysius' hegemony and was thus based upon the philosophic view originating with Plato.[63] On the whole, it seems that the former picture attracted greater popularity and it is this which is likely to have found its way into the writings of the Peripatetic biographers. Unfortunately we know little about the manner in which these writers treated the Sicilian tyrants. We do know, however, that they discussed them, for Phaenias wrote a work on the Sicilian tyrants and Satyrus wrote on the younger Dionysius. We might also deduce from Phaenias' acceptance of the tradition which viewed Philoxenus' *Cyclops* as a satyrical diatribe against Dionysius that that writer was acquainted with, and probably accepted, the hostile tradition regarding Dionysius' relations with the dithyrambic poet. Indeed the grotesque caricature of Dionysius as an antinomian Cyclops is very likely to have been found in Phaenias' pages. That the peripatetics utilised this hostile material is suggested, moreover, by two further facts. First they were gossipy writers, for gossips like Athenaeus preserved their traditions. Secondly, the fashion of the time was to typify lives of luxury and the excesses of absolutism of the tyrants. Phaenias' work on the Sicilian tyrants may thus have anticipated Suetonius' *Caesars*.[64]

To these factors, we must add the general tendency of writers to theorise in a hostile manner with neutral data. This tendency, as Stroheker has shown,[65] can be most clearly seen in the three surviving accounts which we possess of Leptines' death, Plutarch (*De Alex. Fort.* II. 5. p. 338a) ascribing this event to jealousy by the tyrant of his brother, Aelian (*VH* XIII. 45) declaring that Dionysius could have saved Leptines in a sea-fight, while Diodorus (XV. 17. 1) merely observes Leptines' brave death at Cronium, commanding one wing. It follows that the early tradition found in Diodorus, as we shall see, possibly derived from Philistus or from Ephorus, merely stated the fact that Leptines had the weaker force. Later sources elaborated upon the point with the result that Dionysius' placing of Leptines became a deliberate and vindictive cut arising from the tyrant's jealousy of his brother, recalling in a strategic sense King David of Israel's elimination of Uriah the Hittite (2 *Samuel* 11: 14-17). The evidence of Aeneas Tacticus (X. 21 ff), moreover, indicates that the theme of Dionysius' savage treatment of Leptines was widespread. Very likely the variant details about Dionysius' selling of Plato, possibly deriving originally from Aristophanes' *Kokalos*, were similarly inspired, though some historical basis associated with Athenian-Syracusan tension of these years undoubtedly lay at their root.[66] Equally intriguing is the development of anecdotes regarding Dionysius' devices to effect the successful shaving of his beard which, as we have seen, clearly derive from the Athenian comic stage. Hence while Diodorus (XX. 63. 3) states that the tyrant simply let his hair grow as long as possible and, if necessary, singed it, Plutarch (*Dion* IX. 3) records that the tyrant, distrusting the scissors, bade a barber accomplish the job by utilising hot coals. A third variation on this theme is found in Cicero's *Tusculan Disputations* (V. 20. 58), where we read that the tyrant only trusted his daughters to shave him, and that when they grew up, they were obliged to singe their father's hair with walnut shells. The barber theme finally emerges in Plutarch (*De Garrul.* XII. p. 508f) where we encounter the barber who was crucified for boasting that he regularly held his blade near Dionysius' throat.

IV

To sum up our assessment of the validity of the pre-Timaeus hostile tradition regarding Dionysius I, clearly we must regard it as highly questionable in view of the nature of its origins and subsequent development. We must above all be aware of the fact that it arose in Athens from developments following Athens' and Syracuse's failure to cement an alliance in 388 BC and consequently that the material which derives chiefly from Philoxenus' experiences as reflected in that poet's dithyrambic poem, the *Cyclops*, reproduced and elaborated upon in the Athenian comic theatre and utilised by subsequent hostile sources such as Phaenias is essentially Athenian in origin, content and thrust, that it does not constitute in essence Sicilian hostile tradition and therefore can hardly be utilised with confidence as evidence for a repressive Dionysian regime by modern historians, attempting to characterise Dionysius' rule either in constitutional or ethical terms. We should in addition be cognisant of the fact that the objective of Philoxenus and the comic poets was deliberately to distort and overturn the propagandist policies of the Syracusan tyrant and their efforts to characterise Dionysius' rule in the most negative of terms must accordingly be treated with the same degree of scepticism that one generally accords the Aristophanic portraiture of the sophistic Socrates in the *Clouds*. Dionysius' harsh treatment of the literati at his court, moreover, we suggest, should be regarded as a response to a very real and serious danger which negated the successes of Dionysius' propagandist policies both within Sicily and upon the Greek mainland, especially at Athens, attacked Dionysius' supporters in Athens and even threatened the dynastic and oligarchic basis of his empire. We therefore do not share Plutarch's amazement and scepticism at the contrast between Dionysius' actions and theoretical aims as expressed particularly in the dramas (*De Alex. Fort.* II. 5. p. 338c),[67] albeit aware that Plutarch's assessment was also influenced by his acquaintance with a vast body of hostile tradition, including particularly Timaeus' account, and conclude that Dionysius did desire to establish a just regime in par with the ideals of contemporary political theorists; that the sentiments expressed in the tyrant's dramas and in the nomenclature of his daughters were not mere verbiage of a hypocritical dynast; and that the purge of 388-386 BC was from the tyrant's point of view a highly necessary response to the growth of a serious threat to the stability of his regime. Consequently we suggest that it is inadvisable to utilise evidence related to Dionysius' crisis with his literati for a hostile evaluation of Dionysius' regime as a whole.

Having exposed to question the roots of the hostile tradition, we do well to view with caution the main thrust of its two-pronged attack upon Dionysius elaborated upon by subsequent sources. In the first place, since the attack upon the tyrant's literary accomplishments in the *Cyclops* was political in origin, obviously subsequent ridicule of the tyrant's poetical achievements should be treated with some scepticism, though our caution should not necessarily and inevitably imply our recognition of particularly remarkable poetic accomplishment on Dionysius' part. More important, we do well to treat the anecdotal tradition regarding Dionysius' despotic behaviour towards

friends and relatives with a good deal of scepticism, since it originates from the period of Dionysius' crisis with his literati and
derives from Athenian or Athenian-motivated sources who for
political purposes deliberately distorted and totally transformed
Dionysius' political ideals. We have argued, moreover, that
Plato's own testimony in *Epistle* VII as well as fragment 134 of
Theopompus' *Philippica* suggest that Dionysius' hegemony was,
in fact, not the harsh rule depicted by Plato and the Athenian
hostile tradition. Further, we have noted how in the case of the
picture of the rise of the demagogic tyrant in the eighth book of
the *Republic*, Plato's inherent aristocratic bias led the philosopher
to ignore both the popular and oligarchic basis of Dionysius' rule
and thus create the mythical view of Dionysius, the demagogic
tyrant, accepted by Aristotle and reproduced in later hostile
sources. Moreover, to counter those unable to accept our view of
Plato as distorter of historical fact, we have noted Plato's patent
manipulation of historical fact with respect to his claim that
Hipparinus occupied a joint supreme generalship with Dionysius
during the crisis of 405 BC, which resulted in Dionysius' elevation
as Syracusan despot.

And what of the evolution of the hostile tradition following the
demise of Dionysius I? Since we have seen that its basis is
suspect, its development is accordingly open to the same degree
of suspicion. We must stress that the later tradition is also in
essence Athenian and not Sicilian and is ultimately based upon
Athenian comic distortion and the equally untrustworthy philosophic testimony, stemming from the Academy and Lyceum,
highlighting Dionysius' role as demagogic tyrant. Finally we have
seen that the tendency to theorise with neutral data and the
Peripatetic biography increased the distortion, and the scene was
prepared for the vitriolic onslaught upon Dionysius, launched by
Timaeus of Tauromenium.

Notes

1. The early date of Dionysius' intellectual interests is suggested by
Pseudo-Lysias' reference (VI. 6) to Andocides' visit to Dionysius in 402 BC
and by Lysias' reference (XIX. 19) to a certain Eunomus who was guest-
friend of Dionysius in 393 BC and might well have been as Stroheker suggests (K.F. Stroheker, *Dionysios I. Gestalt und Geschichte des Tyrannen von
Syrakus* [Wiesbaden, 1958], p. 87), following J. Kirchner, (J. Kirchner,
Prosopographia Attica [Berlin, 1901], p. 379), the pupil of Isocrates of that

same name. Early intellectual interests, especially in the field of political theory by Dionysius, dated to the middle 390s, may also be deduced from Dionysius' naming his eldest daughter 'Dikaiosyne' (Plut. *De Alex. Fort.* II. 5, p. 338 c; cf. Diod. Sic. XIV. 44). We further note that, since the *floruit* of Philoxenus of Cythera is dated by Diodorus (XIV. 46. 6) to 398 BC (i.e. Olymp. 95. 2) and we assume that the poet's association with Dionysius anteceded the appearance of the hostile *Cyclops* of 389 BC (Aristoph. *Plut.* 290), Philoxenus' initial association with Dionysius is likely to have taken place probably in the late 390s — as we shall see, a period when most of Dionysius' relations with his literati were cemented. Consequently, we should be unwise to interpret literally Diodorus' statement (XV. 6. 1) that only in 386 BC, after the completion of the Punic War of 392 BC, was Dionysius free to devote his time to poetry and deduce from it that the literary tastes of the tyrant are all to be dated to the last two decades of his life — a conclusion also arrived at by the dating of Philoxenus' *Cyclops* to 389 BC (Aristoph. *Plut.* 290) and Plato's first visit to Sicily to 388 BC (Plut. *Dion* V. 3; Plato *Epist.* VII, 324a; Diog. Laert. III. 19; Xen. *Hell.* V. 1).

2. I follow C.A. Folcke, 'Dionysius and Philistus', Dissertation, New York University, 1973, p. 12, who argues from Alexis (F. 36 (Edmunds)/ Athen. 544e).

3. For this possibility, the chief evidence is: (a) Athenaeus (X. 427f-428f) who mentions Xenophon, the son of Gryllos, seated at the table of Dionysius, delivering a Socratic-style discourse on eating when hungry and drinking when thirsty; (b) Xen. *Hell.* III. 1. 2 which refers to the *Anabasis* of Themistogenes of Syracuse who, according to E. Delebecque, *Essai sur la vie de Xénophon* (Paris, 1957), p. 83, is Xenophon the historian whom Plutarch (*De Gloria Atheniensium* I. 345e) mentions feared the publication of Themistogenes' *Anabasis* under his own name. Cf. the Suda, *s.v.* 'Θεμιστογένης', Tzetzes, *Chil.* VII. 937, who claim that Themistogenes was Xenophon's lover. One might also be tempted to attribute importance to the fact that Xenophon's *Hieron* has a Sicilian context, a possible aim being to 'angle for an invitation to Sicily' (thus J.K. Anderson, *Xenophon* [London, 1974], p. 193), or to rally opposition to Lysias after the latter's attack upon Dionysius at the Olympics of 388 BC (thus M. Sordi, 'Lo Ierone di Senofonte, Dionigi e Filisto', *Athenaeum*, vol. 58, nos. 1-2 (1980) pp. 3-13). However, cf. A. Croiset, *Xénophon* (Paris, 1873), 18-19 where the quotation from Semonides on the subject of generosity to the state rather than to the tyrant (*Hieron* XI. 5-6) is viewed as a reflection of Lysias' onslaught. It is furthermore tempting to follow Folcke, 'Dionysius', pp. 51-2, in noting Philistus' influence upon Xenophon by comparing the obviously derived Philistus account of Dionysius' war preparation in Diod. Sic. XIV. 41-6 with Xenophontine passages of a similar nature pertaining to Agesilaus. Thus Agesilaus' war preparations against the Persians while at Ephesus, which include the fostering of the competitive spirit (*Ages.* I. 25; *Hell.* III. 4. 16-17) and Xenophon's general view of Agesilaus as a skilled tactician and organiser (*Ages.* V. 5-6) who toils in a democratic and equal manner with his troops (*Ages.* V, 3), is always in the forefront (*Ages.* VI. 1) and whose life is temperate (*Ages.* V. 1), whence the total obedience and affection of his troops (*Ages.* V. 4; cf. *Cyrop.* I. 6. 8). Parallels between

Dionysius' and Hermocrates' military preparations in *Hell.* I. 1. 30 noted by C. Mossé, *La Tyrannie dans la Grèce antique* (Paris, 1969), pp. 107ff; cf. however Sordi, 'Lo Ierone di Senofonte, Dionigi e Filisto', who, associating the reference in *Hieron* I. 28 to the preferability of marriage with strangers than with equals and one's own citizens with Dionysius' double marriage and viewing the observations on the usefulness of mercenaries (*Hieron* X), the importance of competition (*Hieron* XI. 7) and seeking honour (*Hieron* XI) within a Dionysian context, regards Diodorus' chapters on Dionysius' war preparations as reflective of Xenophon's influence upon Philistus.

4. Though he was associated with the younger Dionysius, the Suda, *s.v.* 'Καρκίνος', dates him to 380 BC (Olympiad 100).

5. If we associate the guest-friend of Dionysius, Eunomus, mentioned by Lysias (XIX. 19) with the pupil of Isocrates of the same name. Thus above, n 1.

6. See F. Jacoby, *Die Fragmente der griechischen Historiker* (Leiden, 1955), vol. IIIb (Komm.), p. 515.

7. See A. Nauck, *Tragicorum Graecorum Fragmenta*, 2nd edn (Leipzig, 1889), pp. 616-19; C.O. Zuretti, 'L'attività letteraria dei due Dionisii di Siracusa', *RFIC*, vol. 25 (1898), pp. 529-57 and vol. 26 (1899), pp. 1-23. For the authenticity of Dionysius' historical *oeuvre*, taking the form of autobiographical self-justification, see Jacoby, *FGH*, vol. IIIb. no. 557 (Komm.), pp. 514-15; A. Lesky, *History of Greek literature*, 2nd edn, translated by James Willis and Cornelis de Heer (London, 1966), p. 629. M.P. Loicq-Berger, 'Le Bruxellensis 11281 et l'activité littéraire de Denys l'Ancien', *RBPH*, vol. 44 (1966), pp. 12-20, emending an alternative Suda text from μισθοφορικὰ to μυθιστορικὰ, argues that Dionysius' histories and dramas betrayed a mythistoric content. Folcke's objection ('Dionysius', p. 13) that Philistus' *oeuvre* rendered unnecessary a historical defence on the part of the tyrant himself is difficult to sustain both because the existence of more than one defence is not unlikely and because, as we hope to show, Philistus' Dionysian history was no mere panegyric and, in fact, in one respect (*viz.* concerning Dionysius' South Italian policy), was decisively negative. The problem of Dionysius' comic works is even more complex: W. Suess, 'Der ältere Dionys als Tragiker', *RhM*, vol. 109 (1966), pp. 299-318, followed by E. Simon, 'Dramen des älteren Dionysios auf Italiotischen Vasen', *ΑΠΑΡΧΑΙ: Nuove ricerche e studi sulla Magna Graecia e la Sicilia antica in onore di Paulo Enrico Arias* (Pisa, 1982), pp. 479-82, views Dionysius as a Euripidean whose dramas contain a mixture of tragic and comic elements and as a forerunner of New Comedy. For the view that Dionysius was in fact a composer of satyr-plays, see Zuretti, 'L'attività letteraria dei due Dionisii di Siracusa', pp. 551, 555ff and Stroheker, *Dionysios I*, p. 215. Aelian's remarks (*VH* XIII. 18) that Dionysius was not φιλόγελως leads us to question the validity of the Suda's reference to Dionysius' comedies, though Athenaeus VI. 249e suggests the contrary. Against the authenticity of both the historical and comic works, see W.E. Weter, 'Encouragement of literary production in Greece from Homer to Alexander', Dissertation, Chicago University, 1953, p. 57.

8. Thus Folcke, 'Dionysius', pp. 18-19.

9. Photius, Suda *s.v.* 'Ρηγίνους'; M. Pinto, 'Il mimo di Senarco contro i Reggini', *Atene e Roma*, N.S. vol. 8 (1927), pp. 69-80 dates it to 394 BC. For the argument that the account in Diod. Sic. XIV. 112 concerning the noble death of Phyton derives from a rebuttal of Xenarchus' account by the Rhegine bloc opposed to Dionysius, see M.P. Loicq-Berger, *Syracuse: Histoire culturelle d'une cité grecque* (Brussels, 1967), pp. 229-30. For the view that this stems from Philistus, see below pp. 57, 127.

10. Thus Stroheker, *Dionysios I*, p. 214; Folcke, 'Dionysius', p. 20.

11. Thus above, n 6.

12. Folcke, 'Dionysius', p. 17.

13. Thus, while Aeschylus' *Eumenides* (744-55, 851-7) culminates in the acceptance of the Erinyes who, in their transformed state, reflect tyrannical or monarchical power, for the suppliant maidens, just as for Io (*Supplic.* 15-18, 40-8, 162-75, 291-324, 350-3, 535-89, 1063-4), submission to the monarchical element in the form of the Egyptians, no matter how harsh, is ultimately imperative (*Supplic.* 194-203, 387-91, 485, 624, 1047-51), and in the *Prometheus Vinctus*, Prometheus cannot escape the yoke of the tyrant Zeus (17, 50, 61-2, 325, 550-1, 1009-10). To Sophocles, on the other hand, Zeus is the protector of kings, giving them his blessing and good fortune, while the gods and Zeus give earthly rule and the divine sceptre (*Ajax* 1291; *Antig.* 174; *Electra* 160; *Oed. Tyr.* 1235). Finally a Euripidean monarchical thrust is seen in his *Supplices* (403), where Theseus is described as the young and noble shepherd, for want of whom many states have perished, while monarchy was also considered in the *Erechtheus* and *Archelaus*. Even more significant is the fact that all these poets emphasised that monarchy had to be just. Hence while in Aeschylus monarchy had to accept the progressive, just and democratic element as epitomised by the causes of Orestes (*Eum.* 696-706, 805, 858-69, 885-91, 911-12, 916-26), Prometheus (*Prom. Vin.* 92, 149, 189, 227, 241-3, 306, 325, 347-67, 403-6; cf. 190-5, 518-25, 755-74, 908-40) and the Danaids (*Supplic.* 1, 26, 77, 192, 340, 343, 359-64, 368, 385-6, 390-1, 395-6, 402-6, 418-37, 478-9, 605-24, 627, 707-9, 733, 942-9, 1071-3), Sophocles' Creon lacks self-control (*Antig.* 478-80, 505-7, 509, 525, 690-1, 706, 710-11, 737-8, 765, 1015), the lawful king being of royal blood, possessing divine authority (*Antig.* 38, 938-41, 948, 981-6). Euripides' *Archelaus*, written after the poet's move to Pella in 408 BC, provides an ideal portrait of the son of Temenus, the fragments portraying a monarch of noble ancestry, possessing a noble soul and suffering like his ancestor Heracles, possessing self-control, justice and piety (Nauck, *TGF²*, F. 237, 250, 254, 255, 256, 258, 259). Finally similar positive *sententiae* on monarchy characterise a fragment from the *Erechtheus* in which the dying king gives his son good advice on how to rule (F. 362, T. 6. F.). See G. Dvornik, *Early Christian and Byzantine political philosophy. Origins and background*, vol. I (Washington, D.C., 1966), pp. 172ff. On the Solonian and Herodotean origin of the 'good' as opposed to the 'bad' or 'tyrannical' ruler, see Stroheker, *Dionysios I*, p. 89; Stroheker, 'Zu den Anfängen der monarchischen Theorie in der Sophistik', *Historia*, vol. 2 (1953/4), pp. 381-412; A. Ferril, 'Herodotus on Tyranny', *Historia*, vol. 27 (1978), pp. 385-98.

14. Aeschylus seems to have paid two visits to Sicily at the express

invitation of Hieron of Acragas and is supposed to have died at Gela. His visits are associated with the *Aetnaean Women* or *Aetna* which seems to have been produced after the eruption of Aetna in 476 BC (*Vit. Aesch.* p. 4 Dindorf) and the second performance of the *Persae* which would have been particularly appealing to the Syracusans after their victory at Himera in 480 BC (*Vit. Aesch.* p. 4 Dindorf; Schol. Aristoph. *Ran.* 1060). For death at Gela, see Plut. *Cim.* VIII. 8; Suda. *s.v.* Αἰσχύλος. Epitaph in H. Weir Smyth, *Aeschylus*, Loeb Classical Library (Cambridge, Mass., 1922), vol. 1, p. xxiii. A possible Sicilian link can be discerned in the *Prometheus Vinctus* (see lines 370-5 on the eruption of Aetna) and the *Supplices*, whose chief theme might have reflected the poet's hospitable reception in Sicily. See Loicq-Berger, *Syracuse*, pp. 94ff; cf. A. Lesky, *Greek tragedy*, 2nd edn, translated by H.A. Frankfurt (London, 1967), p. 58. Euripides' intimate association with Sicily is suggested by the poet's epitaph on the Athenians who had fallen at Syracuse (Plut. *Nic.* XVII. 4) and Plutarch's anecdote (*Nic.* XXIX. 2) regarding the Athenian survivors who saved themselves by reciting the choruses of Euripides. The *Cyclops*, moreover, reflects the poet's interest in the West and its theme was, of course, utilised by Philoxenus of Cythera during his Syracusan sojourn. Finally, possible references to Sicily have been discerned in the *Iphigenia in Tauris*, *Electra* and *Orestes* by P. Green, *Armada from Athens* (New York, 1970), pp. 77, 101, 244-5. See also Athenaeus XII. 544e; Plato *Epist.* I. 309d; Plut. *Tim.* XXXII. 2.

15. See J.M. Edmonds, *Fragments of Attic comedy*, vol. 1 (Leiden, 1957), p. 883; vol. 2 (Leiden, 1959), pp. 146-9, 157-9; T.B.L. Webster, *Art and literature in fourth century Athens* (London, 1956), p. 48; Webster, *Studies in later Greek comedy* (Manchester, 1959), p. 40.

16. Other evidence of Isocrates' less direct, though undoubtedly favourable, stance towards Dionysius includes *Nicocles* (23), written between 372 and 365 BC where Dionysius is praised for his role in saving the Western Greeks and creating a major power; the *Archidamus* (44), written a year after *Epistle* I, where the orator quotes with approval the anecdote regarding Dionysius' steadfastness when told by a companion that royalty is a glorious shroud (cf. Diod. Sic. XIV. 8. 5; Aelian *VH* IV. 8); and the *To Philip* (65, cf. 81) of 346 BC, where the novelty of Dionysius' sea-empire is commented upon. On the other hand, the references in the *Panegyricus* (126, 169) to the slavery of Sicily and laying waste of Italy, as we shall see, suggest an earlier, cooler relationship between orator and tyrant, at a time when relations between Dionysius and Athens were at a low ebb — though Dionysius' friendship with Eunomus, possibly a pupil of Isocrates, might suggest a friendly relationship, even at the very beginning of Dionysius' reign (see Stroheker, *Dionysios I*, p. 108). Finally, despite Isocrates' seemingly favourable comment in the *To Philip* noted above, an apparently neutral comment in the same section where Isocrates refers to Dionysius as of 'no account among the Syracusans in birth, reputation and other respects', perhaps suggests a cooling off, provoked by Isocrates' new interest in Philip II.

17. A.D. Momigliano, *Filippo il Macedone* (Florence, 1934), pp. 183ff; cf. W. Jaeger, *Paideia: The ideals of Greek culture*, translated by G. Highet (Oxford, 1945), vol. 3, p. 94 who suggests that the *Nicocles* is actually a

plea for Timotheus. For a criticism of Isocrates' choice of leaders, see A.W. Gomme, 'The End of the City State', *Essays in Greek history and literature* (Oxford, 1937), p. 227.

18. Isocrates' first peaceful overtures to Philip are encountered in *On the Peace*, 22. See generally S.D. Perleman, 'Isocrates' *Philippus* — a Reinterpretation', *Historia*, vol. 6 (1957), pp. 306-17. The Isocratic historians, Ephorus and Theopompus seem to have followed Isocrates in sacrificing democracy for monarchy. For Ephorus', or rather his son Demophilus', attitude, see Diod. Sic. XVI. 1. 4, 6; cf. A.D. Momigliano, 'La storia di Eforo e le Elleniche di Teopompo', *RFIC* N.S., vol. 13 (1935), pp. 180-204, esp. pp. 195-204. For Theopompus' attraction towards monarchical figures, see Jacoby, *FGH*, vol. IIb, no. 115, F. 88-9 (Cimon), 288 (Alcibiades), 22 (Agesilaus), 295, 259 (Antisthenes); cf. K. von Fritz, 'The historian Theopompus: His political convictions and his conception of historiography', *AHR*, vol. 46 (1941), pp. 765-87. (Reprinted as 'Die politische Tendenz in Theopomps Geschichtsschreibung', *AA*, vol. 4 (1954), pp. 45-64.) On the respective central roles of Lysander and Philip in Theopompus' *Hellenica* and *Philippica*, see A.D. Momigliano, 'Teopompo: Studi sulla storiografia greca del IV secolo A.C.', *RFIC*, N.S., vol. 9 (1931), pp. 230-42, 335-53.

19. Stroheker, *Dionysios I*, pp. 100-7. Cf. W.H. Porter, 'The sequel to Plato's first visit to Sicily', *Hermathena*, vol. 61 (1943), pp. 48ff, esp. pp. 53-4; G.C. Field, *Plato and his contemporaries*, 2nd edn (London, 1948), pp. 17-18; L.J. Sanders, 'Plato's first visit to Sicily', *Kokalos*, vol. 25 (1979), pp. 207-19; M. Sordi, 'Dionigi I e Platone', Φιλίας χάριν. *Miscellanea di studi classici in onore di Eugenio Manni* (Rome, 1980), pp. 2015-22. Diogenes Laertius' reference (III. 21) to subsequent correspondence between Plato and Dionysius has been rightly suspected by Stroheker, *Dionysios I*, p. 106. For Philodemus, see S. Mekler, ed., *Index der Akademiker* (Berlin, 1902), col. 10. 10ff.

20. See Plato *Rep.* 494a, 502a-b, 557a; *Laws* 709e-10d; *Epist.* VII. 324d; *Epist.* VIII, 355e-6c; Stroheker, *Dionysios I*, p. 93; M.I. Finley, *Aspects of antiquity* (London, 1968), pp. 77, 79, 82-5. Diogenes Laertius X. 8 records that Epicurus called the Platonists Διονυσοκόλακες. See G.R. Morrow, *Studies in the platonic epistles* (New York, 1962), pp. 143-4 on the Academy's attraction towards monarchy. On Dion, see H.D. Westlake, 'Dion: A study in liberation', *Essays on the Greek historians and Greek history* (Manchester, 1969), pp. 251-64, who, I believe, correctly bases his view of the undemocratic quality of Dion upon the facts: (a) that only twenty-five or thirty exiles from at least a thousand returned under Dion (Plut. *Dion* XXII. 4; Diod. Sic. XVI. 10.5); (b) that Heracleides, as leader of the navy and admiral, supported a popular land redistribution, which Dion revoked, while removing Heracleides to Messana; and (c) that Dion ultimately became tyrant himself, in the process murdering Heracleides, in turn being murdered himself by another Academician, Callippus. We also follow Westlake in noting the brief and vague nature of Plutarch's account of Dion, suggesting that Plutarch deliberately suppressed hostile information which might lead his reader to conclude that Dion entertained unconstitutional or tyrannical designs — a stance sharply in constrast to Nepos' open hostility towards Dion's dictatorship.

21. See E.R. Goodenough, 'The political philosophy of Hellenistic kingship', *YClS*, vol. 1 (1928), p. 55:

> With his [i.e. Xenophon's] eyes on Cyrus and Sparta alike, his ideal state is clearly that dominated by an absolute ruler who surpasses his subjects in every way, physically, mentally and morally. The sanction of monarchy is the legal, moral and philosophical character of the ruler and his action.

See also W. Weathers, 'Xenophon's political idealism', *CJ*, vol. 49 (1953-4), pp. 317-21, 330; Anderson, *Xenophon*, p. 193. For the late dating of the *Hieron*, see G.J.D. Aalders, 'The date and intention of Xenophon's *Hiero*', *Mnemosyne*, Ser. 6, vol. 4a (1953), pp. 208-15, following J. Hatzfeld, 'Note sur la date et l'objet du *Hiéron*', *REG*, vol. 48 (1946-7), pp. 67ff; Delebecque, *Xénophon*, p. 411; H.R. Breitenbach, *RE* (1967), vol. 9a, col. 1746. For a date c. 338 BC, see G. Grote, *Plato* (London, 1885), vol. 1, pp. 221-2; Sordi, 'Lo Ierone di Senofonte, Dionigi e Filisto', pp. 3-13.

22. On the rise of monarchical figures and monarchical theories in a general sense, see K. von Fritz, 'Conservative reaction to one man rule in Ancient Greece', *PSQ*, vol. 56 (1941), pp. 51-83; V. Ehrenberg, 'The fourth century as part of Greek history', *Polis und Imperium* (Zurich, 1965), pp. 39-40; Stroheker, *Dionysios I*, pp. 88ff; Stroheker, 'Zu den Anfängen der monarchischen Theorie in der Sophistik', pp. 383ff; G. Glotz, *The Greek city and its institutions* (London, 1929), pp. 385-8.

23. See Jaeger, *Paideia*, vol. 3, pp. 84ff.

24. Theopompus, influenced by practical political considerations, seems to have followed Isocrates in demanding superior moral standards from his ideal ruler. See von Fritz, 'The historian Theopompus: His political convictions and his conception of historiography', pp. 765-87; R.T. Connor, *Theopompus and fifth-century Athens* (Cambridge, Mass., 1968); Connor, 'Theopompus' treatment of Cimon', *GRBS*, vol. 4 (1963), 107-14; Momigliano, 'Teopompo: Studi sulla storiografia greca del IV. secolo, A.C.', pp. 230-42, 335-53; M. Grant, *The ancient historians* (London, 1970), p. 139; I.A.F. Bruce, 'Theopompus and Classical Greek Historiography', *HT*, vol. 9 (1970), pp. 86-109, esp. pp. 96 and 105. For the alternative view that Theopompus' attack on prominent political figures derived either from Theopompus' innate cynicism or from purely moral or social disapproval, see G. Murray, 'Theopompus or the Cynic as historian', *Greek studies* (Oxford, 1946), pp. 149-70; R.T. Connor, 'History without heroes. Theopompus' treatment of Philip of Macedon', *GRBS*, vol. 8, no. 2 (1967), pp. 133-54; G. Shrimpton, 'Theopompus' treatment of Philip in the *Philippica*', *Phoenix*, vol. 31, no. 2 (1977), pp. 123-44.

25. E. Barker, *Greek political theory: Plato and his predecessors* (London, 1918), p. 196.

26. This type of picture was adopted by Aristotle who, maintaining a philosophic friendship with the tyrant Hermias of Atarneus, and of course acting as tutor to the young Alexander of Macedon, accepted the possibility one one-man rule, compared his ideal ruler to Zeus and emphasised the virtuous aspect of the monarch, when he likened the

tyrant Hermias to Heracles, the Dioscuri, Achilles and Ajax, all of whom died for virtue's sake. Moreover, Aristotle stated distinctly that kings were Law. See Aristot. *Polit.* 1284a-c; Didymus *De Demosthene Commenta Philippicon*, VI. 22-36, edited originally by H. Diels and W. Schubart, *Berliner Klassikertexte* (Berlin 1904), vol. 1, p. 11, now newly edited by L. Pearson and S. Stephens (Berlin, 1983), cited by Dvornik, *Political philosophy*, vol. 1, pp. 185-6.

27. Cited by Stroheker, *Dionysios I*, p. 160, following A. Alföldi, 'Gewaltherrscher und Theaterkönig', *Late classical and medieval studies in honour of A.M. Friend, Jr.* (Princeton, 1955), pp. 15ff.

28. See Stroheker, *Dionysios I*, pp. 159ff. Oddly enough, major modern authorities argue against Dionysius' utilisation of the royal title. Thus K.J. Beloch, 'L'impero siciliano di Dionisio', *MAL*, ser. 3, vol. 7 (1881), pp. 227-8; E.A. Freeman, *History of Sicily* (Oxford, 1894), vol. 4, p. 7; B. Niese, *s.v.* 'Dionisios I', *RE* (1905), vol. 5a, col. 898; Stroheker, *Dionysios I*, p. 173; F. Sartori, 'Sulla δυναστεία di Dionisio il vecchio nell'opera Diodorea', *CS*, vol. 5 (1966), pp. 57-61. Against these views, see S.I. Oost, 'The tyrant kings of Syracuse', *C. Phil.*, vol. 71 (1976), pp. 224-36. For the view that Dionysius I's official title was *archon* and not *basileus* and that the first Sicilian tyrant to assume the title of king was Agathocles who did so in imitation of the Diadochi, see F.W. Walbank, *A historical commentary on Polybius* (3 vols., Oxford, 1957, 1967, 1979), vol. 2, p. 495 (henceforth cited as *HCP*). Late references to Dionysius as king: Cicero *De Div.* I. 73; *De Nat. Deor.* III. 84; *Tusc.* V. 57, 61; Nepos *Reg.* II. 2; *Tim.* II. 2. Evidence for Dionysius II's emulation of his father in calling himself king: see Diod. Sic. XVI. 17. 2 on the royal παρασκευή; Baton of Sinope (268. F. 4) (see above p. 8); Plutarch *Dion* XIII. 1, on the royal chariot being placed at Plato's disposal; Plutarch *Dion* XXI. 6, on royal honours being paid to the tyrant's sister, Theste, after her husband Polyxenus' flight; late evidence in Nepos *Dion* I. 1; II. 4; V. 5; *Tim.* II. 2; Justin XXI. 1. 3. 7; 2. 8, 9; 5. 9.

29. The fourth-century adulation of Persia can certainly be traced back to Herodotus and Aeschylus. See Aeschylus *Persae* 155ff, 694ff, 759ff; cf. Dvornik, *Political philosophy*, vol. 1, pp. 172ff; H.D. Broadhead, *The Persae of Aeschylus* (Cambridge, 1960), pp. xxvii-xxxii; Herod. I. 131-41; III. 80; cf. Stroheker, *Dionysios I*, p. 90; H.R. Immerwahr, *Form and thought in Herodotus* (Cleveland, 1966), p. 174.

30. Cf. Athenaeus XIII. 545f on the relationship of the younger Dionysius and the Great King.

31. See B. Meritt, 'Athens and Carthage', *HSCPh*, supplementary volume 1 (1940), pp. 247-53; cf. K.F. Stroheker, 'Athen und Karthago', *Historia*, vol. 3 (1954-5), pp. 163-71; R. Meiggs and D. Lewis, *A selection of Greek historical inscriptions* (Oxford, 1969), no. 92; R. Vattuone, 'L'alleanza fra Atene e Cartagine alla fine del V. Sec. a.C. *I.G.I²* 47 = *S.E.G.* X. 136', *Epigraphica*, vol. 39 (1977), pp. 41-50.

32. *Syllog.*, I³ 159; 163; Tod, *Greek historical inscriptions*, vol. 2, nos. 133, 136; Isocrat. *Epist.* I; Xen. *Hell.* VII. 1. 20; Diod. Sic. XV. 70; 1; 74; Tzetz. *Chil.* V. 180; Nauck. *TGF²*, 794. The loss of the main section of Isocrates' letter renders uncertain knowledge of Isocrates' precise intentions with respect to Dionysius. Stroheker (*Dionysios I*, pp. 108-9) cor-

rectly questions whether Isocrates hoped to employ Dionysius as con-
queror of Persian territory. It is also questionable whether Dionysius was
sympathetic enough to Isocratean panhellenism to include his Sicilian
and Italian empire within its sphere. Probably all Isocrates hoped to gain
was the tyrant's service as a stabilising force in Greece with the support of
Athens. Such motivation probably underlies Isocrates' reference to
μεγάλα πράγματα ὑπὲρ τῆς Ἑλλάδος ἀγαθόν.

33. On Dionysius' relations with the Greek mainland, see P. Meloni,
'Il contributo di Dionisio il vecchio alle operazione di Antalcide del 387
a.C.', *RAL*, ser. 8, vol. 4 (1949), pp. 190-203.

34. See G. Grote, *History of Greece*, 2nd edn (London, 1869), vol. 10, p.
312, though cf. Stroheker, *Dionysios I*, pp. 227, 234.

35. See K.J. Beloch, *Griechische Geschichte*, III² (Strasbourg, 1912-27),
vol. 3, pp. 102-6.

36. See Edmonds, *Fragments of Attic comedy*, vol. 1, p. 671. On
Kokalos in Greek mythology see Diod. Sic. IV. 77. 6; 78; 79. 3; Paus. I. 21.
4; VII. 4. 6; 5; Hyg. *Fab.* 44.

37. Edmonds, *Fragments of Attic comedy*, vol. 1, p. 573, n.c.

38. Lysias' intense involvement in Sicilian affairs probably derives
from the orator's paternal connection with Sicily (Dionys. Hal. *Lys.* I;
Plut. *Vit. X. Orat.* 835c; Phot. *Bibl.* 262, p. 488; Suda. *s.v.* 'Λυσίας'; Lys.
XII. 4; Cic. *Brut.* XVI. 63. Thus Stroheker, *Dionysios I*, p. 139. Within this
context, Dionysius' sack of Rhegium of the same Olympic year might
well have been a factor spurring Lysias' ire against the tyrant.

39. See Webster, *Studies*, p. 28; W. Schmid — S.O. Stählin, *Griechische
Literarturgeschichte* (Munich, 1946), I. 4. p. 487.

40. Thus Sordi, 'Lo Ierone di Senofonte, Dionigi e Filisto', pp. 7ff.
Xenophon's sojourn at that time at Skillus near Olympia (*Anab.* V. 3. 7),
as Sordi notes (anticipated by Grote, *Plato*, vol. 1, p. 221) certainly suggests the probability of Xenophon's intimacy with the events of the
Olympics of 388 BC. Moreover, given Xenophon's friendship for
Agesilaus and exile from Athens, Lysias' attack upon Sparta would have
been particularly resented by Xenophon.

41. Cf. Sanders, 'Plato's first visit to Sicily', pp. 207-19 and Sordi,
'Dionigi I e Platone', pp. 2015-22. Plutarch's statement (*Dion* V. 3) that
Plato was sold because a recent decree provoked by the hostilities
between Athens and Aegina had stipulated that Athenians on the islands
were to be sold as slaves certainly gives the anecdote an even more precise
historical context and firmly dates these events between 389 and 387 BC
(Xen. *Hell.* V. 1). For the intriguing suggestion that the enslavement of
Crinnipus' force sent by Dionysius to aid the Spartans in 372 BC (Xen.
Hell. VI. 2. 33-6) was an act of retaliation for the enslavement of Plato, see
Sordi, 'Dionigi, I e Platone', p. 2019.

42. Accounts of Philoxenus' incarceration found in Plut. *De Tran. An.*
471e-d; Cic. *Ad Attic.* IV. 6. 2; Aelian. *VH* XII. 44; Lucian, *Adv. Indoct.* 15.

43. See Lesky, *History of Greek literature*, p. 415; Webster, *Studies*, p.
21; A.W. Pickard-Cambridge, *Dithyramb, tragedy and comedy*, 2nd edn,
revised by T.B.L. Webster (Oxford, 1962), p. 61.

44. Thus Plutarch records that Philoxenus ultimately decided to leave
Sicily because he did not wish to be seduced by the luxury prevalent

there and the Suda states that upon receiving an invitation to return from the tyrant, he wrote the letter O which represented οὐ. Hence arose the Φιλοξένου γραμμάτιον. See J.M. Edmonds, *Lyra Graeca* (London-Cambridge, Mass., 1967), vol. 3, p. 363; Plut. *Vit. Aer. Al., fin.*; Suda *s.v.* φιλοξένου λραμμάτιον; 1 Schol. Aristides 46. 309d; cf. Stroheker, *Dionysios I*, pp. 99ff. Plutarch's note on Sicilian luxury is probably reflective of a Platonic-dependent source, which we shall suggest below masks strong anti-democratic feeling within a moralistic superstructure.

45. An elaboration of this episode is found in Diodorus, recording how Philoxenus, sent to the quarries, released and exposed to a further recitation by the tyrant, asked to be returned to the quarries. There follows a description of Dionysius' amusement and Philoxenus' characterisation of Dionysius' poetry as οἰκτρά, which to Philoxenus meant pitiable and to Dionysius as full of pathos. Plutarch, *De Tran. An.* 471e-d merely sees Dionysius' jealousy of Philoxenus as a cause of the poet's incarceration. Cf. *De Alex. Fort.* II. 334c, whereupon being asked by Dionysius for a critique of the tyrant's drama, Philoxenus cancels the whole work. Folcke, 'Dionysius', p. 8, unilaterally dismisses the basic tradition as apocryphal.

46. The novelty of the Cyclops' dance was first noted by G.R. Holland, 'De Polyphemo et Galatea, commentatio philologica', *LS*, vol. 7 (1884), pp. 184-209. On the Cyclops' dance, see Horace, *Sat.* I. 5. 63; *Epist.* II. 2. 124.

47. Lesky, *Greek tragedy*, p. 142.

48. Holland, 'De Polyphemo et Galatea, commentatio philologica', pp. 184-209. Galatea (Milk White) the sea nymph is first found in Homer (*Iliad* XVIII. 45). She is very popular with pastoral writers (see Theocritus XI; cf. VI. 6; Bion XII; Virgil *Eclogue* IX. 39; cf. II. 19ff; VII, 37; Ovid *Metam.* XIII. 738; Propert. III. 2. 7). The earliest surviving lengthy account of the relationship between Polyphemus and Galatea occurs in Theocritus, where Galatea loves Acis. Polyphemus then serenades Galatea and crushes Acis with a huge stone, after which Galatea turns Acis into the river bearing his name.

49. Loicq-Berger, *Syracuse*, p. 231 doubts the authenticity of the tradition that the tyrant's relations with a mistress were attacked on two grounds: the fact that Athenaeus I. 6e is confused between the royal court and the prison; and that Dionysius' temperate nature, attested to by a variety of sources (as we shall see Plato, Theopompus, Diodorus, Trogus-Justin, Plutarch and Cicero) renders unlikely the view that Dionysius had extramarital relations. To counter these arguments, we note (a) that Athenaeus' confusion in itself cannot prove conclusively that the tyrant's mistress was not attacked and (b) that the evidence pertaining to Dionysius' controlled libido is viewed fundamentally within a political context and that no evidence exists substantiating the view that Dionysius was excessively puritanical in circumstances which did not threaten the security of his regime.

50. See Sartori, 'Sulla Δυναστεία di Dionisio il vecchio nell'opera Diodorea', 3-66; L. Gernet, 'Mariages de tyrans', *Hommage à Lucien Febvre. Eventail de l'histoire vivante* (Paris, 1953), pp. 41-53; M.I. Finley, *Ancient Sicily to the Arab conquest* (London, 1968), pp. 77-8; Stroheker,

Dionysios I, pp. 157-9; H. Berve, *Die Tyrannis bei den Griechen*, vol. I, (2 vols., Munich, 1967), pp. 249-51.

51. Plutarch (*Vit. X. Orat.* 833c) and Philostratus (*Vit. Soph.* I. 15. 3) confuse this Antiphon with the Attic orator, put to death in 411 BC. See Stroheker, *Dionysios I*, pp. 99-100.

52. See Edmonds, *Fragments of Attic comedy*, vol. 2, p. 94 (no 25 Eubulus), p. 222 (Antiphanes) p. 392 (Alexis), p. 157 (Ephippus); cf. Folcke, 'Dionysius', p. 9.

53. Diod. Sic. XIV. 109; XV. 74; Tzetzes, *Chil.* V. 178-85; Cic. *Tusc.* V. 22. 63; Lucian, *Adv. Indoct.* 15; *Cal. Cred.* 14; Athen. III. 98d; Hellad. ap Phot. p. 537b. 32. For Dionysius' use of words for etymological purpose, such as a mouse hole (μυστήριον) deriving from τοὺς μοῦς τηρεῖ, derived from Philoxenus (Athen. 643a) see Hell ad. ap. Phot. p. 532b. For motifs from Dionysius' dramas appearing on South Italian pottery, see 'Dramen des älteren Dionysios auf Italiotischen Vasen', pp. 479-82. Total acceptance of posterity's jaundiced view of Dionysius' literary ability, see Weter, 'Encouragement of literary production in Greece from Homer to Alexander', pp. 53-9.

54. See n 16 above.

55. See Webster, *Studies*, pp. 23-8; Webster, *Art and literature*, p. 34; Folcke, 'Dionysius', p. 10.

56. Thus Field, *Plato and his contemporaries*, pp. 128-9; Barker, *Greek political theory*, p. 300; Berve, *Die Tyrannis*, vol. 1, p. 354; K.F. Stroheker, 'Platon und Dionysios', *HZ*, vol. 179 (1952), pp. 225ff; J. Luccioni, *La Pensée politique de Platon* (Paris, 1958), pp. 78, 80-1, who suggests that Plato's description was also influenced by the philosopher's knowledge of the circumstances of the rise of Pisistratus as well as by his intimate acquaintance with the tyranny of the younger Dionysius, the latter hypothesis implying that the *Republic* was, in fact, revised after 367 BC.

57. See von Fritz, 'The historian Theopompus', pp. 765-87.

58. Thus Stroheker, 'Platon und Dionysios', pp. 225ff.

59. Though even here it is worth nothing, Hipparinus is not mentioned as Aristomache's father, the first reference in Diodorus to Hipparinus as the father of Aristomache and Dion, occurring in XVI. 6. 1-2.

60. The evidence of the letter accepted by B. Niese, *s.v.* 'Dionysios', *RE*, vol. 5a, col. 883; E. Meyer, *Geschichte des Altertums* (Stuttgart, 1902), vol. 5, p. 77; Morrow, *Platonic epistles*, p. 86; and Folcke, 'Dionysius', p. 159. The latter, ignoring the late association of Dionysius and Hipparinus, argues that underlying Diodorus' text is Philistus' deliberate suppression of pro-Dion material. Morrow's claim that the evidence of Aristotle (*Polit.* V. 1306a) and Plutarch (*Dion* III. 4) proves the authenticity of the information does not convince because Aristotle almost certainly based his information upon Plato, and Plutarch is a late source who seems to have used Timaeus who might well have used Plato's epistles. Rejection of the evidence of the *Letter* in Beloch, *Griechische Geschichte*, vol. 2a, p. 410, and A. Holm, *Geschichte Siziliens im Altertums* (Leipzig, 1874), vol. 2, p. 428.

61. Though the dream story cited by Aeschines is not found in Demosthenes *On the Embassy* nor anywhere else in the Demosthenic corpus.

62. These are reflected largely in later sources. Thus the sword of Damocles in Cic. *Tusc.* V. 21, 61; Horace *Odes* III. 1. 17; Amm. Marcell. XXIX. 2. 4; Sidonius, II. 13. 6; Euseb., *Praep. Evang.* VIII, 14. 29, p. 391; Boethius, *Consol. Philos.* III. 5. 15; cf. Damocles and Dionysius II in Timaeus (566), F. 32; cf. B. Niese, *s.v.* 'Damokles' in *RE* (1901) vol. 2, col. 2068; Damon and Phintias in Diod. Sic. X. F. 4; Iamblichus *Vit. Pyth.* 33; Cic. *De Offic.* III. 10. 45 and *Tusc.* V. 22; Val. Max. IV. 7. 1; cf. Wellman, *s.v.* 'Damon' in *RE* IV. 2 (1901), col. 2074. Barber-theme in Diod. Sic. XX. 63. 3; Plut. *Dion* IX. 3; Cic. *Tusc.* V. 20. 58; Plut. *De Garrul.* XII. 508f; murder of Dionysius' mother in Plut. *De Alex. Fort.* II. 5. 338b; Aelian *VH* XIII. 45. On Dionysius' father and son stripping, see Plut. *Dion* IX. 3; Marsyas in Plut. *Dion* IX. 5.

63. Dionysius' murders in Plut. *De Alex. Fort.* II. 5. 338b. Police state in Plut. *De Curios.* XII. 523a; *De Garrul.* XIII, p. 508f; *Reg. Apophth. Dionys. Mai.* X. 176a; Polyaen. V. 2. 3; Quarries in Cicero *Verr.* V. 55; Aelian, *VH* XII. 44. Financial rapacity in Ps.-Aristot. *Oecon.* II, 2. 20a (1349a, 14ff) and 41 (1353b. 20ff); Aristot. *Polit.* V. 9. 5 (1313b, 26ff); Val. Max. I. 1. 3 and VI. 2. 2; Plut. *Reg. Apophth. Dionys. Mai.* V. 175e; Polyaen. V. 2. 11, 19, 21; Aelian *VH* I. 20; Athen. V. 693e; Cic. *De Nat. Deor.* III. 34. 83ff; Lact. *Div. Instit.* II. 4. 16ff; Diod. Sic. XV. 13. 1.

64. See D.R. Stuart, *Epochs of Greek and Roman biography* (California, 1928), pp. 133, 159.

65. Stroheker, *Dionysios I*, pp. 20-1.

66. Viewed with suspicion by Stroheker, 'Platon und Dionysios', pp. 225-59 and U. Karstedt, 'Platons Verkauf in Sklaverei', *WJA*, vol. 2 (1947), pp. 295ff. The anecdote regarded more positively by Porter, 'The sequel to Plato's first visit to Sicily', pp. 46-55 and Sordi, 'Dionigi I e Platone', pp. 2015-22. On Dionysius' financial rapacity see C.H. Bullock, 'Dionysius of Syracuse financier', *CJ*, vol. 25 (1930), pp. 260-76.

67. Cf. Folcke, 'Dionysius and Philistus', p. 19 who accepts Plutarch's testimony as valid.

2

The Pre-Diodorus Historiographical Tradition

I

Ten historians preceding Diodorus appear to have concerned themselves with the reign of Dionysius. With regard to six of them, however, Dionysius I, Alcimus Siculus, Hermias of Methymna, Athanis of Syracuse, Polycritus of Mende and Silenus of Caleacte, scarcely anything at all is known. Dionysius' own history (Jacoby, *FGH*, vol. 3b, no. 557), if indeed we accept its authenticity, as Jacoby suggests, might well have been auto-biographical and have offered a self-justification by the tyrant of his rule, providing in fact a depiction which accorded closely with the sentiments expressed in the tyrant's own dramas. It is even possible that poetic and dramatic elements found their way into Dionysius' history, resulting, in fact, in the creation of a Cornfordian-style mythistoric concoction.[1] With regard to another historical work written by a contemporary of the events described, that of Hermias of Methymna (Jacoby, *FGH*, vol. 3b, no. 558), we know that it was composed of twelve or possibly ten books, was important enough to merit mention by Diodorus and did not cover the whole of Dionysius' reign, ending with the events of 376-375 BC (Diod. Sic. XV. 37. 3/T. 1) — a terminal point perhaps deliberately designed by the author to coincide with the ending of Dionysius' third and penultimate war with Carthage[2] but more likely to be associated with the author's failure to complete the history of Dionysius because of his own physical demise. Beyond this, all that we can say is that the fact that one surviving fragment from Hermias' history (F. 1/Athen. X. 51. p. 438c) seems unfavourably disposed towards Nicoteles, Dionysius' opponent who was slain in 404-403 BC by the tyrant's supporter, Aristus the Spartan (Diod. Sic. XIV. 10. 2-3) whom the author seems to regard as a toper, suggests, if not that Hermias wrote a pro-Dionysius propagandist history,[3] that its account of Dionysius was favourable, and since by Book III, Hermias had only reached 404-403 BC, obviously the account of Dionysius' reign was dealt with in considerable detail and constituted a much fuller work than Philistus' Περὶ Διονυσίου, to which we shall see only four books were allotted.[4] Finally, though the motif of Nicoteles' drunkenness might well have appealed to Theopompus, the latter historian's use of Hermias for his own account of Dionysius can, of course, by no means be proved. As for Athanis' continuation of Philistus' history of the reign of Dionysius II (Jacoby, *FGH*, vol. 3b, no. 562) which, in part, constituted a history of Dion, written in twelve books, continuing to the year 357 BC (T. 2/Diod. Sic. XV. 94. 4) obviously by the very nature of the chronological boundaries imposed upon the work, little was said about the elder Dionysius. From the possible identification of Athanis with the general of the same name who, according to Theopompus (Steph. Byz. *s.v.* 'Δύμη'/F. 194), was chosen στρατηγός with Heracleides at the time of Dion's withdrawal from Syracuse in 356 BC, we might deduce that Athanis was an extreme democrat who was neither favourable to Dion nor to Dionysius II. Consequently we might further suspect that whatever data pertaining to Dionysius I was contained in his history is unlikely to have been favourable to the tyrant.[5] About the accounts Alcimus Siculus (Jacoby, *FGH*, vol. 3b, no. 560) and Polycritus of Mende (Jacoby, *FGH*, vol. 3b, no. 559), we simply do not have a scrap of evidence for formulating even a minimal assessment. There remains the *Sikelica* of Silenus of Caleacte (Jacoby, *FGH*, vol. 2b, no. 175) whose discussion of Dionysius I as of the rest of Sicilian history was characterised by extreme brevity since by Book III, Hieron II was already being discussed (F. 4/Athen. XII. 59, p. 342a). Manni[6] may accordingly be correct in supposing that this book covered the lengthy period from the great Athenian expedition to Sicily to the reign of Agathocles, including therefore Dionysius' reign. For the rest, Folcke's inference from Timaeus-type moderate battle figures of F. 6 (Liv. XXVI. 49) and agreement with Timaeus on Spanish geography of F. 7 (Plin. *NH* IV. 120) that Silenus adopted Timaeus' hostile stance towards Dionysius, cannot obviously be proved and tends to be negated by the difficulty of reconciling the two historians' respective scales of six as opposed to a meagre section of one book devoted to the career of the tyrant.[7]

Of much more substantial fare are the remaining four historians: the purely Siceliot Philistus (Jacoby, *FGH*, vol. 3b, no. 556) and Timaeus (Jacoby, *FGH*, vol. 3b, no. 566) and the more universally inclined Ephorus (Jacoby, *FGH*, vol. 2a, no. 70) and Theopompus (Jacoby, *FGH*, vol. 2b, no. 115), whose accounts of Sicilian affairs merely constituted one element within a much broader canvas of Hellenic history. Of these historians, without doubt the most significant was Philistus, the son of Archonides or Archomenides, depending upon whether we follow the testimony of the Suda (*s.v.* 'Φίλισκος ἢ Φίλιστος'/T. 1. b) or Pausanias (v. 23. 6/F. 57. b).

II

Philistus' history of Dionysius, the Περὶ Διονυσίου, derives its initial importance from the fact that it was written by a contemporary eye witness of Dionysius' tyranny. Certainly Plutarch's statement (*Nicias* XIX. 6/T. 2) that Philistus witnessed Gylippus' liberation of Syracuse suggests that, while Philistus was an intelligent observer of these events, he was too young to partake of them in a practical military or political sense. Consequently we may agree with De Sanctis that Philistus must have been at least ten years of age by 414-413 BC and therefore at least in his late teens by 406 BC when he threw in his lot with Dionysius. Philistus was accordingly undoubtedly younger than his ideological mentor, Thucydides, and older than his political and ideological rival, Plato.[8]

Even more significant is the fact that Philistus was a close associate of Dionysius, intimately acquainted with Syracusan military and governmental affairs. Hence while the Suda (*s.v.* 'Φίλισκος ἢ Φίλιστος'/T. 1a) considered him a συγγενής of Dionysius, to Cicero (*De Orat.* II. 15. 7/T. 17b) he was *familiarissimus* with the tyrant.[9] Philistus was certainly a member of Dionysius' inner cabinet of advisers, the φίλοι and commander of Ortygia until his banishment (Diod. Sic. XIII. 91. 4; XIV. 8. 5; XV. 7. 3; Plut. *Dion* XI. 5/T. 3a. 4. 5b. 5c). He played a key role in the events leading to the establishment of Dionysius' tyranny by paying the fines which were imposed upon the future ruler of Syracuse by Dionysius' opponents (Diod. Sic. XIII. 91. 4/T. 3a). In the description of Dionysius' consultation with his friends after the revolution of

404-403 BC we find Philistus opposing Polyxenus' advice and counselling Dionysius to maintain the power which he had obtained as long as possible (Diod. Sic. XIV. 8. 5-6/T. 4).[10] Plutarch (*Dion* XI. 4/T. 5c) associates Philistus with the role of phrourarch and it is likely as Gitti has suggested that it was in this capacity that he played a major role in Syracusan colonisation projects in the Northern Adriatic, ultimately aimed at the creation of a protectorate in Northern Italy against the Illyrians or possibly to establish Gallic contacts.[11] Because of Diodorus' sketchy account of Dionysius' Northern Adriatic activity and lack of reference to Philistus' role within this context, we actually have very little evidence to rely upon — in fact, essentially Pliny's reference to the *fossa Philistina* (*Nat. Hist.* III. 121) which Gitti has associated with a vast hydraulic system bearing Philistus' name as a tribute to the historian's important role as administrator of this region and including the Philistina Branch of the Po and Philistina canal.[12] It is also curious and perhaps not accidental and hence suggestive of Philistus' important contribution to Dionysius' northern policies that colonisation activity seems to cease with Philistus' exile in 384 BC and resumes again upon his return from exile upon the Elder Dionysius' death (i.e. Diod. Sic. XVI. 5). If we associate this evidence with that of Diodorus (XV. 13) and to a lesser extent Polybius (I. 6) and Justin (XX. V. 4) concerning Dionysius' northern colonising activity, we must date these colonising projects, together with Philistus' hydraulic schemes, to the period 388-384 BC,[13] and by associating Philistus with them, postdate Philistus' exile from Syracuse, dated by Diodorus (XV. 7. 3-4/T. 5b) to 386 BC to 384 BC. The latter transposition is not unreasonable in view of a similar dating error found in the same passage of Diodorus with respect to Lysias' attack upon Dionysius which, as we have already noted, also involves a transposition date — in this case from 386 to 388 BC.[14]

Philistus' exile was spent in Epirus (Plut. *De Exil.* XIV. 605c/T. 5a). The reference in Plutarch's *Dion* (XI. 4/T. 5c) to εἰς τὸν ᾿Αδρίαν does not pertain to Adria but to the Adriatic coastal area in a broad sense since Adria in the masculine always refers to the sea.[15] Nor can confidence be placed in Diodorus' location of the exile at Thurii (XV. 7. 3/T. 5b) since this notice is suspect on account of its association with what we shall perceive as an erroneous reference to an early joint recall of Leptines and Philistus from exile.[16] The exile was indeed a long one, lasting in fact to the end of Dionysius' reign, despite the contrary assertion of Diodorus (XV. 7. 3/T. 5b) who might well have confused the recall of Leptines, Dionysius' brother with that of Philistus by assuming wrongly that a similarly dated banishment implied a similarly dated recall. Certainly Leptines had to have been recalled to fight and indeed die at the battle of Cronium of 383 BC or thereafter (Diod. Sic. XV. 17. 1), whereas Philistus was less needed in a military capacity at this particular juncture. On the other hand, in contrast to Cicero (*De Orat.* II. 57/T. 17b) who asserts that Philistus composed his history in his spare time, Plutarch (*Dion* XI. 4/T. 5c) as well as Nepos who read Philistus' own history personally (*Dion* III. 2/T. 5d), assert quite categorically that Philistus only returned upon Dionysius I's death. Pausanias (I. 13. 9/T. 13a) confirms this testimony in what admittedly might well be a *post-eventum* reconstruction, by arguing that Philistus wrote his Περὶ Διονυσίου with the express purpose of obtaining his pardon and return to the Syracusan court. Moreover, Plutarch's wording with respect to Philistus' exile,[17] Philistus' lament for Leptines' daughter (Phil. *Tim.* XV. 10/F. 60) and the unlikelihood of a life of intense political activity accompanying the composition of Philistus' history renders unlikely both the view of a short exile on the part of Philistus and the compromise solution offered by Jacoby, negated in any case by the fact that Ἀδρία in the masculine always refers to the sea and that Plutarch elsewhere (*De Exil.* XIV. 605c/T. 5a; cf. Plut. *Dion* XI/T. 5c) supplies Epirus as the place of exile, to the effect that Philistus, after a brief genuine exile was recalled and induced to accept an honorary exile as governor of Adria in a manner resembling Miltiades' honorary exile in the Hellespontine region.[18] Finally when Jacoby argues that Philistus must have received an early recall from exile, for otherwise he could not have described the latter part of Dionysius' reign in detail in his Περὶ Διονυσίου, we retort that there is in fact no evidence to suggest that Philistus placed equal emphasis upon the earlier and later parts of Dionysius' reign in his Dionysian history. Indeed the contrary is suggested by Diodorus' narrative which, even if in accord with the scholarly consensus we regard as directly derived from Timaeus, is certainly reflective ultimately of Philistus who, as we shall see, was utilised by Timaeus, albeit in a highly biased and distorted manner. Hence since fragment 28 (Theon *Progymn.* II. 68, Sp.) indicates that the first book of Philistus' history covered the preparations for the great conflict between Dionysius and Carthage, it is not unreasonable to assume that the period from the establishment of Dionysius' tyranny down to the actual outbreak of open hostilities between Dionysius and Carthage in 398 BC in Diodorus' text derives ultimately from the first book of Philistus' Περὶ Διονυσίου. Judging by the detailed account which follows in Diodorus, it is further logical to conclude that the great conflict itself occupied the next two books, Book II dealing primarily with the capture of Motya and Book III centring around the destruction of the Punic host. Judging further by the relatively small scale of Diodorus' subsequent narrative, it would seem that details regarding the rest of Dionysius' reign, including presumably the description of Dionysius' war with Rhegium and the Italiot League, the last three wars with Carthage, Dionysius' Northern Adriatic ventures, his relations with mainland Greece and with the literati at his court, and Dionysius' death must have all been crammed into the fourth and final book of the Περὶ Διονυσίου. Thus while three books covered the period 405-396 BC, the rest of Dionysius' reign to 367 BC probably occupied one book.[19] Moreover, we note that after Diodorus discusses the Italian war, his narrative diminishes considerably, in fact becoming a mere sketch, and as we shall see an inaccurate one at that, and that apart from a few odd references to Dionysius, dated to 380-379, 374-373 and 369-368 BC, placed in a broader context of Hellenic as opposed to purely Sicilian affairs (XV. 23. 5; 47. 7; 70. 1) and a curious chapter on Siculo-Punic hostilities (Diod. Sic. XV. 24), dated to 379-378 BC, which might either be appended to the account of Dionysius' third Punic War, dated by Diodorus (XV. 15-17) to 383 BC, or to that of the tyrant's final conflict with Carthage of 368-367 BC (Diod. Sic. XV. 73), we have no reference at all to the events of the last sixteen years of Dionysius' reign until the narrative of Dionysius' last year, describing his last war with Carthage and his death (XV. 73-4). It is accordingly not unreasonable to regard this phenomenon as reflective of Philistus' long seventeen-year exile which separated the historian from the central theatre of political activity at Syracuse and hence robbed him of data indispensable for the construction of a coherent and full narrative.

In 367 BC upon the elder Dionysius' death and the accession of Dionysius II, Philistus returned to Syracuse to play once again a major political role at the Syracusan court, above all to assume the leadership of the anti-Plato faction there (Plut. *Dion* XI. 4; Nepos *Dion* III. 2./T. 5c, 5d). In concrete terms, as we shall see in the course of our discussion of Philistus' political ideas as

enshrined in his Dionysian history, this implied the maintenance
of a strong centralised Syracusan power, operating from a broad
popular base, commanding the support of both the *demos* and the
nouveau-riche oligarchy, from whom derived the tyrant's φίλοι, and
opposition to the Platonic conception of government of a traditionally narrow oligarchic type, conducive to *stasis*. At the same
time, a resumption of colonising activity upon Philistus' return
(Diod. Sic. XVI. 5), after a twenty-year break which coincided
with Philistus' exile, implies a key role in these developments on
the part of Philistus. One important consequence of Philistus'
return to the Syracusan court was, of course, his renewed
acquaintance with directly and easily available data indispensable for a historian writing about the Syracusan tyranny.
Hence the appearance of the two books dealing with Dionysius II
which on account of Philistus' renewed political interests, which
must have limited the time available for historical activity, and
the abrupt and violent demise of the historian, only dealt with
part of the younger Dionysius' reign and had to be completed by
Athanis of Syracuse who may accordingly be regarded as the
Syracusan Xenophon to the Thucydidean Philistus (Diod. Sic.
XIII. 103. 3; XV. 89. 3; XV. 94. 4/T. 11a, b, c).[20] The final event
recorded about Philistus before the narrative of Philistus' death at
the head of a naval squadron in 356 BC (Plut. *Dion* XXXV/T. 9d)
concerns Dionysius II's reading of a letter sent by Dion to
Carthage to Philistus (Plut. *Dion* XIV. 4/T. 6a) — evidence certainly indicative not only of Philistus' deep intimacy with the
younger Dionysius and of his strong opposition to the Platonic
reformist element but also of the historian's important role as an
executant of foreign policy under Dionysius II and of the key
diplomatic role which Philistus might well have assumed not only
with Carthage but as we shall see also with the Italic peoples with
whom in the course of his sojourn in Northern Italy he is likely to
have come in contact — though in view of the Greek reluctance
to learn the languages of their barbarian neighbours, we may
doubt whether Philistus had actually mastered the Punic, Gallic
or numerous Italic tongues.[21]

These biographical details, albeit sketchy, do suggest to us the
fundamental tenor which is likely to have characterised Philistus'
Περὶ Διονυσίου. In the first place a positive stance towards
Dionysius would be expected from a senior public servant, sup-
portive of the Syracusan tyranny and intimate with the two
Dionysii. The two favourable portents recording the dream of

Dionysius' mother while pregnant concerning the future greatness of her son, testified to by the Galeatae (F. 57a/Cic. *De Div.* I.
39), and the miraculous swarm of bees encircling Dionysius'
horse while stuck in a bog (F. 58/Cic. *De Div.* I. 75), deriving
probably from the introduction to Philistus' first Dionysian book
and ushering in Philistus' account of Dionysius' reign,
accordingly come as no surprise to us. We might further deduce
from the phenomenon of Philistus' military and political service
on behalf of the two tyrants that the Περὶ Διονυσίου provided a
canvas resplendently rich in political and military details at least
for the period preceding the historian's exile. The vivid military
descriptions which the work is likely to have contained would
explain the fact that Philistus' history — and we would presume
that the Περὶ Διονυσίου is here indicated — was the one historical
work which Plutarch (*Alex.* VIII. 3/T. 22) tells us was sent by Harpalus to Alexander in Asia. For while we may question whether
Alexander consulted the work to learn about the West for possible future involvements there, as Wilcken and Brown suggest,
the data contained in the Περὶ Διονυσίου concerned with the
creation of a mighty empire which faced a hostile eastern power,
Carthage, and as we see from fragment 28 (Theon. *Progymn.* II.
68. 17sp) with a colourful description of new weapons, ships and
fortifications devised by the tyrant, would have been particularly
appealing to Alexander and indeed have foreshadowed in the
Macedonian monarch's eyes his own military and imperialistic
ventures.[22] In particular, we surmise that Alexander would have
regarded as particularly appealing Philistus' description of
Dionysius' Motyan mole (cf. Diod. Sic. XIV. 47. 4; 49. 3; 51. 1)
which might have appeared to him by virtue of the series of
χώματα to have anticipated Alexander's own Tyrian mole.
Equally appealing and prophetic of Alexander's own military and
political experimentation, moreover, must have been Dionysius'
employment of mercenaries, the Sicilian tyrant's establishment
of military colonies in both Sicily and Italy and the transference
of populations from one zone to another. Similarly it is surely not
coincidental that another campaigner, Cicero's brother Quintus,
while in Gaul with Caesar who was engaged at the time in
military and imperialistic ventures, should have read upon the
strong recommendation of his brother, and found particularly
appealing, Philistus' history of Dionysius I (*Ad Quint. Fratr.* II. 11.
4/T. 17a).[23] Obviously the overt military and imperialistic tone of
the work which, in light of our discussion pertaining to the likely

allocation of material in the Περὶ Διονυσίου, is particularly likely to have been emphasised in the context of Philistus' treatment of Dionysius' first Punic War of 398-396 BC, must have exercised considerable appeal upon the two campaigners.

Though Philistus' likely involvement in Dionysius' colonisation activity in the Northern Adriatic and construction of an immense hydraulic system in that area might induce us to suspect that his history provided a detailed narrative of these events in which Philistus was a guiding force and that it furnished significant material pertaining to the economic structure of Dionysius' *arche*, we are obliged to concede that the evidence to substantiate such a thesis, somewhat enigmatic and inconclusive, tends in a contrary direction. Thus while a few fragments from Philistus' fourth book of the Περὶ Διονυσίου, relating to Etruscan and Samnite cities (Steph. Byz. *s.v.* 'Μυστία', 'Τύρσητα', 'Νουκρία'/ F. 41, 42, 43) do suggest that Philistus did indeed write about Dionysius' colonisation projects in the last Dionysian book, Diodorus' testimony regarding Dionysius' Northern Adriatic policy (Diod. Sic. XV. 13-14) survives in a very sketchy format with no reference to Philistus' role in these ventures preserved at all. While we might certainly be tempted to argue that Diodorus' meagre testimony is reflective either of Diodorus' use of a source other than Philistus or that detailed discussion and mention of Philistus' role therein was made in what now constitutes a lacuna, we note that the bulk of Diodorus' Sicilian narrative in Books XIII and XIV, which most source-critics attribute at least indirectly to Philistus, pays scant attention to economic data, being primarily concerned with war and politics conceived of in personal psychological terms. This in itself need not surprise us, since as is well known, Thucydides, Philistus' spiritual mentor, for all his interest in, and impressive knowledge of, economics (I. 2; 4; 7; 8. 3-4; 9. 2-5; II. 1-2; 13. 1, 5; 83. 2; 100; 141. 5; IV. 105. 1; V. 103; VI. 24. 3-4; 34. 2)[24] did not allow this knowledge to percolate through into the main body of his narrative and thereby indeed established a clear precedent for subsequent pre-Marxian historiography. Hence war and political strife were in Thucydides' view caused by personalities and their differences, either individually or collectively, and not explicable within the context of economic considerations.[25] Consequently we suggest, admittedly tentatively, that Diodorus' sparse testimony pertaining to Dionysius' Northern Adriatic activity and lack of information concerning his own important role therein might well be reflective of Philistus' lack of interest in these ventures as fitting subjects for his history with its political and military slant.

We are clearly on firmer ground in attempting to assess the political philosophy contained in the Περὶ Διονυσίου. Obviously the overtly monarchic tone of the Περὶ Διονυσίου suggested by the very title of the work, dealing with the career of an individual who by his daring, initiative and willpower anticipated Alexander by a couple of generations, whence the work's appeal to the Macedonian monarch and to Cicero who, we emphasise, for all his republicanism was at the time he recommended Philistus' second *syntaxis* to his brother, entertaining the possibility of one-man rule,[26] suggests that the Περὶ Διονυσίου contained in its pages a highly relevant philosophy of absolutism for subsequent eras. Even more to the point are the facts that according to the Suda (*s.v.* ῾Φίλισκος ἤ Φίλιστος᾽/T. 1a, 1b), Philistus was a student of the sophist Euenus of Paros who in fragment 4 spoke of the advantages accruing to the daring and wise individual; that Philistus might well have been an associate of the sophist Antiphon, the open advocate of the supremacy of φύσις over νομός;[27] and that Cornelius Nepos, who read Philistus' history at first hand (*Dion* III. 2/T. 5d) in the context of a discussion of a conflict of political ideals between Plato and Philistus, should describe Philistus as 'hominem amicum non magis tyranno quam tyrannidi' (Nep. *Dion* III. 2/T. 5d) — a statement which, to be sure, some scholars have interpreted to mean that Philistus was the type of subservient individual who would have supported any tyrant but which more likely constitutes evidence to the effect that the allegiance of Philistus could have been gained by any despot and not merely by Dionysius, precisely because Philistus favoured tyranny as an ideal form of government by conviction.[28]

That the chief distinguishing feature of Philistus' work was its patent espousal of despotism is confirmed by the phenomenon of the Philistus revival in Rome in the first century BC. As we shall see, second-century Roman writers, imbued by the republican spirit of contempt for the eastern monarchs whom Roman armies had so easily vanquished, were to find the 'republican' antimonarchist Timaeus of Tauromenium much more to their liking than the tyrant-lover Philistus. However, by the first century BC, as a result of the civil wars and the rise of military despots, when the problem of absolutism began increasingly to occupy men's thoughts, we find ever-increasing references to Philistus prevalent in Diodorus (XIII. 103. 3; XV. 89. 3; 94. 4; XIII. 91. 4; XIV. 8. 5; XV. 7.3/T. 11a, b, c, 3a. 4. 5b), Nepos (*Dion* III. 2/T. 5d; cf. *De Reg.* II.

2), Dionysius of Halicarnassus (*Ad Pomp.* IV./T. 16b) and Cicero (*Ad Quint. Fratr.* II. 11. 4; *De Orat.* II. 57; *Brut.* 66; *De Div.* 39, 73/ T. 17a, b, 21, F. 57a. 58) and we note with particular interest how a writer like Dionysius of Halicarnassus, essentially concerned with Philistus' style, regards Philistus as a model of rhetorical style, to be classed with Thucydides, Xenophon and Theopompus, all significantly historians who were concerned with problems of monarchy and absolutism: Thucydides the champion, as we shall see of the despotic and tyrant-like figures of Pericles, Hermocrates and Archelaus of Macedon and defender of the reputation of the Pisistratidae; Xenophon, author of the *Cyropaedia, Agesilaus* and *Hieron*; and Theopompus, author of the *Hellenica* and *Philippica*, centred around the monarchic figures of Lysander and Philip II of Macedon. It is further hardly accidental that Cicero, the adherent of Pompeius Magnus should have been particularly attracted by the Dionysian books in a period in which he began to theorise about a *princeps* who would restore the harmony of the Roman World, so rudely shattered in the century following the tribunate of Tiberius Gracchus. Nor do we hasten to add it is unlikely, given the parallel which has been traced by Sordi between Cicero's dream foretelling Octavian's future role as avenger preserved in Augustus' autobiography (*De Vita Sua* F. 2. Peter; Tertull. *De Anim.* 46; Suet. *Div. Aug.* XCIV. 9) and a possible Philistus' passage to which Timaeus, F. 29 constituted a rebuttal, that the Emperor Augustus himself read Philistus' Περὶ Διονυσίου which constituted a source of encouragement for his own role as avenger of Jove.[29]

Philistus accordingly emerges as a typical representative of fourth-century sophistic thought whose attraction to monarchy and absolutist regimes, perhaps already imbued in him by his teacher Euenus, parallels similar phenomena encountered in other literati of the era, including Isocrates, Xenophon and Plato, also intimates of Dionysius' circle. In Philistus' particular case we might surmise that consideration of the political collapse of Syracuse and other Siceliot cities subsequent to the ejection of the Deinomenid tyrants which the historian had obviously already considered in his Περὶ Σικελίας, a subject perhaps reflected in relevant sections of Diodorus' eleventh and thirteenth books (XI. 86. 3, 5; 87. 5; 88. 4; 91. 2; 92. 3; XIII. 33. 1; cf. Polyaen. I. 43. 1) influenced the historian's train of thought, particularly when a further contrast was effected between Sicilian triumph against Athens under Hermocrates and subsequent Syracusan and

Siceliot disaster in the course of the conflict with Carthage in the last decade of the fifth century BC. The latter comparison, moreover, suggests the attribution of an avenging role to Dionysius *vis-à-vis* Carthage by Philistus. Indeed given the somewhat favourable context of Himeraean homage to Dionysius provided by Valerius Maximus I. 7. 6 for the Himeraean lady's confrontation with Dionysius — a context which clearly jars with the rest of the surrounding narrative and contrasts markedly with the clearly hostile evidence of the scholion on Aeschines II. 10 which associates the episode with Dionysius' appearance with his bodyguard — it is not unlikely as Sordi suggests, that this narrative is reflective of a passage in Philistus' history which depicted Dionysius most favourably as an avenger and liberator of Himera probably within the context of Dionysius' capture of Himera in 396 BC (Diod. Sic. XIV. 47. 6; cf. XIII. 75. 5; 80. 1; 114. 1) to which Timaeus' fragment constituted a response.[30]

More significant direct comprehension of the basis for Philistus' sympathies towards absolutism can, however, be ascertained by consultation of Plutarch's summation of the main thrust of Philistus' argument in the Περὶ Διονυσίου (*Dion* XXXVI. 2/T. 23a) to the effect that Philistus admired the luxury, wealth and marriage alliances of Dionysius, particularly if we follow these sentiments in detail as reproduced in Diodorus' account of Dionysius' preparations for war in 398 BC (Diod. Sic. XIV. 41-6) — a passage which scholars so correctly observe obviously derives from Philistus, first since Diodorus' data relating to the Syracusan regime's military inventions and constructions bear eloquent testimony to the material prosperity of Dionysius' regime and in the case of the marriage alliance actually contain the material referred to by Plutarch, and secondly because fragment 28 (Theon *Progymn.* II. 68. 17 sp.) of Philistus states specifically that Philistus in Book Eight of his history (i.e. Book I of the Περὶ Διονυσίου) dealt with Dionysius' preparations for war against Carthage, discussing the arms, ships and instruments of war, precisely the topics which are discussed in Diodorus' narrative at this point as well and which, we suggest, were probably regarded by Philistus as evidence of the very prosperity of Dionysius' regime.

Obviously then the pomp, wealth, luxury, power, vitality and sheer inventiveness of Dionysius' regime as expressed in the tyrant's invention of new military and naval weapons and devices of war, the double marriage alliance with the Syracusan Aristomache and the Locrian Doris and above all in Dionysius' cham-

pionship of Western Hellenism against Persian aggression during
the tyrant's first confrontation with Carthage was particularly
representative of Philistus' sophistic ideal of absolutism and
indeed lay at the heart of Philistus' history, though the possibility
that these ideals were summed up at the work's conclusion cannot be excluded.[31] What must be emphasised, however, is that it
was not simply the power of Dionysius' regime by itself but its
very basis which the historian seems to have appreciated and
emphasised in these passages. In the first place, we should note
how Plutarch's statement that Philistus' chief interest was the
luxury, wealth and marriage alliances of Dionysius is comprehensible within the context of the fact that Dionysius' government possessed a clear oligarchic character, being composed of a
new oligarchic element or aristocracy of wealth who either, like
the independently wealthy Philistus, appear to have invested
their inherited wealth in it with the prospect of receiving handsome political and economic dividends (Diod. Sic. XIII. 91. 4/T.
3a) or who, like the poverty-stricken Hipparinus, threw in their
lot with Dionysius in order to rectify their pecuniary embarrassment (Arist. *Polit.* 1306a, 39).[32] The oligarchy, technically called
δυναστεία,[33] from which was drawn Dionysius' cabinet of φίλοι, in
typical oligarchic and tyrannical fashion, were bound to the
tyrant through marriage alliance (Diod. Sic. XIII. 96. 3; XIV. 44;
XV. 7. 4; XVI. 6. 2; Plut. *Dion* VI. 2; XXI. 4-6), whence the significance of Philistus' emphasis upon Dionysius' marriage alliances, noted by Plutarch and reproduced in Diodorus' crucial
Philistus-derived chapters.[34] It would accordingly appear that
what particularly appealed to Philistus was not merely the phenomenon of Dionysius' power but its source of strength as well,
to be found in the support given Dionysius by his governing oligarchy, a class to which incidentally Philistus himself belonged
and of which the historian was indeed the foremost
representative.

Equally significantly, Diodorus' chapters emphasise, on the
one hand, the popular basis of support being given the tyrant as
manifested in the common effort (XIV. 41. 4, 6; 42. 1; 43. 1; 46. 4)
and declaration of war on Carthage (XIV. 46. 5; 47. 1-2) and on
the other, the crucial role of Dionysius in gaining the co-
operation of the *demos*, by his mixing with them, inspiring their
patriotic zeal and persuading them to give of their patriotic best
(XIV. 41. 4, 6; 42. 1; 44. 3; 45. 1-2, 4; 46. 1). It would accordingly
appear that Philistus, as well as appreciating the significance of

the oligarchic character of Dionysius' tyranny and of the support which the oligarchy gave the tyranny, was also cognisant of the important role played by the populace of Syracuse, subject at the same time to the restraints imposed upon it by the tyrant which enabled it to give of its political best.

Thus the emphasis, in Diodorus' chapters describing Dionysius' preparations for war in 398 BC, laid upon the close association of the Syracusan *demos* as a whole with Dionysius, the Pisistratean-democratic nature of Dionysius' tyranny, the wealth of the tyranny enabling the tyrant to spend so lavishly for war, the pomp of the double marriage — all suggest that the despotism's appeal to Philistus derived to a considerable extent from its broad base of support which included the *demos* as well as the new aristocracy of wealth — a sharp contrast, we might add, from the divisive and narrow oligarchical structure favoured by the Platonists. We note further that the full significance of this phenomenon will be appreciated within the context of our later consideration of Philistus' Thucydidean legacy.

While Dionysius' campaign against Carthage in 398-396 BC was obviously treated positively by Philistus, the events which followed, especially the tyrant's wars against the Rhegine bloc in South Italy, we suggest, were regarded with less significance and treated with a more jaundiced eye by the historian, and Philistus' negative attitude towards these ventures, we further suggest, might well have provoked his exile. The source of these sentiments can be found in the data associated with Philistus' exile, for which event we possess two accounts: Diodorus (XV. 7. 3/T. 5b) associating it with the tyrant's madness as a result of his failure at the Olympic games and his attacks on the other literati at his court; Plutarch (*Dion* XI. 4/T. 5c) viewing Philistus' marriage to Leptines' daughter as the cause.[35] While quite clearly, as Diodorus indicates, we have to view Philistus' exile to a certain extent within the context of Dionysius' overall crisis with the literati, following, we have suggested above, the collapse of the peace negotiations between Dionysius and Athens of the late 390s and early 380s, this explanation does not alone totally satisfy, since both Diodorus and Plutarch clearly connect Philistus with Leptines who did not belong to the company of Dionysius' literati, Diodorus by noting, as we have seen, a concurrent brief exile to Thurii and subsequent joint recall to Syracuse for the two men (Diod. Sic. XV. 7. 3) and Plutarch by delineating as a cause of exile, Philistus' marriage to Leptines' daughter (Plut. *Dion* XI.

4). Obviously then Dionysius' suspicion and harsh treatment of Philistus possessed more complex origins, associated in some manner with Philistus' relationship with Leptines. The marriage alliance, of course, as we have seen, is likely to have endangered the complex web of oligarchic alliances which characterised Dionysius' government, paralleling to some extent Philoxenus' rash liaison with the tyrant's mistress Galatea and his publicising of it in the *Cyclops*. And yet we should not necessarily view these events as a palace plot cemented by Philistus' marriage to Leptines' daughter, since, following Gitti, we note that a party alliance should not be equated with an open conspiracy. Moreover, the question still remains: what lay at the basis of the alliance between Leptines and Philistus? Hence such considerations draw us towards the likelihood that common political and ideological sympathies underlie the Philistus-Leptines entente against Dionysius and led ultimately to the marriage alliance. More specifically we suggest in line with Gitti that the rift between Dionysius and his brother in alliance with his chief minister primarily concerned differing views regarding Syracusan conduct towards the Italiot Greeks. Certainly we know that Leptines opposed Dionysius' belligerency towards the Italiots by reconciling Italiots and Lucanians (Diod. Sic. XIV. 102. 3) — an act for which the Italiots accordingly honoured him but which cost him his command since it directly foiled Dionysius' projects of conquest by a policy of 'divide et impera'.[36] Dionysius' acute sensitivity to interference with his Italiot policies is underlined, moreover, by the fact that Heloris, one of the tyrant's φίλοι, after suffering banishment at the hands of Dionysius, immediately in 389 BC moved into the camp of the Italiot opposition against the tyrant (Diod. Sic. XIV. 103. 5). Further, it would be unwise to make light of Leptines' intervention in Dionysius' Italiot war on the grounds of Leptines' adherence to a policy of sentimental philhellenism. His union with Philistus, the practical political animal, considered as we shall see by some authorities as a Thucydidean, negates the viability of such a theory. Moreover, a substantial body of evidence testifies to the wide-ranging character of the rift between Dionysius and Leptines (Diod. Sic. XIV. 59. 7; 60. 2; Aen. Tact. X. 21; Polyaen. VI. 16. 1; Front. *Strat.* II. 5. 11).

The question, however, remains, what evidence do we possess indicating that Philistus shared Leptines' pro-Italiot views? Our evidence is, in fact, threefold: the parallel exile of the two men

and Diodorus', albeit erroneous, view of a common place of exile
for the two men at Thurii and their joint return; the marriage alliance; and finally Philistus' Northern Adriatic policies in the years
immediately preceding his exile, which obviously favoured the
establishment of peaceful relations with Northern Italy by colonisation activity and the construction of hydraulic works — a
policy, moreover, which seems to have been terminated with
Philistus' departure from Syracuse and only revived upon his
return, which not insignificantly coincided with the establishment of two new colonies in Apulia (Diod. Sic. XVI. 5).

Moreover, it is not difficult to conjecture why Philistus would
have been sympathetic to the Italiots and opposed to Dionysius'
imperialism in Magna Graecia, while at the same time supporting his anti-Carthaginian imperialistic ventures, especially as
manifested in 398-396 BC. The period from the late 390s to the
early 370s could certainly be interpreted as years of less substantial success than that which characterised the period immediately preceding, marked as they were by Dionysius' fierce war
in Southern Italy with the hostile Rhegine bloc, the frustrations
which Dionysius met in his attempt to court Athens and win over
the literati at his court in support of his propagandist policies,
and above all the relative failure which characterised Dionysius'
later conflicts with Carthage — that of 394-392 BC involving
Dionysius' loss of Selinus, Gela and Camarina,[37] the third conflict
resulting in the loss of Selinus and Acragas and the payment to
Carthage of an indemnity of 10,000 talents (Diod. Sic. XV. 17. 5).
Thus the only real successes during what can only be termed a
period of serious political failure on Dionysius' part were the
Northern Adriatic colonisation ventures in which Philistus was
probably deeply involved. Obviously then Dionysius' policies
with respect to the Italiots must have been seriously questioned
by the historians who would have concluded that it would have
been better for the tyrant to have concentrated his military power
and hostility upon Carthage, avoiding belligerency with the
Italiots while at the same time espousing a policy involving the
establishment of peaceful relations with the Greeks of Magna
Graecia and colonisation and irrigation ventures which in turn
would provoke economic prosperity in Italy and the establishment of a protectorate against the Illyrians. One can only surmise
that Philistus considered hostilities between Dionysius and
Siceliots and other native elements in Sicily unavoidable within
the context of the tyrant's relations with Carthage, while with

Italiots, he concluded that the circumstances were probably very different, meriting a very different type of approach.

Moreover, we do possess some evidence to suggest that Philistus' disfavour towards Dionysius' hostilities with the Italiots was reflected in the pages of Philistus' history and hence was echoed in Diodorus' narrative of the period following the destruction of the Punic host in 396 BC. In Diodorus, the depiction of the second decade and beginning of the third decade of Dionysius' rule is not only dealt with more summarily — witness the sketchy account of Dionysius' Second Punic War of 394-392 BC (Diod. Sic. XIV. 90. 2-4; 95. 1; 96. 4), a war arguably of greater significance than the previous encounter between Dionysius and Carthage, given the Siceliot-Sicel alliance which it entailed — but we are also confronted with what appears to constitute the first manifestation of open hostility to the tyrant in the depiction of the Italiot and Third Punic Wars. Hence in the description of Dionysius' hostilities with the Italiots, we are introduced to the anecdote pertaining to the Rhegine offer of marriage to Dionysius of the public executioner's daughter (Diod. Sic. XIV. 107. 2-3) and the tyrant's cruelty to Phyton is stressed as an act meriting divine vengeance (Diod. Sic. XIV. 112) — a motif hitherto applied to the Punic foe alone — while in the narrative of the Third Punic War, Leptines' bravery and distinction in combat is highlighted *vis-à-vis* that of his brother — a portrait of Dionysius, contrasting markedly with that found in Diodorus' description of the great war of 398-396 BC (Diod. Sic. XV. 17). Moreover, we note uncharacteristic praise being accorded Carthage in this war — Magon for falling ἀγωνισάμενος λαμπρῶς, his son and successor eulogised for his ambitions and courage, and the Punic army for its competence (Diod. Sic. XV. 15. 3; 16. 2), while the deity, having previously sided with the Siceliots, now changes sides and accords victory to the Barbarians at Cronium (Diod. Sic. XV. 16. 3). Further we note recognition of Punic nobility in that state's bearing success humanely and in willingness to grant Dionysius an opportunity to end the war (Diod. Sic. XV. 17. 5). Finally in the chronologically imprecise twenty-fourth chapter of the fifteenth book, which might either pertain to Dionysius' Third or Fourth Punic War, we observe an uncharacteristic praise of the Punic State for its restoration of Hipponium to its citizens and total absence of the motif of divine retribution accompanying the account of the plague which struck the Punic camp — a depiction in its ethical stance totally at variance with Diodorus' description of the great plague of 396 BC. Now what is noteworthy is that the dating of the Italiot and Second Punic Wars antecedes the date of Philistus' exile which we have ascribed to 384 BC; that there is as we shall see in the following chapter, virtually no manifestation of direct hostility to Dionysius which might be construed as reflective of Timaeus' hostility to be found in Diodorus' text preceding the description of Dionysius' war with the Italiots; and that the data in Diodorus relating to the Italiot and Second Punic Wars might accordingly well derive ultimately from Philistus' pen and reflect, on the one hand, Philistus' pro-Italiot sympathies and, on the other, the historian's disfavour towards Dionysius, as testified by the lack of enthusiasm and insipid depiction of Dionysius' Second Punic War.[38] If, moreover, Diodorus' depiction of the Third Punic War derives ultimately from Philistus — though as we shall see below, this cannot be proved conclusively — it could be conjectured that the hostility of Dionysius which it contains represents a further manifestation of hostility towards the tyrant from the Syracusan historian.

The view which we are presenting of Philistus as a singularly independently-minded individual, willing even to challenge Dionysius in matters pertaining to public policy and echo this bone of contention in the pages of his history appears to be challenged by the evidence of Dionysius of Halicarnassus, Plutarch and Pausanias who all seem to have shared the view that Philistus' slavish mentality rather than any serious reflection on the virtues of totalitarianism *per se* on his part drew the historian to the Syracusan tyrant, Dionysius of Halicarnassus (*Ad Pomp.* IV; Πμίμ., III. 2/T. 16b, 16a) claiming that Philistus displayed a character which was obsequious, subservient, mean and petty, while to Plutarch (*Dion* XI, XXXVI; /T. 5c, 23a) Philistus was the greatest lover of tyrants alive, Pausanias even going further by arguing (I. 13. 9/T. 13a) that because Philistus wanted to be recalled from exile, he left out the worst deeds of the tyrant.[39] Nor have modern historians been impervious to such influences. Hence Columba and Laqueur interpreted Nepos' comment regarding Philistus' attraction towards tyrants in a highly negative light: the former viewing Philistus as a despot's lackey who would just as easily have supported any tyrant and who kept silent about the tyrant's crimes, offering in the Περὶ Διονυσίου an apology for Dionysius' atrocities; the latter assuming that because Timaeus hated tyrants for highly personal reasons, Philistus must have adulated them.[40]

Little confidence can, however, be placed in these assessments for we must be aware of the fact that Dionysius of Halicarnassus, Plutarch and Pausanias lived between three and five centuries after Philistus and hence had access to the vast body of hostile tradition originating in the Athenian Comic theatre and Academy and ultimately enshrined in the popular western history of Timaeus of Tauromenium which, amongst other things as we shall see, systematically distorted Philistus' account of Dionysius and attacked Philistus' reputation with the utmost vigour. Consequently, the real possibility presents itself that, confronted particularly with Timaeus' hostile and distorted portrait of Philistus and his historical work and what appeared to them the strange fact that Philistus, who had by then been popularly regarded as a tyrant's lackey, had portrayed in a favourable light the man who had become through the ages the classic example of the tyrant in the later Greek, and indeed modern, sense of the word, these writers opted for the hostile tradition regarding Dionysius and his retinue and swallowed whole the hostile stance adopted towards Philistus. Certainly evidence for Plutarch's and Dionysius of Halicarnassus' utilisation of the hostile tradition is not lacking. Hence we note how Plutarch (*Dion* XXXVI/F. 154) read Timaeus and accepted much of the hostile testimony (*De Alex. Fort.* II. 5. 338b; *De Garrul.* XIII. 508f; *Dion* III. 3; XI. 3), while Dionysius of Halicarnassus (*Ant. Rom.* XX. 7. 3) seems to be reflecting a hostile source, possibly Timaeus, though as we have seen, very likely Philistus, when he refers to the κάκωσις suffered by the Italiot cities under Dionysius which placed them in a state of constant suffering, being unable to choose whether to join Dionysius or the barbarians.

Since, however, as we have seen, the very basis of the hostile tradition is open to suspicion and, as we shall see, Timaeus' assault upon Philistus' reputation in the Dionysian books was dictated by personal motives, and his account of both Philistus and Dionysius was consequently devoid of all objectivity, and since Plutarch himself warned his readers to avoid adopting *in toto* Timaeus' assessment, advising them to adopt a middle course between excessive adulation of Philistus and vilification of Timaeus (Plut. *Dion* XXXVI. 1/Jacoby, 556. T. 23a; cf. 566. F. 154), obviously the negative evaluations of Philistus delineated by Dionysius of Halicarnassus, Plutarch and Pausanias deserve to be regarded with a good deal of scepticism.

Besides, the evidence which we have cited thus far does not, in fact, indict Philistus as an obsequious lackey of Dionysius. In the first place, a man such as Philistus, wealthy enough to pay the fine inflicted upon Dionysius out of his own pocket at the time of Dionysius' coup and hence deriving from a family of material substance would have been expected to have thrown in his lot with his natural allies, the opponents of Dionysius, were he made of lesser mettle, and not support as he did the opponents of the oligarchs. Moreover, Philistus' firm commitment to tyrannical power both in a practical and theoretical sense renders most unlikely sympathy on Philistus' part towards Dionysius' theoretical aims of establishing a just regime on a par with that enunciated by the great fifth-century tragedians and fourth-century political theorists. Above all, a leader of men in his capacity as navarch and phrourarch who possessed the initiative and daring to persuade Dionysius to seize and later hold on to the tyranny of Syracuse in the face of the most serious internal crisis, who was involved in impressive irrigation and colonisation projects in Northern Italy to the extent of having his name associated with them, a man who was in Gitti's words 'l'artefice della fortuna di Dionisio',[41] and who assumed the leadership of the anti-Plato faction upon the elder Dionysius' demise, does not impress us as a weak, subservient lackey of tyrants but as a forceful director of policy, himself capable of claiming the allegiance of others in most hazardous and complex circumstances. Obviously such an individual, during the period of Dionysius' crisis with his literati, when the very governmental-aristocratic structure was endangered and when Dionysius' policies with regard to Italy as well as Athens were being vigorously assaulted, must have represented a particularly insidious threat to the tyrant and to the stability of his regime, particularly when viewed within the context of Philistus' own successes in Northern Italy and his marriage to Dionysius' niece and hence, as we have seen, have clearly merited in Dionysius' eyes a much lengthier exile than that allotted to Leptines.

It is within the context of our reconstruction of Philistus' political ideals as expressed in the historian's career as well as in the Dionysian history that we can readily appreciate the verdict of later classical writers — Cicero (*Ad Quint. Fratr.* II. 11. 4; *De Orat.* II. 57; *Brut.* LXVI/T. 17a, 17b, 21), Dionysius of Halicarnassus (*Ad Pomp.* IV/T. 16b) and Quintilian (*Instit. Orat.* X. 1. 74/T. 15c) to the effect that Philistus was a Thucydidean.[42] And while many of the epithets employed by these writers to describe Philistus suggest that the comparison rested upon stylistic considerations,[43] Cicero's reference to Philistus as 'doctus et diligens' (*De Div.* I. 39/T. 24) and Dionysius of Halicarnassus' description of the historian (*Ad Pomp.* IV/T. 16b) as mediocre and cheap (μικρός and εὐτελής) suggests that broader comparisons relating to content and including within their sphere political considerations are also involved. That Cicero's favourable estimate of Philistus as a 'pusillus Thucydides' rested very much upon political considerations is, moreover, indicated by that author's emphasis upon the close relationship existing between Philistus and Dionysius[44] and upon the political experience and cunning of Dionysius.[45] Furthermore, the fact that Cicero recommended the Dionysian books to Quintus while on campaign in Gaul and in Caesar's service and while Cicero himself was experimenting with monarchical ideas suggests as we have seen that the work's content, especially the military and political details and its political message appealed strongly to Cicero. And while with respect to Philistus' acceptance of the portents, foreshadowing Dionysius' future greatness (Cic. *De Div.* I. 39; 73/F. 57a, 58), we are certainly inclined to suspect that Philistus abandoned the highest Thucydidean standards of historiography, we should not exaggerate the extent of this departure from Thucydides' precedent and be cognisant of the facts that Thucydides himself presents natural disasters as portents and manifestations of calamitous happenings without finally committing himself to a path of scepticism (Thuc. II. 8. 3; I. 23. 3), that he refers to *tyche* as the unknown in contrast with the known or γνώμη (Thuc. IV. 17. 4; 64. 1; 64. 1; II. 64); and that although he professes the opinion that oracles are often misinterpreted, he does not openly reject their veracity, if correctly interpreted (I. 118. 3; II. 17. 1-2; 21. 3; 47. 4; 54. 1-3; V. 26. 3-4).[46] Finally while it is certainly true that Philistus, by prefacing his 'contemporary' Dionysian history by seven books on early Sicilian history from earliest times to the capture of Acragas in 406 BC (Περὶ Σικελίας) (Diod. Sic. XIII. 103. 3/T. 11), might appear to have again abandoned the strict Thucydidean standards as found in Thucydides' *Archaeology* which stipulated the eschewal of detailed consideration of past history and presentation in its place of fragmentary data (τεκμήρια or σημεῖα) for confirming the present,[47] this apparent lapse into Herodotean practice should also not be exaggerated,[48] since it is clear from the fact that by Book III Gelon was already being discussed (Schol. Pind. *Olymp.* 5. 19c/F. 15) that while the early history of Sicily was telescoped into the first two books of the Περὶ Σικελίας, the period 480-405 BC was contained in Books III to VII, and that of these five Books, the last two actually discussed events of which Philistus was contemporary,[49] while Books IV and V dealt with events of the generation immediately preceding Philistus, knowledge of which Philistus himself could easily have ascertained by oral communication with his elders.[50] Moreover, we may deduce from *PSI* 1283 (Jacoby, *FGH*, vol. 3b, no. 577. F. 2) — probably a genuine fragment of Philistus — that the strength of Philistus' narrative, even in the Περὶ Σικελίας, *vis-à-vis* Thucydides' narrative of parallel events, rested upon superior acquaintance with accurate local political and military data, obviously derived from eyewitness accounts.[51]

We should, of course, not make too much of Dionysius of Halicarnassus' theory that Philistus emulated Thucydides by deliberately leaving his work incomplete (Dion. Halic. Π. μίμ. III. 2/T. 16a). The historian's demise in battle constitutes a perfectly reasonable explanation. Nor should the fact that both Thucydides and Philistus suffered exile be attributed too much importance since exile proved to be an occupational hazard of the most prominent historians of classical antiquity, affecting Theopompus, Ctesias, Timaeus, Polybius and Poseidonius as well as Philistus and Thucydides.[52] Besides, the cause and effects of the two historians' exiles were markedly different. While Thucydides' was due simply to the historian's military incompetence and failure to prevent the capture of Amphipolis (IV. 104. 4; 105. 1; V. 26. 5), Philistus' was, as we have seen, the by-product of profoundly differing political stances on the part of the historian and tyrant and of a general crisis between Dionysius and the literati at his court, provoked by the anti-Syracusan forces centred at Athens. And while, as we have seen, to Philistus, exile imposed severe limits upon the degree to which the historian could present a coherent and fully detailed narrative of the whole of Dionysius' reign, to Thucydides, on the contrary, exile extended considerably the range and variety of source material available for the historical reconstruction which he was attempting (Thuc. V. 26). More to the point though is the fact that while both historians, though emanating from established wealthy families, shunned the company of their natural allies, the oligarchs. Thucydides by eschewing his Philaïd connections[53] and Philistus by opposing, as we have seen, the *Chariestatoi*, they both at the same time, as we shall observe, remained committed to regimes with distinct oligarchic colouring.[54] With regard to the subject matter and thought of the two historical works, moreover, we note that just as to Philistus, the historian's overriding interest was focused upon power, in this particular case, the power of Dionysius' regime as especially manifested during the war with Carthage between 398 and 396 BC, so too Thucydides' history revolved around the subject of the power of Athens.[55] Since to Thucydides, the Athenian empire constituted the final and culminating manifestation of power-growth in the Greek world, it is not inconceivable that a similar evaluation marked Philistus' appraisal of the Syracusan empire under Dionysius, and though we cannot actually prove the point, it is more likely that the theme of a gradually increasing power-growth of Syracuse characterised the Περὶ Σικελίας and that the latter work served accordingly as a prologue to the Περὶ Διονυσίου — in fact in a loose sense as a Thucydidean-type *archaeology* — the penultimate example of power concentration, taking place under Hermocrates in the period of the great Athenian expedition to Sicily, Hermocrates within this context serving as a blueprint for Dionysius.[56] Certainly we note how Dionysius of Halicarnassus (*Ad Pomp.* 5/T. 12) regarded the Περὶ Σικελίας and Περὶ Διονυσίου as a unity. Further, judging by what can be salvaged of Philistus' thought from its ultimate reproduction in Diodorus and from the fragments, a similar evaluation of economic data seems to have characterised the two historians. Thus we have noted how it seems unlikely that Philistus attributed much importance to Dionysius' northern colonisation ventures, despite his own involvement therein. Further, while, on the one hand, the bulk of Diodorus' narrative regarding Dionysius in Books XIII and XIV, like that of Thucydides, pays scant attention to economic phenomena as causative agents in hostilities and views warfare merely in terms of pure power, devoid of an economic base and its resulting tensions created between political leaders and members of states which they represent, as we have seen, particularly from Plutarch's comment (*Dion* XXXVI. 3/T. 23a) with regard to Philistus' admiration for the wealth and luxury of Dionysius' empire and from the crucial chapters in Diodorus describing the preparations of Dionysius for war in 398 BC, Philistus does seem to have emphasised at this point of the narrative which constituted an introduction to the description of the great war of 398-396 BC, the material basis of Dionysius' power, reflecting in a sense the Thucydidean emphasis upon material wealth in the *Archaeology*. What must be emphasised, however, is that in characteristic Thucydidean fashion, Philistus does not appear to have allowed the latter consideration to infiltrate into the bulk of his Dionysian narrative.

Philistus' obsession with power which drew him towards Dionysius, the individual who most epitomised and was the driving force behind the Sicilian concentration of power is similarly reflective of Thucydides' interest in and favour towards tyrants and governments of a tyrannical type. Hence the earlier historian's favourable estimate of Archelaus of Macedon (Thuc. II. 100. 2),[57] his defence of the government of the Pisistratidae as constitutional, and his proposition that the conspiracy of Harmodius and Aristogeiton was due simply to an erotic coincidence (δι'ἐρωτικὴν ξυντυχίαν) rather than to an oppressive government (Thuc. VI. 54-60),[58] and above all the historian's obviously positive depiction of the tyrannical or monarchical Pericles as the first man, the most powerful of those leading the state, less led by the people than leading them, ruling a city which is nominally a democracy but is in reality the rule by the first man (Thuc. I. 127. 3; 140. 1, II. 22. 1; 34. 8; 60; 65), a man who can declare unhesitatingly with respect to the Athenian empire (II. 63. 2) ὡς τυραννίδα γὰρ ἤδη ἔχετε αὐτήν..., which Gomme is surely correct to translate, 'it is now like a tyranny, which we know it is a crime in popular opinion to seize but which it is very dangerous to let go.'[59] And lest it be asserted that Thucydides' estimation of the Periclean regime as tyrannical is reflective more of the historian's own highly personal estimate than of historical reality[60] and that no valid comparison between the Athens of Pericles and the Syracuse of Dionysius can be effected,[61] in support of the Thucydidean thesis, we retort, that Athenian politics from 460 to 429 and particularly from 446 onwards, following the expulsion of Thucydides the son of Melesias, were directed by one man whose hand could be seen behind the election of generals except at moments of crisis, whose position as general, in fact, clearly anticipated that of the later *strategos autokrator*, an individual, moreover, who by his wealth, popularity and pride and association with intellectuals, foreigners and strange women clearly conjured up before the Athenians a Pisistratean image but who by virtue of his sheer ability, command of speech and persuasive powers could effectively mask his tyrannical hold — a man, in short, in Ehrenberg's phraseology whose *auctoritas* was greater than his *potestas*.[62] It is such a phenomenon which renders comprehensible Spartan emphasis upon the Alcmaeonid curse on the eve of the Peloponnesian War (Thuc. I. 127. 1), the contemporary equation of Pericles with the tyrannical Zeus in Cratinus' *Cheirones* (F. 241) and *Ploutoi* and Plutarch's attempt in the *Pericles* to evaluate Pericles' monarchical position,[63] all of which evidence renders plausible the modern theses maintaining that tension between the Athenian democratic tradition and the figure of the tyrant Pericles underlines both Sophocles' *Oedipus Tyrannus* and *Antigone*[64] as well as Herodotus' comments on tyranny in the famous debate of the Persian grandees following the overthrow of the Magi (III. 80-2).[65]

We should, of course, expect that Thucydides with his totalitarian sympathies, within the context of his discussion of Sicilian history, would view favourably Hermocrates the Syracusan, the most prominent Western Greek politician flourishing during the period of the Peloponnesian War who, according to Diodorus' testimony, was distrusted by the Syracusan populace for his tyrannical aspirations and who ultimately proved correct the reality of these fears by actually attempting to seize the tyranny of Syracuse (Diod. Sic. XIII. 75. 5-9) — an occurrence about which Thucydides was undoubtedly well informed, whence the reference to τυραννίδας δὲ ἔστιν ὅτε (VI. 38. 3). In fact to Thucydides, Hermocrates' position within the Greek world was second only to that held by Pericles.[66] We should not, however, be misled into accepting as a total and well-rounded portrait, Thucydides' depiction of Hermocrates, particularly in the speech at Gela in 424 BC and in the altercation with Athenagoras (IV. 59-64; VI. 33-34; cf. VI. 36-40) as a figure of courage, enlightenment, integrity and principles who, unlike the Cleon-type Athenagoras, betrayed no interest in gratifying the mob and who obviously at the same time did function within a democratic state (Thuc. VI. 20. 3; VII. 55. 2; VIII. 96. 5) and indeed be aware that Thucydides' sympathy for Hermocrates sprang from his innate sympathy for politicians with distinct totalitarian traits.[67] Hence in support of our contention, we note in Thucydides, Hermocrates' advocacy of the reform reducing the Syracusan high command to three generals with absolute powers and the negligible obscurity which characterised Heracleides and Sicanus, Hermocrates' two colleagues (Thuc. VI. 72-5; 96. 3),[68] the accusation launched against Hermocrates and his followers by Athenagoras as seekers of office before legal age (Thuc. VI. 38. 5); the reference to the ever-present distrust towards Hermocrates (ὀλίγον δ'ἦν τὸ πιστεῦον τῷ

Ἑρμοκράτει) contrasted with the description of Athenagoras as popular leader (δήμου τε προστάτης) (Thuc. VI. 35. 1); and finally the ultimate deposition of Hermocrates and his colleagues which significantly was not accompanied by the overthrow of Hermocrates' reform measures — evidence surely of a very real confidence in the reforms on the part of the people coupled with their most real distrust of Hermocrates himself (Thuc. VI. 103. 4).[69]

Thucydides' sympathy towards an individual of such pronounced despotic inclinations as Hermocrates, moreover, gains particular significance when viewed within the context of the parallel paths taken by Hermocrates and Dionysius, who was Hermocrates' follower (Diod. Sic. XIII. 75. 9), in pursuance of their political aims, evidence which in turn serves to render Philistus' Περὶ Διονυσίου a Thucydidean work in a most precise thematic sense. In the first place we should note how surprisingly similar the rise to power of the two men was: Hermocrates' reforms limiting the number of generals to three amongst whom Hermocrates ruled supreme, paralleling closely Dionysius' replacement of the generals by a new board of generals including his own person, followed by the total elimination of his new colleagues and Dionysius' appointment as *strategos autokrator* (Diod. Sic. XIII. 94. 5). Dionysius' championship of Siceliot nationalism against Carthage, particularly in the war of 398-396 BC may, moreover, be compared with Hermocrates' 'patriotic' incursions into Punic territory and championship of the bones of Himera (Diod. Sic. XIII. 63, 75). Nor should we forget that the exiles for whose return Dionysius pressed (Diod. Sic. XIII. 92. 4-7) were originally the followers of Hermocrates and that they aided in the establishment of the despotate of Dionysius. Finally lest we utilise Athenagoras' attack upon Hermocrates and the young aristocrats to distinguish what might appear to be aristocratically-inclined Hermocrates from Dionysius the opponent of the *Chariestatoi* (Diod. Sic. XIII. 91. 4), we should note that the subsequent murder of Dionysius' wife, Hermocrates' daughter, by the oligarchs (Diod. Sic. XIII. 112. 4) suggests that the links between Hermocrates and the aristocrats were hardly close and that whatever tenuous connections prevailed during the period of the Athenian invasion were probably severed immediately preceding Hermocrates' demise. Moreover, as we shall see, Dionysius' opposition to the *Chariestatoi* did not preclude his support of a new aristocracy.

In two further respects, the theses on imperialism entertained by both Thucydides and Philistus seem identical. In the first place, for all their interest in power and the process of its growth, both historians clearly distinguished between what they conceived of as practical and justified imperialistic acts and what appeared to them as less practical and consequently unwarranted ventures. Thus while as we have seen to Philistus, Syracusan military imperialism within a Punic and Sicilian context was more than justified, no such recommendation was forthcoming from the historian with respect to the hostilities waged by Dionysius with the Italiots. Quite clearly Philistus, a direct participator in Dionysius' Northern Adriatic ventures, favouring peaceful means of maintaining suzerainty in Italy aimed at promoting economic prosperity and a protectorate against the hostile Illyrians, regarded Dionysius' belligerency in Southern Italy in a less positive light since it negated both the spirit implied by the northern ventures in which Philistus played a major role and perhaps more importantly in a practical sense weakened the basic military potential of the Syracusan state by diverting from it forces which should rightly have been concentrated upon the narrower and more specific area of Sicily and directed against the Punic foe — hence particularly, Dionysius' failures in the Second and Third Punic Wars. Such sentiments undoubtedly echo in a broad sense Thucydides sober reflections on the virtues of Periclean limitations of imperialistic ventures, above all with respect to acquisition of a sea rather than a land empire (Thuc. I. 144. 1; II. 65. 7; IV. 17. 4; 21. 2; VI. 24. 4; 31. 6; VII. 75. 7)[70] and that historian's condemnation of the ambitious demagogues of the post-Periclean era, epitomised by the pre-eminent Cleon (Thuc. V. 43. 2; VI. 15. 2; III. 36. 3; 45. 4; IV. 39. 3; cf. II. 60. 5; 65. 5; III. 82. 2).[71] Consequently we suggest that what appeared in Thucydides as the imperialistic ambitions of post-Periclean Athens,[72] in Philistus' Dionysian history took the form of a condemnation of post-396 BC Syracusan policies. It should be added that the fact that both Thucydides and Philistus suffered the disgrace of exile precisely at the time that policies which were regarded unfavourably by them were being pursued by the states upon which they focused their attention may be no more than coincidental but certainly constitutes a phenomenon which might well have strengthened in the eyes of some the Thucydidean connection of Philistus.

No less significantly, Philistus' favourable estimate of what the historian conceived to be the broad base of support, giving strength to Dionysius' tyranny and embracing within its sphere both the oligarchic wealthy elements who, tied to Dionysius by financial benefits, marriage alliances and administrative and political roles, constituted the government and the *demos* whose role in the state was a positive one, albeit distinctly controlled by the tyrant, seems to echo political and constitutional ideals found in Thucydides' history, especially with regard to Periclean Athens. Thus we note how the earlier historian seems to favour a very limited democracy where the *demos* can most definitely express itself politically and constitutionally but where real power appears to reside in the hands of an oligarchy at whose head stands a *princeps*, Pericles himself. Hence we observe with respect to the *demos*' real but limited role the importance played upon the restraining hand of a Pericles (Thuc. II. 65. 2) which can even prevent the summoning of the *ecclesia* (Thuc. II. 22. 1) and which is contrasted with the processes of corruption, violence, unreason and cynicism under the demagogues (Thuc. III. 40. 5, 7; 39. 6; 38. 3-7; 37. 1-5).[73] We also note how, in the *Epitaphios* (II. 35-46), far from being the document *par excellence*, testifying to Thucydides' pro-democratic stance, emphasis is placed not upon constitutional details but upon Athens' cultural pre-eminence and the moderation of her laws — both features quite easily identifiable with a Periclean aristocratically-dominated state. In fact the precise wording which we find in the *Epitaphios* is more applicable to an aristocratically-governed state and hence suggestive of Thucydides' favour to this aspect of the Athenian state: the emphasis placed upon the state's uniqueness recalling Xenophon's praise of Sparta and Aelius Aristeides' of Rome; the contrast of ... δέ implied by ὄνομα μέν, implying in turn that the Athenian democracy was a democracy in name alone; the reference to ἰσονομία as equality in private disputes contrasted with the oligarchic qualification of *arete* in public office; and finally the lack of reference to the central democratic principle of sortition.[74] Other evidence of Thucydides' pro-aristocratic stance is extensive: the historian's favour towards the oligarchs Phrynichus (VIII. 27) and Antiphon (VIII. 68. 1) as well as towards Theramenes (VIII. 68. 4) whose Constitution of Five Thousand with its abolition of pay for office holders and restriction of the franchise to five thousand citizens suitably endowed with property, was in fact more of an oligarchy than the moderate democracy it is often claimed to have been; and finally Thucydides' favourable estimate of Hermocrates who was denounced so decisively by the democrat

Athenagoras for identifying himself with those possessing pro-oligarchic leanings (Thuc. VI. 36-9). Finally, it is surely not insignificant and hence suggestive of Thucydides' favour towards oligarchically run states where the voice of the *demos* is distinct but limited, that Thucydides in the course of his digression on the Pisistratidae (VI. 54-60) whose government he favoured, should emphasise that the only respect in which the government was unconstitutional was the tendency of the tyrants to keep their own men in office (VI. 54. 6). Now since we know that under the Pisistratidae, the archonship was actually filled by men of aristocratic origin, it would seem that what particularly appealed to Thucydides in the Pisistratid tyranny, apart from the tyrannical or monarchical position of the Pisistratidae themselves was, on the one hand, its utilisation of the aristocracy, albeit as instruments of the tyranny in an executive and probouleutic capacity, as archons and areopagites, and, on the other hand, its non-interference with the traditional organs of government — the Areopagus council, archonship, and, perhaps more importantly, the *ecclesia* and *heliaea* where the popular voice expressed itself in a limited form.

We can accordingly readily appreciate why later writers considered Philistus a Thucydidean. Parallels abound: the two historians' exile and criticism of the policies of regimes which caused their exiles; their paradoxical opposition and favour towards oligarchical regimes in the states upon which they concentrated their attention; the common emphasis placed upon power concentration as expressed in military and political activity; both historians' awareness of the economic basis of power coupled with their refusal to consider adequately this factor within the overall political and military framework; the overwhelming emphasis of the two historians upon contemporary history as opposed to history of the distant past; the common attraction towards individuals with a distinctly tyrannical bent; Thucydides' particular interest in Hermocrates the Syracusan, Dionysius' former leader who anticipated Dionysius in entertaining the possibility of seizing the Syracusan tyranny and whose policies Dionysius emulated closely; both historians' convictions with regards to the necessity of restraints being applied to imperialistic ventures in order to ensure military and political concentration upon a clearly defined and reasonable objective; above all, the common sympathy manifested by the two historians towards regimes where an aristocracy was involved in the actual tasks of government while the participation of the *demos*, albeit concrete, was distinctly controlled.

From what has been heretofore discussed, two further conclusions may be derived. First we can readily appreciate why Plato and Philistus assumed diametrically opposed political stances and in the process confirm our conclusion of the previous chapter to the effect that the crux of the dispute between Plato and Dionysius I on an intellectual and theoretical level did not concern the issue of the acceptance or rejection of despotism as such, but rather that pertaining to the particular character which despotism in the eyes of Plato and Dionysius should assume at Syracuse. Obviously Philistus' Thucydidean promotion of a definite, albeit limited, constitutional role for the *demos* and Dionysius' effecting of this policy concretely would hardly have appealed to Plato who in the *Republic* (VI. 494a) banished the *demos* allegedly because of its inability to become philosophical as an effective political force from his ideal state and for whom in the same work, the demagogic tyrant, rising to power with the support of the masses (VIII. 565ff), as we have seen, clearly reflective of Dionysius' rise to power, was anathema. Moreover, as we have seen, Plato's disfavour towards Syracusan and Siceliot hedonism in the *Seventh Letter* (326b-327b) suggests quite clearly that what merited Plato's disfavour in the Syracusan regime of Dionysius was its very liberality or democratic character which we have seen proved particularly amenable to Philistus. As for Dionysius' support for a new oligarchy of wealth which included Philistus and rejection of the old oligarchy of *Chariestatoi*, this too could obviously have alarmed a scion of the old Athenian aristocracy such as Plato for whom an oligarchy of wealth marked a distinct deterioration from one of birth and whose ruling element in the *Republic* (III. 416. E-417A) was obliged to surrender all economic interests to the apolitical acquisitive third social class of inferior mettle.

Finally, given the real but limited power of the *demos* which contrasted so noticeably with the more concrete administrative and political role of the aristocracy prevalent at Syracuse which Philistus favoured and depicted positively in his Dionysian history, we can easily comprehend that Cicero's interest in the Περὶ Διονυσίου derived not simply from the depiction of despotism which that work contained but from broader considerations as well relating to the precise social character of the Syracusan regime under Dionysius. Cicero, after all, favoured a mixed constitution (*De Rep.* I. 45; 69; II. 41; 65), where the role of the populace was heavily curtailed[75] and where, despite the guiding hand of the *princeps*, real power lay in the hands of the aristocracy. The aristocracy of the Ciceronian ideal, moreover had to incorporate into its midst men of wealth, stemming from the equestrian order (*Ad Attic.* I. 14. 1; 16. 6) — men, in fact, who closely resembled Cicero himself, for whom Philistus and Hipparinus as well as other φίλοι of Dionysius might well have appeared as distinct prototypes. Finally Philistus' Italian connections and resulting sympathy for the Italiots might equally well have foreshadowed in Cicero's eyes, Cicero's own favourable stance towards Italy (*Philip.* VII. 23; *Pro Sestio* XVI. 36; *Ad Quint. Fratr.* I. 2. 16; *Ad Attic.* IV. 1; *Ad Fam.* I. 9. 16) whence many of the newly incorporated aristocrats hailed.[76]

III

In contrast with Philistus' Περὶ Διονυσίου, Ephorus' account of Dionysius I can hardly be regarded as a contemporary work, even though its composition followed Dionysius' death by scarcely two decades. At the same time, the seriousness of this deficiency should not be overstressed since Isocrates' direct relationship with Dionysius renders it most probable that Isocrates' pupil had access to material which he had received personally from Isocrates himself. More significant is the fact that the value of the material contained in Ephorus' account can hardly be compared with that which was found in Philistus' history since it was not derived as was Philistus' from the pen of a close associate and collaborator of Dionysius' tyranny. Nor is it probable that a pupil of Isocrates would have found appealing and hence availed himself of data contained in the *oeuvre* of a Thucydidean historian like Philistus, despite the favour of Ephorus towards Philistus (Plut. *Dion* XXXVI. 2/F. 220), Ephorus' utilisation of Philistus for the former historian's account of Daedalus' flight to King Kokalos (Theon. *Progymn.* II. p. 66, 26 sp./F. 57) and the likely use of Philistus' account of the Athenian expedition to Sicily by Ephorus.[77] Two distinct limitations would, in fact, have characterised Philistus' worth in Ephorus' eyes: its lack of interest in moral evaluations of its central character and its pre-eminent concern with the period 405-396 BC and resulting lack of interest in the later period of Dionysius' role when the tyrant sought to assume a more universal role in Greek affairs and forge links with the states of the Greek mainland, especially with Athens and its pro-Dionysian element, pre-eminent amongst whom was Ephorus' mentor Isocrates.

That Ephorus did not utilise Philistus' Περὶ Διονυσίου is clearly indicated by his error in detail in referring to the Syracusan suburb of Tyche as an island (Steph. Byz. *s.v.* 'τύχη'/F. 66; cf. Diod. Sic. XI. 68. 1; Cic. *Verr.* IV. 119) — an error unlikely to have stemmed from an accurate and local source like Philistus, as we have seen a Thucydidean to wit — and by the fact that Ephorus' figures for Punic forces in Books XIII and XIV of Diodorus diverge dramatically from those supplied by Timaeus (Diod. Sic. XIII. 54. 5; 60. 5; 80. 5; XIV. 54. 5/Jacoby, *FGH*, vol. 3b, no. 566. F. 103, 104, 25, 108; vol. 2a, no. 70, F. 201, 202, 203, 204) — a historian who we shall see quite clearly utilised Philistus' account and hence was here reproducing Philistus' figures.[78] Also pertinent is a distinct divergence of viewpoint between Ephorus and Diodorus who, we shall see, seems to have used Philistus either directly or, as scholarly consensus suggests, indirectly via Timaeus with respect to the date of the inauguration of Dionysius' tyranny, Diodorus dating it to 406 BC (XIII. 96. 4) and Ephorus (F. 218/Polyb. XII. 42. 3) to 410-409 or possibly to 408-407 BC in agreement with the *Marmor Parium* (Jacoby, *FGH*, vol. 2b, 239A, 62).[79] The unlikelihood of Ephorus' use of Philistus is further suggested by the facts that whereas Philistus, as we have seen, spent four books discussing Dionysius, Ephorus seems to have spent only two on the tyrant.[80] Hence we note how Entella which was given to the Campanian allies of Dionysius in 403 BC and later, after these Campanians had rejoined Carthage, was attacked and destroyed by Dionysius (Diod. Sic. XIV. 9. 9; 48. 5; 53. 5), is associated in fragment 68 (= Steph. Byz. *s.v.* "Ἔντελλα') with Book Sixteen of Ephorus' history, while references to Pharos, Dionysius' colony of 385 BC (Diod. Sic. XV. 13. 4; 14. 2) and to the city Herbita which was attacked by Dionysius in 403 BC (Diod. Sic. XIV. 15-16) are attributed to Book Twenty-eight (Steph. Byz. *s.vv.* 'Φάρος, Ἔρβιτα'/F. 89, 91).[81] We should also note that since Ephorus' sixteenth book followed the discussion of the Peloponnesian War in Books Thirteen to Fifteen, it is likely that the description of the two Punic invasions of Sicily of the last decade of the fifth century BC as well as Dionysius' reign, were contained in Book Sixteen. This contrasts markedly with Philistus' decision to devote a whole book of the Περὶ Σικελίας,

Book VII, to a description of these same events, while the events following the capture of Acragas and centring around Dionysius' rise to power were placed quite logically in the first book of the Περὶ Διονυσίου or Book VIII of the total *oeuvre*.[82]

In view of the likely association of the events of 410-409 BC and 406-405 BC with the first Dionysian book of Ephorus and the fact that two books were devoted to Dionysius, it is further logical to conclude that the chief theme of Ephorus' sixteenth book was Punic-Siceliot hostilities leading up to and including Dionysius' reign — the most important phase of which came to an end in 392 BC. Henceforth Dionysius' interests were centred as much upon his war with Rhegium in South Italy, his Northern Adriatic colonisation projects and moves against the Illyrians and his attempts to forge firm links with mainland Greece, as with hostilities with Carthage — events fully meriting equal space to the earlier period contained in Book Sixteen and hence probably contained in Book Twenty-eight. That the year 392 BC constituted the dividing line between the two Dionysian books of Ephorus' history is, moreover, confirmed by the fact that, as we shall see,[83] Theopompus' account of Dionysius' reign in his *Philippica* also appears to have begun in 392 BC. Finally in favour of the view that as much space was devoted to the post-392 BC period as to the pre-392 BC period in Ephorus' history, we should note that it is also likely that Ephorus, with his universalistic approach derived from Isocrates, would pay much more attention to the later phase of Dionysius' career than Philistus — a period, after all, during which Dionysius attempted to play a greater role than before in the affairs of mainland Greece and when he was in direct contact with a party whose most prominent spokesman was Ephorus' teacher, Isocrates himself.

On the basis of these considerations we conclude that Ephorus' data on Dionysius, though more equally spread over the whole of Dionysius' reign, covered in far less detail than Philistus the early years of Dionysius' reign leading up to and including the great encounter with Carthage in 398-396 BC. More specifically we suggest that the details concerning Dionysius' preparations for war, the siege of Motya and the destruction of the Punic host contained in Diodorus' narrative, which we have suggested derived ultimately from Philistus, is unlikely to have occupied as important a place in Ephorus' as in Philistus' history. Less detail, we moreover suggest, implies less factual accuracy to the extent, for example, that Ephorus might well have followed his mentor Isocrates (*Archid.* VI. 44) in inaccurately placing Heloris' notorious comment to Dionysius, pertaining to the meritoriousness of dying clad in the robes of tyranny within the context of Dionysius' struggle with Carthage rather than within that of Syracusan *stasis*.[84] We further suggest that Ephorus' second Dionysian book dealt with Dionysius' later career in more detail than Philistus, since a pupil of Isocrates who was in contact with Dionysius is likely to have possessed more information for this period than Philistus who was forced to endure exile and hence be deprived of valuable information which would have enabled the historian to formulate a coherent and full narrative of the later part of Dionysius' reign.[85] A further conclusion which follows is that, while the bulk of Philistus' narrative emphasised Dionysius' achievements within a Siceliot context, it is likely, given Ephorus' probable emphasis upon Dionysius' attempts to forge close links with mainland Greece, Ephorus' general Isocratean-derived interest in universal Greek history and Isocrates' favour towards various political alternatives during the course of his lengthy career, that Ephorus' narrative stressed Dionysius political and military achievement within a wider Hellenic panorama than within a narrowly Sicilian context. Such a Panhellenic line of thought is likely to have permeated both the narrative of Dionysius' Punic War, and the campaign in Southern Italy and possibly even that of the tyrant's Northern Adriatic ventures. Consequently the negative tone found in Diodorus' description of the events after 396 BC, echoing we have suggested Philistus, is unlikely to have been prevalent in Ephorus' narrative at all. The details of this application of a universalistic approach on Ephorus' part to Dionysius' reign can for want of substantial detailed evidence only be surmised. We should expect to discover in Ephorus' sixteenth and twenty-eighth books an emphasis on Europe as opposed to Asia, which seems to have appeared in Ephorus' narrative of the events of mainland Greece in the fourth century BC.[86] One purpose of Ephorus' inflated figures of barbarian troops in contrast with those of Timaeus' derived from Philistus, moreover, was probably to emphasise the magnitude of the forces aligned against the Siceliots and hence magnify the Siceliot achievement and indeed, in fact, convert a Siceliot success into a universal Greek one. Finally, despite fragment 211 (Schol. Aristeid. p. 294, 13, Dindorf) which discusses the imperialistic schemes of Dionysius II and the Great King against the Greeks, we should not be wrong to conclude that Ephorus' account was marked by distinct favour towards Dionysius. Certainly, since Ephorus lived before the full development of the hostile tradition with respect to Dionysius and was sympathetic to the Siceliots in the face of overwhelming forces threatening them and since Isocrates throughout most of his life was sympathetic towards Dionysius, we can surmise that Ephorus would have been sympathetic towards Dionysius, the champion of the Syracusans against Carthage. A moderate form of favour towards Dionysius on Ephorus' part is, moreover, suggested by Ephorus' favourable attitude towards Philistus in contrast with Timaeus who attacked the Syracusan historian (Plut. *Dion* XXXVI. 2/F. 220). What form Ephorus' favour towards Dionysius took can only be guessed and though he might well have praised in typical Isocratean manner Dionysius' personal qualities, just as he praised those of his other historically important personages,[87] all that can be categorically stated is that praise was probably accorded Dionysius' successes against Carthage and the Italiots, which resulted in the creation of a great power bloc which attracted itself to Isocrates in the course of his search for a champion of Hellenism against Persia. Further, given Isocrates' distinct favour towards monarchically or aristocratically governed states and his relative lack of enthusiasm towards democratically guided republics,[88] it is unlikely that any favour towards, or interest in, the clear democratic basis of Dionysius' power such as Philistus favoured and described was to be found in Ephorus' history. Finally in view of Ephorus' likely detailed and sympathetic treatment of Dionysius' attempt to establish closer relations with mainland Greece and Isocrates' and Ephorus' likely favour towards the maxims contained in Dionysius' propaganda policies, it is logical to conclude that Ephorus' serious consideration of, and favour towards, these policies was echoed in the pages of his history.

IV

Theopompus' treatment of Dionysius I in the *Philippica*, like Ephorus' Dionysian material, can hardly be viewed as a contemporary testimony, though as in the case of Ephorus, it is most probable that the work of a pupil of Isocrates contained within its pages a fair amount of contemporary Isocratean data. Theopompus' account, however, is likely to have been much fuller than Ephorus', since Theopompus was the much more arduous researcher of the two historians, particularly in the field of Western affairs. Indeed the three or three-and-a-half books of the Sicilian excursus in the *Philippica*, Books Thirty-nine to Forty-one or to the beginning of Book Forty-two (Diod. Sic. XVI. 71. 3/F. 184), following significantly an account of Macedonian operations in Epirus (Steph. Byz. *s.v.* 'Αἰθικια'/F. 183) were part of a broader digression on Western history, their being followed in turn by close to two further books, Books Forty-two to Forty-three, which discussed Western affairs from a broader perspective, including within their confines, from the point of view of Greek historiography, a quite unique detailed discussion of Punic affairs, which was probably utilised by Trogus Pompeius in the nineteenth and twentieth books of his own *Philippica*.[89] At the same time, despite Photius' conjecture that Theopompus attacked Philistus (F. 25/Phot. *Bibl.* 176. p. 120b. 30), like Ephorus, Theopompus, not merely because of his probable Isocratean disfavour towards the Thucydidean characteristics of Philistus' history, is unlikely to have utilised Philistus' full account directly;[90] for in the first place only three books of the *Philippica*, or at the most three-and-a-half, discussed Dionysius, as opposed to Philistus' four books (Diod. Sic. XVI. 71. 3/F. 184) and there is no direct evidence to prove that the *Hellenica* contained any Dionysian material at all.[91] More significant is the fact that the Sicilian excursus in the *Philippica* does not appear to have discussed the whole of Dionysius' reign and the part which it does seem to have covered was precisely that which seems to have been most summarily perused in Philistus' Περὶ Διονυσίου. This certainly seems to be implied by Diodorus' notice (XVI. 71. 3/F. 184) to the effect that the excursus covered a fifty-year period from the beginning of the tyranny of Dionysius to the expulsion of the younger Dionysius; for since this time span from 405 to 343 BC is actually a sixty-year period, it is more likely that the excursus began in 392 BC — a particularly appropriate point of time since it witnessed the completion of Dionysius' intensive period of hostilities with Carthage and the establishment of Dionysius' empire and in Ephorus' scheme constituted the dividing line between the two Dionysian books.[92] Further, Dionysius' endeavours to play a major Panhellenic role and establish contact with a party whose most notable representative was Theopompus' mentor, Isocrates, enables us to appreciate only too well, as in the case of Ephorus, why the later phase of

Dionysius' career was so appealing to a universal Isocratean historian like Theopompus. Finally, the unlikelihood of Theopompus' utilisation of Philistus is suggested by the fact that Theopompus' excursus in the *Philippica* does not seem to have been essentially concerned with Dionysius I but with Dionysius II. Hence we note how despite the fact that Dionysius' reign covered three-fifths of the excursus period, only two fragments (Athen. X. 47. p. 436a, b/F. 186, 187) which belong to the Sicilian books mention Dionysius and they merely note the fact that he was the father of Hipparinus and Nysaeus. The remaining fragments, moreover, refer to events which took place under Dionysius II and not under the elder Dionysius. Thus one fragment from Book XXXIX refers to the intemperance of Apollocrates, the eldest son of Dionysius II and his estrangement from his father (Athen. X. 47. p. 435f-436a/F. 185). Since Dionysius II was born after 398 BC (Diod. Sic. XIV. 44. 6-7), it is clear that Apollocrates belonged to the generation which flourished after Dionysius I's death. We should also observe that fragments 192 and 194 (Athen. XII, 51. p. 536b-c, Steph. Byz. *s.v.* 'Δύμη') refer to events occurring in Book Forty, after Dionysius II's withdrawal and that by Book Thirty-nine, the first book of the excursus, the reign of Dionysius II appears already to have been discussed (F. 185/Athen. X. 47. p. 435f-436a). Further it does seem significant and suggestive again of the fact that the Elder Dionysius was not Theopompus' chief interest in the *Philippica* that the one fragment which we possess concerning Dionysius I directly, which attacks Dionysius for promoting luxury and debauchery (F. 134/Athen. VI. 77. p. 261a-b), should stem from Book Twenty-one and from a section which contained a general attack upon Greek tyrants, including Pisistratus (F. 135, 136/Athen. XII. 44. p. 532f-533a; Harp. Sud. s.v. 'Λύκειον'), while no mention is made of an attack upon Dionysius deriving from the Sicilian excursus, despite the fact that Athenaeus, the source of this quotation, was perfectly well acquainted with the excursus of Books Thirty-nine to Forty-one (F. 185-188, 192, 193/Athen. X. 47. p. 435f-436a; X. 47. p. 436a; X. 47. p. 436a-b; X. 47. p. 435e-f; XII. 51. p. 536b-c; VI. 20. p. 231e-232b). Finally, the fact that a notice pertaining to Dionysius' establishment of Adria (F. 128C/ Schol. Lycophr. 631) derives from the twenty-first book of the *Philippica* which discusses countries on the Adriatic seaboard and not from the Sicilian excursus, suggests at the very least minimum coverage of Dionysius' Adriatic colonisation ventures and more probably no coverage at all in the Sicilian excursus. Clearly then Dionysius himself was not the central interest of Theopompus in his Sicilian excursus, even though the chronological span technically allotted to this section would initially suggest that this was in fact not the case.

On the contrary, the terminal date of 343 BC attributed to the excursus suggests that Theopompus' chief theme in the Sicilian excursus seems to have been the collapse of the empire of Dionysius I rather than a consideration of the career of Dionysius I as a whole. The evidence for this phenomenon appears to have been found in the dissolute character of Dionysius II; for the latter's moral failings appear to have been emphasised in this section of the *Philippica*. Hence we note that the excursus was Athenaeus' source for gossip regarding the reign of Dionysius II (Athen. X. 435a-436b/F. 185-188, 283) and that Aelian (*VH* VI. 12), who significantly quotes the same story as Athenaeus (X. 47. p. 435d) from Theopompus regarding Dionysius II's infirmity of the eyes, caused by excessive drinking (F. 283a, b), like Theopompus attributed the collapse of Dionysius II's empire to the instability of temperament and violence which reduced Dionysius to a life of abject poverty. It is also noteworthy that Trogus Pompeius whose use of Theopompus is illustrated by the very title of his work, the *Philippica*, the lack of hostility to Dionysius I, placement of Sicilian affairs within a wider Western context (Justin. XIX-XX) and finally utilisation of the story attributing Dionysius II's blindness to excessive indulgence, though not specifically to drunkenness (Just. XXI. 2. 1; cf. Aelian *VH* VI. 12), essentially concentrates his attention upon the dissolute career of Dionysius II (Just. XXI. 2-3; 5).[93] The data found in the Sicilian excursus from a thematic standpoint accordingly corresponded closely to that found in other sections of the *Philippica* and focused attention upon a central thesis of Theopompus' work, which above all was applied to the central figure of the work, Philip II, namely the negative effect which immoral behaviour exerted upon political success.[94]

Since Theopompus concentrated his hostility upon the younger Dionysius, it would appear that his attitude towards Dionysius I was not basically unfavourable. That this was, in fact, the case is proved by fragment 134 where Dionysius was not attacked for his own personal moral deficiencies but for his encouragement of dissoluteness in others. In the light of Dionysius of Halicarnassus' remarks (*Ad Pomp.* VI/T. 20) on the thoroughness of Theopompus's research into the moral failings of the chief figures of his histories, it would appear that the historian did not discover a great deal of negative evidence relating to Dionysius I.[95] It would, moreover, be expected that a pupil of Isocrates who we also know was unfavourable to Plato (Athen. XI. 118, p. 508c-d; Arrian, *Epict. Diss.* II. 17. 5-6/F. 259, 275) would provide a positive portrait of Dionysius whose relationship with the philosopher could hardly be described as a happy one, ultimately providing the grotesque portrait of tyranny in the eighth book of the *Republic* (VIII. 565ff). Only in one respect, as we have seen, do Plato and Theopompus seem to have agreed in their assessments of Dionysius' tyranny. Both viewed with acute disfavour what they interpreted as a too liberal or democratic form of government prevailing at Syracuse — precisely the characteristic which the Thucydidean Philistus seems to have found most appealing, since it proved to be a fundamental source of strength to the Syracusan tyranny.

Finally, in order to comprehend what Theopompus' attack upon the moral deficiencies of Dionysius II implied, we reiterate our earlier observation with respect to fragment 134 relating to Dionysius I's promotion of vice in others, that in Theopompus' and indeed Plato's terminology, moral deficiency denoted democratic weakness. Consequently we conclude that Theopompus' chief objection to Dionysius II lay in the fact that he was infected by the democratic vices which his father, the elder Dionysius, though personally immune to himself, had provoked in his subjects.

V

Turning from Ephorus and Theopompus to Timaeus, we again find ourselves in the company of a historian for whom Dionysius' reign constituted a central rather than a peripheral topic of interest. Notwithstanding, however, this similarity, the chief thrusts of Philistus' and Timaeus' narratives were markedly different — a fact attributable as much to the personal historical circumstances of the two historians as to the environments in which they flourished. Certainly the vicissitudes suffered by both Timaeus and his father exercised a profound influence upon the direction taken by Timaeus in his evaluation of Dionysius. Thus we note how Timaeus' father, Andromachus, described by

Diodorus as a man 'well known for his high mindedness and wealth' — sentiments without doubt ultimately reflective of Timaeus himself — had quite obviously pitted himself against the Dionysii early in his political career by gathering together the Naxian survivors whose town had been destroyed by the elder Dionysius and by superintending the colonisation of Tauromenium (Diod. Sic. XVI. 7. 1/T. 3a). Subsequently he had thrown his support behind Timoleon and thereby manifested open opposition to the Sicilian tyrants — a move which obviously paid handsome dividends in view of the fact that, while Andromachus had certainly been a tyrant and traditionally Timoleon was a hater of one-man rule who was even prepared to murder his brother for aspiring to the tyranny of Corinth (Diod. Sic. XVI. 65), according to Marcellinus (*Vit. Thuc.* XXVII/T. 13), Timaeus praised Timoleon immoderately because he had not overthrown the one-man rule of his father Andromachus.

Timaeus' own personal experiences are likely to have reinforced his antagonism towards the Dionysii. Banished from Sicily by Agathocles for a fifty-year period spent in exile at Athens (Diod. Sic. XXI. 17. 1; Polyb. XII. 25h; Plut. *De Exil.* XIV/T. 4a, F. 34, T. 4e), his view of the Sicilian tyrants, epitomised by Agathocles is hardly likely to have been a positive one. Moreover, the strong anti-monarchical spirit, stemming from antagonism towards the Hellenistic monarchs, particularly Macedon, which prevailed at Athens combined with the long-standing anti-Dionysian tradition, which we have seen is likely to have characterised Athenian sources and have been found in Athens' libraries, which Timaeus is accordingly likely to have utilised for his depiction of Dionysius, rendered Timaeus' opposition to Dionysius as well as to other Sicilian tyrants in his Western history both inevitable and absolute.[96] Hence we should not be surprised to note that, while Agathocles and Dionysius I were castigated vigorously in Timaeus' history (Polyb. VIII. 10-12; XII. 15; Diod. Sic. XXI. 17. 3; Schol. Aesch. II. 10; Plut. *Quaest. Conv.* VIII. 1. 1. p. 717c/F. 124a, b, d, 29, 105),[97] excessive praises were heaped upon Timoleon.[98] Certainly Polybius (XII. 23. 4/F. 119a) found it difficult to reconcile Timaeus' exaltation of Timoleon with the same historian's criticism of Callisthenes for flattery, while Cicero (*Ad Fam.* V. 12. 7/F. 119c), writing to L. Lucceius the historian, expressed the wish that someone should do for him what Timaeus had done for Timoleon and Herodotus for Themistocles, and Plutarch (*Tim.* XXVI. 2/F. 119b), explicitly citing Timaeus and therefore obviously echoing him, declared that apart from the distressing incident about Timoleon's brother, Sophocles' words, 'O gods, what love and affection were joined in him', might well be applied to Timoleon.

The method employed by Timaeus to blacken the reputation of the Dionysii was varied. On the one hand, living in Athens with its long-standing hostility towards monarchs as well as specifically towards Dionysius, Timaeus would have been expected to avail himself of such Athenian testimony unfavourable to the tyrant, obtained both by a process of oral communication and by utilisation of data from Athens' libraries. Thus we are not surprised to note a common emphasis upon Dionysius' luxurious lifestyle both in Timaeus (F. 111/Polyb. XII. 24. 3) and in the Athenian comic writer Polyzelus (F. 11/Schol. Aristoph. *Plut.* 550) as well as development of the motif of Dionysius' association solely with flatterers, found originally in Eubulus' *Dionysius*, in an anecdote likely derived from Timaeus concerning the flatterer who obligingly laughed whenever the tyrant laughed, though unable to hear the joke (Athen. VI. 249e).[99] Similarly Timaeus appears to have availed himself of the distinctly hostile Athenian negative assessments of Dionysius' literary pretensions, found originally in Philoxenus, Antiphon, Eubulus, Antiphanes, Alexis and Ephippus, when he commented, no doubt adversely, upon the peculiar vocabularly, proverbs and aphorisms encountered in Dionysius' tragedies (Athen. III. 98d).[100] Since the evidence, moreover, indicates that Timaeus was forced to leave Sicily at an extremely early age[101] and does not suggest that Timaeus ever returned to Sicily before his death,[102] the likelihood of recourse on the part of the historian to more favourable oral native Sicilian tradition is extremely unlikely. Timaeus' history of Dionysius is accordingly likely to have contained within its pages a formidable array of anecdotal material, hostile to the tyrant, stemming ultimately from the Academy, Athenian comic stage and Peripatetic biography. Since as we shall demonstrate below, Timaeus obtained most of his historical data from Philistus' history, albeit adapted in a highly distorted manner, and since Timaeus spent six, as opposed to Philistus' four, books on the tyrant,[103] it would be logical to conclude that the extra material in Timaeus consisted essentially of anecdotal material added to Philistus' basic narrative. Nor should the possibility be gainsaid that Timaeus incorporated his own or his father's personal hostile sentiments towards Dionysius into his history.[104] Certainly from such varied likely sources derived Timaeus' summation of Dionysius' rule as an unadulterated tragedy for Sicily, epitomised by the equation of the death of the tragedian Euripides with the birth of Dionysius, the epitome of tragedy (Plut. *Quaest. Conviv.* VIII. 1. 1. p. 717c/F. 105),[105] and the description of the ominous dream of the Himeraean lady, significantly already current in Athens in the mid-fourth century BC (Aesch. *On the Embassy* II. 10), prophesying Dionysius' role of destruction in Sicily and Italy, the publicising of which, we are told, ultimately provoked the murder of the woman at the express command of the tyrant (Schol. Aesch. II. 10/F. 29).[106] Close perusal of the latter fragment, moreover, enables us to determine clearly the considerable extent to which Timaeus modified the material which he received to accord its content a contemporary relevance. Thus following Vattuone[107] we note that Timaeus deliberately transformed a priestess (Aesch. *On the Embassy* II. 10) into a Himeraean lady to underline, on the one hand, the contrast between Gelon's victory at Himera in 480 BC and, on the other, Himera as the birthplace of Sicily's latest scourge, Agathocles. By effecting such a transformation of personage from an ordinary priestess to a Himeraean woman, Timaeus was thus in effect decisively establishing Himera as a symbol of Western Greek suffering at the hands of her local tyrants and foreign oppressors. Further, noting a correspondence of thought between the epithets utilised by Timaeus to underline Dionysius' barbarity and those employed by the same historian to describe Agathocles[108] and the oracle in Diodorus XIX. 2-3, foretelling Agathocles' future destructive role in Carthage and Sicily, which seems to echo the sentiments of both F. 29 and F. 105 and thus derive from Timaeus, we may conclude that the depiction of Dionysius which Timaeus sought to propagate was in fact more Agathoclean than Dionysian in content and thrust. It is accordingly distinctly possible that the lowly origins attributed to Agathocles by Timaeus (Polyb. XV. 35. 2/F. 124c) were held against Dionysius as well — though this point cannot obviously be proved.[109]

Timaeus' concern with blackening Dionysius I's reputation led the historian to launch an equally savage indictment upon the tyrant's chief supporter, historian and propagandist, Philistus. After all, in order to present a negative portrait of the tyrant, it was necessary to obliterate the influence of the most prominent historical authority who had ventured to present a favourable portrait of Dionysius. In Plutarch's words, Timaeus' chief concern was to slander Philistus because the latter was zealous and faithful to tyranny (*Dion* XXXVI. 1/556. T. 23a; 566. F. 154). But an equally important factor[110] underlined and intensified Timaeus' need to launch an assault upon Philistus: the frustrations which Timaeus must have experienced, deriving from the fact that, for all his hostility towards Philistus as a lackey of tyrants, he was utterly dependent upon the latter historian for his own account of Dionysius I, since little concrete data for his purposes could be derived from Ephorus' and Theopompus' works in contrast with Philistus' Περὶ Διονυσίου which certainly provided a detailed exposition, albeit merely for the first couple of decades, of Dionysius' reign. Thus we have seen how Ephorus' history, constituting a somewhat sketchy document in two books as opposed to Timaeus' eight for the period 410 to 368 BC, did not utilise Philistus' detailed work and betrayed little interest in the minutiae of governmental and military affairs, viewing Sicilian history merely within the broad context of Isocratean universal Greek history. Theopompus, on the other hand, though a thorough researcher, seems to have been less concerned with Dionysius I than with the latter's son and successor and hence can hardly have appealed to Timaeus as a chief source for factual information regarding Dionysius I.[111]

While Timaeus' criticism of Philistus for the latter's apparent tediousness and clumsiness (Plut. *Nic.* 1/566. T. 18; 556. T. 23b; cf. Porphyr. *Quaest. Hom.* p. 286. 19ff/556. T. 26) and error in assuming the Sicani to have been the original inhabitants of Sicily (Diod. Sic. V. 6. 1/566. F. 38; 556. T. 23c) or believing together with Thucydides that the Syracusans were responsible for the deaths of Nicias and Demosthenes rather than their own hands (Plut. *Nic.* XXVIII. 4/566. F. 101; 556. F. 55; cf. Thuc. VII. 86. 2) suggests that stylistic and non-Dionysian data marked Timaeus' assault upon Philistus as well, undoubtedly the main thrust of the later historian's polemic against his predecessor was directed against the latter's historical evaluation of Dionysius. Thus to Philistus' observation in the concluding book of the Περὶ Διονυσίου regarding Dionysius' lavish funeral fitting the tyrant's greatness (Theon *Progymn.* II. 68. 175 sp./F. 28), Timaeus probably added the comment that its pomposity or brilliance marked a fitting conclusion to the tragedy of Dionysius' tyranny[112] — an interpretation which not only accorded well with Timaeus' equation of the birth of Dionysius with the death of Euripides

(Plut. *Quaest. Conviv.* VIII. 1. 1. p. 717c/F. 105) but which was accepted erroneously as authentically Philistan in origin by no less an authority than Plutarch himself (Plut. *Pelop.* XXXIV. 1/556. F. 40b). Similarly, probably as a direct response to Philistus' dream foretelling Dionysius' future greatness (556. F. 57a) and possibly as a response to a passage in Philistus' history depicting Dionysius as liberator of Himera, Timaeus incorporated the dream of the Himeraean woman (F. 29/Schol. Aesch. *On the Embassy* II. 10).[113] More serious manipulation of evidence or indeed total distortion of his predecessor's data characterised Timaeus' claim that Dionysius' physicians murdered the tyrant (Plut. *Dion* VI. 2/F. 109) since the earlier tradition — undoubtedly Philistus', though not specifically mentioned as such — simply claimed that Dion failed to confer with Dionysius in the interest of Aristomache's children because of the intervention of the physicians who wanted to gain the confidence of the younger Dionysius.[114]

Timaeus' hostile evaluation of Dionysius, of course, is not to be viewed in isolation but, as Truesdale Brown has indicated,[115] should rather be seen within the context of a broader thesis presented in Timaeus' history on the failures of later Siceliot Society in contrast with the glories of its earlier times, testimony for which is above all provided by the striking contrast which we note between Polybius' statement that Timaeus glorified the Sicilian past by his depiction in speeches and deeds of Siceliot wisdom and Syracusan statesmanship on the one hand (Polyb. XII. 26b, 4-5/F. 94) and Timaeus' unmerciful castigation of figures from its more recent past on the other — figures such as the pre-eminent Acragantine, Empedocles, who was attacked by Timaeus for his quick temper (Diog. Laert. VIII. 63/F. 134), arrogance (Diog. Laert. VIII. 66/F. 2) and plagiarism (Diog. Laert. VIII. 54/F. 14), while stories about his miraculous death were seriously questioned (Diog. Laert. VIII. 67/F. 6). Similarly while as we have seen, Dionysius was regarded by Timaeus as a tragedy and a source of destruction for Sicily (Plut. *Quaest. Conv.* VIII. 1. 1. p. 717c; Schol. Aesch. II. 10/F. 105, 29), Agathocles' lowly origins were held against the tyrant (Polyb. XV. 35. 2/F. 124c) and he too seems to have been regarded as a source of distress for both Sicily and the Carthaginians (Diod. Sic. XIX. 2-3; cf. F. 105, 29). Finally in his discussion of Acragantine luxury (Diod. Sic. XIII. 81. 4-84),[116] emphasis was clearly placed by Timaeus upon the weakness stemming from that city's very wealth, which accounted for the Punic victory over Acragas and ultimately produced the tyranny of Dionysius.[117] It would therefore appear that the tragedy which was manifested by Dionysius' career constituted in Timaeus' eyes merely one element of the wider crisis of Siceliot decline. The importance, moreover, which Timaeus attributed to this period of decline and its following recovery under Timoleon is indicated by Timaeus' devotion of two thirds of his *opus* to it, beginning in Books XIV and XV with the Punic invasions of Sicily of the last decade of the fifth century BC,[118] continuing with an account of Dionysius I's reign in Books Sixteen to Twenty-one,[119] and of the period of Dionysius II, Dion and Timoleon from 366 to 317 BC in Books Twenty-two to Thirty-Three, which accordingly averaged an Olympiad per book, culminating in a relatively brief perusal of Agathocles' reign in Books Thirty-four to Thirty-eight — an average of five-and-a-half years being devoted to each book (Diod. Sic. XXI. 17. 3/F. 124d).[120]

Timaeus' history of the Western Greek world attained instant success in the Graeco-Roman world of the third and second centuries BC, essentially because of the Western Greek historian's early recognition of the political importance of Rome (Dion. Halic. *Ant. Rom.* I. 6. 1/T. 9b)[121] and the appeal which the history accordingly exerted upon members of the philhellenist Roman aristocracy,[122] whence derived Polybius' resolve to begin his history at the point where Timaeus concluded his work (Polyb. I. 5. 1/T. 6a) and, following the lead of Istros and Polemon,[123] undoubtedly from motivation of personal jealousy, to assault mercilessly the work of his illustrious predecessor, devoting indeed no less than one half of his twelfth book to this endeavour.[124] Consequently, given the overall popularity of Timaeus in the Graeco-Roman world of the third and second centuries BC, it follows that the popular viewpoint regarding Dionysius I which flourished at that period of time was Timaeus' — a depiction hostile and anecdotal in character whose origins, as we have seen, were to be found essentially in the Athenian comic theatre, Academy and Peripatetic biographical school. The only notable exception in the Graeco-Roman world of the second century BC who, as far as one can deduce from a favourable comment about Dionysius recorded by Polybius (XV. 35. 6), made the acquaintance of Philistus' Περὶ Διονυσίου and approved of Philistus' work, was the elder Scipio Africanus — a figure whose absolutist sympathies, echoed in the *Somnium Scipionis* of Cicero, well qualified that political figure to appreciate the overall tone and message of the Περὶ Διονυσίου and for whom Timaeus' republican stance probably constituted a less alluring phenomenon. In the first century BC, however, possibly Theopompus' assessment of Dionysius I and certainly Philistus' Περὶ Διονυσίου appear to have come once again into their own essentially because of the renewed significance which monarchical figures and monarchical theorising once again attained, and it is accordingly hardly surprising to encounter Dionysius of Halicarnassus (*Ad Pomp.* IV. 11/556. T. 16b; 115. T. 20a) highlighting such monarchically inclined historians as Theopompus and Philistus, albeit within a stylistic context. With respect to Theopompus, the evidence is admittedly meagre since, as we shall see, Diodorus' claim to have read Theopompus' excursus (XVI. 71. 3/F. 184) is not supported by the data found in Diodorus' narrative. However, Justin's lack of interest in Dionysius' early career and consideration of it only within the context of Punic history as a whole and more specifically within the context of Himilcon's failure in Sicily in 396 BC (Justin, XIX. 2) suggests that Trogus had access to Theopompus' Western excursus and hence probably to the Sicilian excursus which it preceded as well. Further, Nepos' sketch of Dionysius (*De Reg.* II. 2), with its emphasis upon Dionysius' lack of vice, might owe something to that biographer's perusal of Theopompus. The evidence for a full scale revival of Philistus is, of course, more extensive. As we have seen, Augustus himself does not seem to have been immune to Philistus' influence. More importantly, Diodorus on numerous occasions (XIII. 91. 4; 103. 3; XIV. 8. 5; XV. 89. 3; 94. 4) mentions Philistus both within a historiographical and political context, and, as we shall argue in the following chapter, admittedly contrary to scholarly consensus, seems essentially to have followed that historian's account for his description of the reign of Dionysius I. Cicero, as we have seen, significantly appears to have encountered Philistus and have looked favourably upon the Syracusan historian's *oeuvre*, especially the Dionysian books (*De Orat.* II. 57; *Ad Quint. Fratr.* II. 11(13). 4; cf. *Brut.* XVII. 66; *De Div.* I. 39) at the very time when he was seriously considering the possibility of one-man rule for Rome in the *De Republica* (*Ad Quint. Fratr.* II. 14; *Ad Attic.* IV. 16) and when its potential was being amply demonstrated by the career of Pompey and Caesar — a fact which, however, did not prevent his acceptance of Timaeus' hostile account as well (*Tusc.* V. 57ff; *De Offic.* II. 7. 25).[125] Further, when Cicero writes about

Dionysius, 'de hoc homine a bonis auctoribus sic scriptum accepimus, summam fuisse eius in victu temperatum' (*Tusc.* V. 20. 57) he seems to be referring to the estimates of both Theopompus and Philistus. Finally Nepos, whom we have seen certainly read Philistus (*Dion* III. 2/T. 5d), describing Dionysius (*De Reg.* II) as a brave and skilful commander, averse to sensuality, luxury and avarice, covetous of nothing except imperial pursuits, able to preserve his power with good fortune and live to over sixty without witnessing the funeral of any of his offspring, preserving a domain in flourishing condition, reveals himself as a biographer totally immune to the hostile anecdotal tradition concerned with the tyrant's negative relationship with his family and wider Syracusan community and undoubtedly deeply influenced by Philistus' Περὶ Διονυσίου.

For the subsequent fate of Dionysius' reputation under the Empire, the evidence is certainly meagre. Jacoby's collection of fragments reveals acquaintance with Philistus' total *oeuvre* on the part of Plutarch, Quintilian and Pollux, while forty-one fragments — all relating to place names — from a total of seventy-six derive from Stephanus of Byzantium who lived in the fifth century AD. Subsequently in the tenth century AD, the Suda (T. 1a, 1b) had confused Philistus with other writers similarly named. Data from the hostile tradition must obviously have found its way into a full-scale biography of Dionysius written by a certain Amyntianus which was ominously appended, together with a parallel life of Domitian, to Plutarch's lives (Phot. *Bibl.* 131. p. 97a).[126] Plutarch, on the other hand, our fullest late source for Dionysius after Diodorus, living in a world which delighted in contrasting 'good' Antonine-type rulers with 'bad' Julio-Claudian despots, was perhaps inevitably drawn both to the hostile and favourable traditions, illustrating as they did two antithetical types of absolute rulers. Thus while, on the one hand, we should not be surprised to discover in his pages anecdotes concerned with Dionysius' less than positive relations with his barber, his father and son, his strangulation of his mother, his murder of ten thousand citizens, the police regime and the tyrant's financial rapacity (*Dion* IX. 3; *De Garrul.* XII-XIII, 508f; *De Alex. Fort.* II. 5. 338b; *De Curios.* XII. 523a; *Reg. Apophth. Dion. Mai* V. 175e; X. 176a), we should be equally cognisant of the facts that he warned his readers against the excesses of Timaeus' bias against Dionysius (Plut. *Dion* XXXVI. 1-2) and accepted the tradition favourable towards Dionysius, stemming probably from both Philistus and Theopompus — a fact manifestly illustrated by his reference to Dionysius' censure of his son for violating the wife of a Syracusan citizen on the grounds of such action being politically unwise rather than morally culpable. Similar echoes of Theopompus and Philistus seem, moreover, to characterise Dionysius' sober advice to his son that 'drinking cups do not make a friend; that resolute action is necessary; that the soul when relaxed is like a bow which breaks when too tightly stretched'. Finally, when we read of Dionysius' greater fear of sober than of drunken men and of Philip II and Dionysius II praising Dionysius I's avoidance of strong drink, we are again obviously dealing with the favourable tradition regarding Dionysius, stemming either from Philistus or more likely Theopompus and possibly from both combined (Plut. *Reg. Apophth. Dion. Mai.* 175e; 176a; *Ad Princ. Iner.* 782c; *An Seni Resp. Ger. Sit* 792c; *Tim* XV. 4).[127]

VI

To sum up, our investigation of the pre-Diodorus historiographical tradition regarding Dionysius I has revealed that Philistus, Ephorus, Theopompus and Timaeus, the four most important historians covering the despot's reign, produced profoundly different narratives and assessments of the individual upon whose career they focused their attention. On the whole, less complex and consequently less interesting designs and thought-patterns appear to have characterised the works of Ephorus and Timaeus. The six books of Timaeus' history of the Western Greek world dealing with Dionysius, the only significant overtly hostile historiographical account of the tyrant, constituted little more than a hostile and distortionist invective, launched against Dionysius and Philistus, the tyrant's chief minister and historiographer, in retaliation for experiences suffered by both Timaeus and his father, supplemented by hostile data found in Athens' libraries by Timaeus which in origin derived essentially from the comic theatre, Academy and Peripatetic biographical school.[128] Whatever of value was found in Timaeus' account is likely to have been found in a less corrupt and distorted form in Philistus' history. As for Ephorus' account, which appears to have dealt with the events preceding 392 BC more briefly than Philistus and with that following in greater breadth, while the evidence suggests that it considered Dionysius in a highly superficial manner in two books which emphasised Dionysius' universal role within the Hellenic world and opposition to the Punic enemy as well as the moral rectitude which fitted Ephorus' central figure for such a task, little concern with the underlying causes of Syracusan power-growth is likely to have been manifested. Thus the external show of power itself rather than its causes, origins and basis were probably discussed by Ephorus and whatever at all was considered pertaining to such topics of causation is likely to have been couched in superficial Isocratean moralising terminology.

The works of Philistus and Theopompus, on account of the former historian's eclipse at the hands of Timaeus and the latter's works' sheer bulk, perhaps less influential in classical antiquity than those of Ephorus and Timaeus, yet judged in terms of quality, far more significant, were particularly antithetical in design, emphasis and political doctrine pursued. On a most general level, while Philistus' concern was centred upon the first decade and to a lesser extent upon the second decade of Dionysius' rule, Theopompus appears to have begun his consideration of Dionysius with the year 392 BC and hence concerned himself only with the last twenty-five years of Dionysius' reign. Further, while Philistus' chief concern was Dionysius and his *arche*, Theopompus seems on a surface level to have been more concerned with Dionysius II than with his illustrious father. In actual fact, as we have seen, Theopompus' interest in Dionysius II was dictated by a desire to explain the causes of the collapse of Dionysius I's empire. Hence, in contrast with the Thucydidean Philistus, who was to a large extent concerned with the power of Dionysius' regime and its social and economic base, Theopompus' chief interest was focused upon its dissolution, which the historian viewed not within the context of political, social and economic causation favoured by Philistus, but in the patently Isocratic terms of the disastrous political consequences of the moral failings of the younger Dionysius — moral deficiencies, moreover, which in Theopompus' terminology were to be equated with democratic malaise, evidence of which Theopompus already discerned in Dionysius I's empire. With respect to the latter point, of course, Theopompus' assessment differed considerably from that of Philistus who maintained that the very real, if limited, political liberality which characterised Dionysius' government constituted together with the support furnished by Dionysius' new oligarchy, a very basic source of strength of the Syracusan regime. As far as the decline of Dionysius' empire was concerned, moreover, Philistus' assessment differed widely from Theopompus' in that he seems to have viewed the failure of the *arche* within the context of Dionysius' pursuit of a divisive and unnecessary war with the Italiots centred around Rhegium which sapped the empire's strength and diverted from the more reasonable Punic conflict and Northern Adriatic projects much needed resources.

Perhaps the most striking contrast characterising these sources is that which marked off Timaeus' savage indictment of Dionysius' rule as a tragedy bringing terror, destruction and loss of liberty to Syracuse and to the West from Philistus' positive depiction of Dionysius' *arche* as one based upon a broad consensus of support within Syracuse from the new oligarchy of wealth, on the one hand, and the *demos* with its democratic role intact, on the other. Given these two contradicting theses, it is accordingly incumbent upon us to determine which of them approximates more closely to historical reality. Obviously mindful of the caution of Plutarch (*Dion* XXXVI. 1/556. T. 23a; cf. 566. F. 154), Timaeus' evidence, which is after all essentially non-Sicilian in origin and reflective of various Athenian anti-Dionysian and anti-monarchical tendencies of the fourth and third centuries BC, emanating from such highly distorted and hence unreliable historical sources of information as the Academy, Athenian comic theatre and Peripatetic biography, supplemented by highly subjective invective against and distortion of Philistus' narrative on Timaeus' own part, must be approached with a considerable degree of caution. Even so, these facts by themselves cannot motivate us to accept Philistus' testimony as necessarily valid and trustworthy and we do well to ask whether any other confirmatory argumentation can be advanced supportive of Philistus' reliability in a broad sense and more specifically pertaining to his claim that Dionysius' regime possessed a decidedly liberal and democratic character.

Certainly, in support of Philistus' general validity as a source, three arguments can, in fact, be advanced. First we should note that Philistus, for all his favour towards Dionysius, as we have attempted to demonstrate, furnished in his Περὶ Διονυσίου much more than a mere panegyric of the tyrant and was clearly not above criticising Dionysius' policies if he felt, as in the case of those policies directed against the Italiots, that they were misdirected and indeed harmful to the overall success of his imperialistic ventures. Thus to delineate a rigid contrast between a fawning tyrant's lackey Philistus, on the one hand, and the tyrant hater, on the other, whose hostility in both cases was based upon highly personal motivation, represents a hypothesis hardly supported in Philistus' case by any accurate and reliable evidence. Secondly we note that Theopompus, for all his seeming inability to discover any substantial negative data pertaining to Dionysius I, did not eulogise the tyrant and offered distinct criticism of one aspect of Dionysius' rule in fragment 134 even though the main thrust of his criticism was directed against the despot's son, the intemperate Dionysius II. We should also note that Ephorus' notice with respect to Dionysius II's and the Great King's threat to partition the Greek world amongst themselves (Schol. Aristeid. p. 294, 13. Dindorf/F. 211) constitutes a less than positive assessment of the Syracusan tyranny, perhaps echoing fears by Athenians of a more 'democratic' persuasion, of the type that rallied around Lysias in his opposition to Dionysius at the Olympic games of 388 BC. Accordingly, the three sources offering quite different assessments of Dionysius' regime from Timaeus can hardly be faulted for providing purely positive eulogistic portraits, devoid of a sense of criticism. Evidence for their objectivity is, in fact, far more substantial than for Timaeus. Thirdly, we emphasise that Theopompus' failure to discover data injurious to Dionysius' moral reputation *per se*, when contrasted with the thoroughness of Theopompus' research into the private failings of individuals elsewhere in his historical *oeuvre*, suggests to us that the historian of Chios could not find any data at all pertaining to Dionysius' moral laxity comparable to the highly unreliable material which Timaeus appears to have located in the Athenian libraries and incorporated into his own history, simply because such evidence did not exist.

Finally, turning to Philistus' proposition that the constitutional organs of the Syracusan democracy were very much in evidence and testified to the liberality manifested by Dionysius' regime, we emphasise first that the fact that Philistus' favour towards the Syracusan democracy was less motivated by propagandist considerations of the type that probably were echoed by Dionysius' other literati than based upon what the historian perceived as the Syracusan democracy's efficiency under a Pisistratean-style despot, would appear to excuse Philistus of suspicious motivation for inventing such a phenomenon. Secondly, we do well to recall that Theopompus and Plato, who in other respects were politically poles apart, agreed with Philistus on the one point, that a great deal of democratic freedom prevailed at Syracuse — a judgement whose validity is strengthened by the fact that both were hardly partial towards this phenomenon. Thirdly, we observe that Dionysius' avoidance of the title τύραννος and use of the appellation ἄρχων Σικελίας for international purposes indicates a very real desire on the tyrant's part to mask his tyrannical position and emphasise the constitutionality of his regime. Finally, we should note that the fact that epigraphic and numismatic evidence suggest the very real existence and functioning of both *boule* and *ecclesia* at Syracuse appears to validate Philistus' evidence to the effect that the broadest type of political liberty characterised the Syracusan regime under the elder Dionysius.[129]

Notes

1. See Chapter 1, n 7.
2. Thus Meyer, *Geschichte des Altertums*, vol. 4. 1. p. 268, though of course this interpretation rests on the assumption that Diodorus' terminal date for the war of 383 BC in XV. 17 is wrong and that hostilities continued for some years afterwards — a fact certainly suggested by Diodorus XV. 24 which dates hostilities to 379 BC.
3. Jacoby, *FGH*, vol. 3b (Komm.), p. 515.
4. See Jacoby, *FGH*, vol. 3b (Komm.), p. 515; K. Meister, 'Die Sizilische Geschichte bei Diodor von den Anfängen bis zum Tod des Agathokles. Quellenuntersuchungen zu Buch IV-XXI'. Dissertation, Munich, 1967, pp. 72-3.
5. See Morrow, *Platonic epistles*, p. 22.
6. E. Manni, 'Ancora a proposito di Sileno-Diodoro', *Kokalos*, vol. 16 (1970), p. 74. F. 5./Phot. Sud. *s.v.* 'Σαρδόνιος γέλως' suggests that a fourth book, dealing with other western lands followed. See Folcke, 'Dionysius', p. 38.
7. Thus Folcke, 'Dionysius', p. 38.
8. G. De Sanctis, *Ricerche sulla storiografia Siceliota* (Palermo, 1958), p. 17. Cf. Jacoby, *FGH*, vol. 3b (Komm.), no. 556, p. 497, who puts Philistus at between twenty and twenty-five in 406 BC. Cf. also R. Zoepffel, 'Untersuchungen zum Geschichtswerk des Philistos von Syrakus', Dissertation, Freiburg, 1965, p. 9.
9. For gossip regarding Philistus' supposed love affair with Dionysius' mother found later in Tzetzes *Chil.* X. 829 and doubted by Plutarch, see Plutarch, *Dion* XI. 5./T. 5c.
10. Whether the dictum that a tyrant should not flee but be dragged

by the leg in fact derived from Philistus' mouth as Diodorus (XIV. 8. 5./T. 4) maintains is, of course, questionable in view of its attribution to Megacles, Dionysius' brother-in-law in another passage of Diodorus (XX. 78. 3). Plutarch's attribution of this remark of Philistus to the authority of Timaeus rather than to that of Philistus (*Dion* XXXV. 2/T. 9d, F. 59. Cf. no. 566. F. 115), moreover, suggests that two different viewpoints did, in fact, exist. Though, see Chapter 3, p. 142.

11. Thus A. Gitti, *Studi su Filisto* (Bari, 1953), p. 30; Gitti, 'Ricerche sulla vita di Filisto, Adria ed il luogo dell'esilio', *MAL*, Ser. 8a, vol. 4. 4 (1952), pp. 225-73, esp. p. 268 — a conclusion implicit in Diod. Sic. XV. 13. 1, though associated with a simplistic thesis regarding Dionysius' aim to plunder Delphi. See below p. 144. Gallic alliance in Justin XX. 5. 4.

12. Objections to this thesis are, in our view, difficult to sustain. Against the view of F. Altheim, *Geschichte der lateinischen Sprache* (Frankfurt, 1951), p. 54, advocating an Illyrian origin of the word *Philistina*, see A. Gitti, 'Sulla colonizzazione greca nell'alto e medio Adriatico', *PP*, vol. 7 (1952), p. 174 and Stroheker, *Dionysios I*, p. 227. More serious is the objection voiced by I. Calabi, 'Review of Gitti, *Studi su Filisto*', *Paideia*, vol. 40 (1954-5), pp. 55-7, to the effect that in contrast to the situation in the Roman Empire, within the context of Greek tyrannies, officials could not give their names to public monuments — an objection which provokes the hypothesis that the word *Philistina* constitutes a nickname attributed to buildings which arose at the time of Philistus' Miltiades-style honorary exile in the Northern Adriatic. To this hypothesis, we retort that Dionysius' tyranny can hardly be conceived of as a traditional tyranny but rather as a blueprint for Hellenistic monarchy; that, as we shall see, the theory of an honorary exile which has been linked with a hypothesis of an early recall from exile, is not only not supported but actually contradicted by the ancient testimony; and finally, as we shall also demonstrate, that the very power and influence which accrued to Philistus from his northern activity is likely to have constituted an important factor contributing to the historian's exile. On Dionysius as a proto-Hellenistic monarch, see J.G. Droysen, *Geschichte des Hellenismus* (Tübingen, 1953), vol. 2, p. xxi; Droysen zum Finanzwesen des Dionysios von Syrakus, *SKAWB* (1882), p. 1013, reprinted in *Kleine Schriften zur Alten Geschichten* (Leipzig, 1894), p. 306; Holm, *Geschichte Siziliens* vol. 2, p. 155; E.A. Freeman, *History of Sicily* (Oxford, 1894), vol. 4, pp. 4ff; Beloch, *Griechische Geschichte*, vol. 3a, p. 127; J.B. Bury, 'Dionysius I of Syracuse', *Cambridge Ancient History* (Cambridge, 1927), vol. 6, p. 135; Bury, *History of Greece*, 4th edn, revised by R. Meiggs (London, 1975), p. 405; Finley, *Ancient Sicily*, p. 78.

13. Thus following Gitti, 'Ricerche sulla vita di Filisto, Adria e il luogo dell'esilio', pp. 268ff, we note (a) that Justin XX. 5. 4 associates Dionysius' alliance with the Gauls with the time of the war against Croton in 389 BC and the Gallic destruction of Rome of 387-386; cf. Polyb. I. 6. 1-2 who mentions Dionysius' defeat of the Italiots and siege of Rhegium in connection with the Gallic sack of Rome in 387-386 BC; (b) that contemporary with, or slightly earlier than, these events was the foundation of Lissos (Diod. Sic. V. 13. 4); (c) that Diodorus associates the year 385-384 with Dionysius' foundation of Pharos and war against

Illyrians and Etruscans (Diod. Sic. XV. 13); and (d) that the alliance with
Alcetas is dated by Diodorus a year earlier. Clearly the possible foundation of Issa (Diod. Sic. XV. 13. 3; 14. 2), Ancona (Strabo V. 4. 2. c 241),
Numana (Pliny *NH* III. 13) and Adria (*Etymologicum Magnum s.v.* "Αδρίας᾿
and Schol. *Ad Lycophr.* 631) must be placed within this period. For the
extent of Dionysius' empire, see Gitti, 'Sulla colonizzazione greca
nell'alto e medio Adriatico', pp. 161-91 supported by A.J. Graham,
Colony and mother city in ancient Greece, 2nd edn (Illinois, 1983), p. 208; cf. A.G.
Woodhead, 'The Adriatic Empire of Dionysius', *Klio,* vol. 52 (1970),
pp. 503-12.

14. See Chapter 1, n 34.

15. Thus see citations in Gitti, 'Ricerche sulla vita di Filisto, Adria e il
luogo dell'esilio', pp. 243-4.

16. We might add that given Leptines' prestige among the Italiots
(Diod. Sic. XIV. 102. 3), his exile to Thurii is more likely than Philistus'.
Thus Folcke, 'Dionysius', p. 182.

17. τὸν δὲ Φίλιστον ἐξήλασε Σικελίας φυγόντα παρὰ ξένους τινὰς εἰς
τὸν 'Αδρίαν.

18. Thus Jacoby, *FGH*, vol. 3b (Komm.), no. 556, p. 497; cf. Gitti,
'Ricerche sulla vita di Filisto, Adria e il luogo dell'esilio', pp. 239ff, esp. p.
244: 'l'ospitalità ricevuta da chiunque sia nel suo esilio, mostra
all'evidenza che Filisto è un vero bandito, un esiliato, un φυγών.' Cf. also
R.L. Beaumont, 'Greek influence in the Adriatic Sea before the fourth
century', *JHS*, vol. 56 (1936), p. 203, who we, however, suggest in view of
our association of the *Fossa Filistina* with Philistus and postdating of
Philistus' exile to 384 BC, wrongly concludes that Philistus was not
governor and that Dionysius did not control the whole of Adriatic Italy as
opposed to the shore.

19. I essentially follow W. Koerber, 'De Philisto Rerum Sicularum
Scriptore', Disseration, Breslau, 1874, pp. 24ff and G.M. Columba,
'Filisto storico del IV. secolo', *ASS,* vol. 17 (1892), p. 284. Cf. Stroheker,
Dionysios I, p. 192 (cf. p. 119) who, though agreeing that the emphasis of
Philistus' work was laid upon the great Punic War, suggests tentatively
that only Book II dealt with this war and that while the narrative of the
Italian War to 386 BC appeared in Book III, the meagre details in
Diodorus XV were derived from Philistus' fourth book. Cf. Zoepffel,
'Untersuchungen', p. 18.

20. Of course we have suggested that Athanis' political sympathies
are unlikely to have accorded with those of Philistus. Cicero (*Ad Quint.
Fratr.* II. 11. 4/T. 17a) by referring to the two corpora of Philistus' history
(the Περὶ Σικελίας and Περὶ Διονυσίου) seems totally oblivious of
Philistus' swan-song.

21. As illustrated by A.D. Momigliano, *Alien wisdom. The limits of
hellenization* (Cambridge, 1975).

22. See T.S. Brown, 'Alexander's book order (Plut. *Alex.* VIII)',
Historia, vol. 16 (1967), pp. 366ff; U. Wilcken, *Alexander the Great,* trans-
lated by G.C. Richards (London, 1967), pp. 225-6; Freeman, *History of
Sicily,* vol. 3, pp. 603-4. For the view that the Περὶ Διονυσίου was read by
Dionysius with an eye to his eventual conquest of the Western Mediter-
ranean, see M. Sordi, 'Alessandro Magno e l'eredità di Siracusa', *Aevum,*

vol. 57, no. 1 (1983), pp. 14-23. The fact that another work sent to Alexander by Harpalus was the dithyrambic corpus of Philoxenus who, of course, frequented Dionysius' court might also suggest that Alexander's literary interests at the time were dictated somewhat by Western interests. Plutarch's notice (*Alex.* VIII. 2) that Alexander employed the *Iliad* as a handbook for the art of war would tend to support the view herein entertained to the effect that Philistus' work served a practical purpose in Alexander's eyes. We follow Zoepffel ('Unter suchungen', p. 72) in adopting the view that Philip of Macedon's interest in Dionysius I (Plut. *Tim.* XV. 4; Aelian, *VH* XII. 60) renders it likely that Alexander's interest in Philistus probably derived from a similar interest in the Syracusan historian on the part of his father. Sordi's suggestion ('Alessandro Magno e l'eredità di Siracusa', p. 20) that the presence at Syracuse of Cleon 'from Sicily' (Curt. VIII. 5. 8), a possible exile from the court of Dionysius II, and the demise of Alexander, the Molossian — an event which, according to Justin XII. 3. 1 deeply affected Alexander — were factors which served to stimulate Alexander's interest in Philistus and the West, though intriguing, can hardly be substantiated.

23. See Stroheker, *Dionysios I*, p. 29; Zoepffel, 'Untersuchungen', p. 40.

24. See S.B. Smith, 'The economic motive in Thucydides', *HS Phil,* vol. 51 (1940), pp. 267-301; A. Zimmern, 'Thucydides the Imperialist' in *Solon and Croesus* (Oxford, 1928), p. 98; G.F. Abbot, *Thucydides. A study in historical reality* (London, 1925), pp. 59-62.

25. The old view of F.M. Cornford, *Thucydides mythistoricus* (London, 1907), pp. 15-51 and G.B. Grundy, *Thucydides and the history of his age* (London, 1911), pp. 315-32, 366ff, to the effect that the Peloponnesian war was occasioned by economic rather than political considerations and that Thucydides was in error in ignoring this, occasionally resurfaces. Thus C.H.V. Sutherland, 'Corn and coin. A note on Greek commercial monopolies', *AJPh*, vol. 64, no. 2 (1943), pp. 129-47; Green, *Armada from Athens*, pp. 12-35; Green, *Shadow of the Parthenon* (London, 1972), pp. 27, 81-2; H. Bengtson, *Griechische Geschichte*, 4th edn (Munich, 1969), p. 225; A.R. Burn, *Pericles and Athens* (London, 1948), p. 181; R. Sealey, 'The causes of the Peloponnesian War', *CPhil*, vol. 70 (1975), pp. 101-2. Though against this view see G. Dickins, 'The true causes of the Peloponnesian War', *CQ*, vol. 5 (1911), pp. 238-48; Abbot, *Thucydides*, pp. 49ff, 61-2; E.J. Bickermann, 'Review of Bengtson, *Griechische Geschichte*', *AJPh*, vol. 74 (1953), pp. 96-9; H. Wentker, *Sizilien und Athens. Die Begegnung der Attischen Macht mit den Westgriechen* (Diss. Heidelberg, 1956), pp. 12-13, 62-3); G.K. Jenkins, 'A note on Corinthian coins in the West', in H. Ingholt (ed.), *Centennial Publication of the American Numismatic Society* (New York, 1958), pp. 367-79; M. Kraay, 'Hoards, small-change and the origins of coinage', *JHS*, vol. 84 (1964), pp. 76-91, esp. pp. 79-80; J. Hasebroek, *Trade and politics in ancient Greece* (New York, 1965), pp. 99-105; K.J. Dover, *Thucydides' books VI and VII* (Oxford, 1965), p. xxiii; D. Kagan, *The outbreak of the peloponnesian war* (Ithaca, 1969), pp. 239-41; G.E.M. De Ste. Croix, *The origins of the peloponnesian war* (London-New York, 1972), pp. 215-21, 262; E.F. Bloedow, 'Corn supply and Athenian imperialism', *AC*, vol. 44, no. 1 (1975), pp. 20-9.

26. Thus we note in the *De Republica*, the discussion in Books V and VI of the *princeps*; the favour in Book I as expressed through the mouth of Scipio Aemilianus to monarchy (I. 54; 69; cf. I. 64; III. 47; II. 43); the eleven chapters devoted to monarchy (I. 54-64) as opposed to the two to democracy (I. 49-50) and the three to aristocracy (I. 51-53); and the particular emphasis upon individuals who in times of crisis have led the people to act correctly (II. 16-32). Also pertinent within this context is Cicero's approval of Scipio Aemilianus' interest in Xenophon's *Cyropaedia (Ad Quint. Fratr.* I. 1. 23). See F. Solmsen, 'Die Theorie der Staatsformen bei Cicero *De Republica* I', *Philologus*, vol. 88 (1933), pp. 326-41; Dvornik, *Political philosophy*, vol. I, pp. 172ff; J.R. Dunkle, 'The Greek tyrant and Roman political invective of the Late Republic', *TAPhA*, vol. 48 (1967), pp. 151-73.

27. For Antiphon the Sophist's views on νομός and φύσις, see K. Freeman, *Ancilla to the pre-Socratic philosophers* (Oxford, 1948), p. 147. Given Plutarch's confused synthesis of orator, sophist and tragedian Antiphon (*Vita X. Orat.* 833c), a decisive association of the tragedian Antiphon present at Dionysius' court with the sophist of that name is certainly questionable. For Euenus, see J.M. Edmonds, *Greek elegy and iambus*, Loeb Classical Library (London, 1931), vol. 1, p. 473.

28. See Zoepffel, 'Untersuchungen', pp. 40, 67-73, esp. p. 69.

29. Cicero's first mention of Philistus occurs in the *De Oratore* of 55 BC (II. 57/T. 17b) and in the next year when Cicero first mentions that he is working on the theme of the *De Republica (Ad Quint. Fratr.* II. 14; *Ad Attic.* IV. 16) he recommends Philistus to Quintus' attention (*Ad Quint. Fratr.* II. 11. 14/T. 17a). The later two references (*Brut.* XVII. 66/T. 21; *De Div.* I. 39/T. 24) are dated on the basis of the dating of the *De Divinatione* and *Brutus* to 46 and 44 BC (*Brut.* 266, *De Div.* I. 119; II. 23, 99). On the Philistus revival see Zoepffel, 'Untersuchungen', p. 25; Jacoby, *FGH*, vol. 3b (Komm.), no. 556, p. 502; doubted by Brown, 'Alexander's book order (Plut. *Alex.* VIII)', p. 365 on the grounds of the unpopularity of tyranny. On Augustus and Philistus, see M. Sordi, 'Il fr. 29 Jacoby di Timeo e la lettura augustea di un passo di Filisto', *Latomus*, vol. 43 (1984), pp. 534-9. Augustus as avenger of Jove in Horace *Odes* I. 2. 29-30, 44, 51; cf. *Res Gestae* I. 1.

30. Thus Val. Max. I. 7. 6: 'Himeraeorum moenia inter effusam ad officium et spectaculum eius turbam intrantem ut aspexit . . .'. Thus M. Sordi, 'Il fr. 29 Jacoby di Timeo e la lettura augustea di un passo di Filisto', pp. 535-6. Philistus, of course, was not the only figure for whom the despotic character of Dionysius' tyranny exercised an allure. Besides Alexander already noted (Plut. *Alex.* VIII. 3), others include Hieronymus, the grandson of Hieron II in 214 BC (Liv. XXIV. 5. 4), Clearchus of Heracleia (364-352 BC), (Diod. Sic. XV. 81. 5), Mamercus of Catana (340 BC) who probably emulated Dionysius' poetical endeavours (Plut. *Tim.* XXXI. 1); Philip II of Macedon (Plut. *Tim.* XV. 4; Aelian, *VH* XII. 60) and the father of Philip II, Amyntas III (Isocrat. *Arch.* 46).

31. Thus Folcke, 'Dionysius', p. 188.

32. See Gernet, 'Mariages de tyrans', pp. 41-53; Stroheker, *Dionysios I*, pp. 157-9; Sartori, 'Sulla δυναστεία di Dionisio il vecchio nell'opera Diodorea', pp. 3-66; Finley, *Ancient Sicily*, pp. 77-8; Berve, *Die Tyrannis*,

pp. 249-51.

33. See especially Sartori, 'Sulla δυναστεία di Dionisio il vecchio nell'opera Diodorea', pp. 3-66.

34. We particularly note Diodorus' statement (XIII. 96. 3) to the effect that when Dionysius married Hermocrates' daughter and gave his sister (Theste) to Polyxenus, the brother of Hermocrates' wife and consequently his bride's uncle, he deliberately aimed at the creation of a governing class.

35. For what follows I am largely indebted to Gitti, *Studi*, followed by Folcke, 'Dionysius', p. 179.

36. See Gitti, *Studi*, p. 13; Stroheker, *Dionysios I*, p. 244, n. 96; De Sanctis, *Ricerche*, p. 20.

37. See Diod. Sic. XIV. 96. 4 for treaty; cf. XIII. 114. 1. Evidence for these cities supporting Dionysius in 397 BC in Diod. Sic. XIV. 47. 6. Loss of Himera in 396 BC in Diod. Sic. XIV. 56. 1; desertion of Acragas from Dionysius in 394 BC in Diod. Sic. XIV. 88. 5.

38. Cf. Folcke, 'Dionysius', pp. 140ff who sees Timaeus as the source for Dionysius' campaigns in Southern Italy.

39. Cf. the remarks of Zoepffel, 'Untersuchungen', p. 50. Philistus' pro-Dionysius bias is also suggested by Plutarch, *De Herod. Malign.* III. p. 855c/T. 13b and reflected in Marcellinus (*Vit. Thuc.* XXVII/T. 13c).

40. Columba, 'Filisto storico del IV. secolo', p. 286; R. Laqueur, *s.v.* 'Philistos', *RE*, vol. 19 (1938), col. 2409ff.

41. Gitti, *Studi*, p. 23; cf. Laqueur, *s.v.* 'Philistos', *RE* col. 2411ff; Stroheker, *Dionysios I*, p. 227, n 116.

42. That the verdict did not rest upon Philistus' simply copying Thucydides as is suggested by Theon's comment (*Progymn.* II. 63. 25 sp./ T. 14) on the historian's treatment of the Athenian siege of Syracuse is suggested by Plutarch's clear notice that he utilised both the accounts of Thucydides and Philistus (Plut. *Nic.* I/F. 54) and by the vivid testimony of *P.S.I.* 1283 on which see below n 51.

43. Cicero's (*Ad Quint. Fratr.* II. 11. 4/T. 17a) *creber, acutus* and *brevis* and Dionysius' (*Ad Pomp.* IV/T. 16b) comments on the historian's neatness (στρογγύλος), fine construction (πυκνός), stylistic logic, and inferior stylistic beauty(ἐνθυμηματικός, καλλιλογία). Correspondence of thought can, moreover, clearly be traced between the two assessments, whence the association between the πυκνός of Dionysius' and Cicero's *brevis* and *creber* and between Dionysius' ἐνθυμηματικός and Cicero's *acutus*.

44. 'Hunc [Thucydidem] consecutus est Syracosius Philistus qui cum Dionysi tyranni familiarissimus esset, otium suum consumpsit in historia scribenda, maximeque Thucydidem est ut mihi videtur imitatus' (*De Orat.* II. 57/T. 17b).

45. 'Me Magis de Dionisio delectat; ipse est enim veterator magnus et perfamiliaris Philisto Dionysius' (*Ad Quint. Fratr.* II. 11. 4/T. 17a).

46. See S.I. Oost, 'Thucydides and the Irrational', *CPhil*, vol. 70 (1975), pp. 186-96. Oost is obviously correct to note that what particularly appalled Thucydides about Nicias' superstition was its 'overbaked' quality. Hence the τι of Thuc. VII. 50. 4. We also note with sympathy M.I. Finley's reticence to state categorically the nature of Thucydides' views in 'Thucydides the moralist', *Aspects of antiquity* (London, 1968), p.

48. Cf. N. Marinatos, 'Thucydides and Oracles', *JHS*, 101 (1981), pp. 138-40.

47. See the comments of Jaeger, *Paideia*, vol. 1, 2nd Engl. ed. (Oxford, 1947), p. 385; J.H. Finley, *Thucydides* (Michigan, 1963), pp. 82-92; D. Grene, *Greek political theory. The image of man in Thucydides and Plato* (Chicago, 1950), pp. 49-53; Lesky, *History of Greek literature*, p. 458.

48. I follow De Sanctis, *Ricerche*, p. 25 and Zoepffel, 'Untersuchungen', pp. 17-19 and disagree decisively with T.S. Brown's comment ('Alexander's book order (Plut. *Alex.* VIII)', p. 365) that only by Book Eight (i.e. Book I of the Περὶ Διονυσίου) was Philistus a contemporary of the events which he described.

49. I.e. the great Athenian invasion and the two Punic invasions of Sicily of the last decade of the fifth century BC. Hence the Suda's statement (*s.v.* 'Φίλισκος ἢ Φίλιστος'/Τ. 1) that the chief theme of the Περὶ Σικελίας was the struggle with the Greeks (ἔγραψε Σικελικά [ἐστι δὲ τὰ πρὸς Ἕλληνας αὐτοῖς πραχθέντα διαφόρως]).

50. The Suda's statement leads us to surmise that a large part of Book V presumably dealt with the Athenian intervention during the Archidamian War, meriting a discussion we further suggest on the basis of *P.S.I.* 1283 of far greater detail than Thucydides' narrative. Given the fact that Book III dealt with the tyrants, we maintain that the overthrow of the tyrants and Ducetius' career were discussed in Book IV and possibly part of Book V.

51. G. Coppola, 'Una pagina del Περὶ Σικελίας di Fllisto in un papiro fiorentino', *RFIC*, vol. 58 (1930), pp. 449-66; A.D. Momigliano, 'Il nuovo Filisto e Tucidide', *RFIC*, vol. 58 (1930), pp. 467-70; I. Perrota, 'Il papiro fiorentino di Filisto', *SIFC*, vol. 8 (1930), pp. 311-15; V. Bartoletti, 'Rileggendo Filisto', *SIFC*, vol. 24 (1950), pp. 159-60. Against the scepticism of A.W. Gomme, *Historial Commentary on Thucydides* (henceforth cited as *HCT*) (Oxford, 1956), vol. 2, p. 390, see L. Pearson, 'Some new thoughts about the supposed fragment of Philistus (*P.S.I.* 1283)', *BASP*, vol. 20, nos. 3-4 (1983), pp. 151-58. Generally see S. Mazzarino, 'Tucidide e Filisto sulla prima spedizione ateniese in Sicilia', *BSC*, vol. 17 (1939), pp. 5-72, and R. Lauritano, 'Ricerche su Filisto', *Kokalos*, vol. 3 (1957), pp. 98-122.

52. A.D. Momigliano, 'History and Biography' in M.I. Finley (ed.), *Legacy of Greece. A reappraisal* (Oxford, 1981), p. 165.

53. On Thucydides' Philaïd connections, see J.H. Finley, *Thucydides*, pp. 9-20.

54. For Thucydides' oligarchic sympathies, see R. Syme, 'Thucydides', *PBA*, vol. 48 (1960), p. 40; M.F. McGregor, 'The politics of the historian Thucydides', *Phoenix*, vol. 10 (1956), p. 102; H. Lloyd-Jones, *The justice of Zeus* (California, 1971), p. 205, n 68; G.W. Bowersock, 'The personality of Thucydides', *AR*, vol. 25 (1965), p. 137; Abbot, *Thucydides*, p. 100; F. Wasserman, 'The speeches of King Archidamus in Thucydides', *CJ*, vol. 48 (1953), pp. 193-200; J.H. Finley, *Thucydides*, pp. 9-35. The historian's attachment to any one party questioned by H.D. Westlake, 'Nicias in Thucydides', *CQ*, vol. 35 (1941), pp. 58-9.

55. See esp. Thuc. I. 76. 3; II. 63. 1; 64. 4; 8. 4. On the Athenian power drive, see J.H. Finley, *Thucydides*, p. 143; J. de Romilly, *Thucydides and Athenian imperialism*, translated by P. Thody (Oxford, 1963), pp. 19ff.

56. As argued by Mazzarino, 'Tucidide e Filisto sulla prima spedizione ateniese in Sicilia', pp. 5-72. Mazzarino (ibid., pp. 59-60) further suggests that the evidence of Hermocrates' speech (Thuc. IV. 59-64) which does not harmonise with the narrative of events of 427-424 BC indicates that the Athenian historian ultimately came to a similar viewpoint as was later maintained by Philistus with respect to Hermocrates' important role as unifier of Sicily. Our acceptance of this thesis, of course, strengthens the Philistus-Thucydides thematic link which we are advocating.

57. Contrasting markedly with Plato's negative estimate (*Gorgias* 471a-d).

58. See V. Hunter, 'Athens Tyrannis: A new approach to Thucydides', *CJ*, vol. 69, no. 2 (1973-4), pp. 120-6.

59. Gomme, *HCT*, vol. 2, p. 175 on Thuc. II. 63. 2.

60. As argued by McGregor, 'The politics of the historian Thucydides', pp. 97-8 and W.G. Woodhead, *Thucydides on the nature of power* (Cambridge, Mass., 1970), p. 89.

61. Thus Jaeger, *Paideia*, vol. 1, pp. 409-10.

62. Thus I follow G. Busolt, *Griechische Geschichte* (Hildesheim, 1967), vol. 3. 1, p. 499; K.J. Beloch, *Die Attische Politik seit Perikles* (Stuttgart-Leipzig, 1884), pp. 19-22; H.T. Wade-Gery, *Essays in Greek History* (Oxford, 1958), p. 260; V. Ehrenberg, *Sophocles and Pericles* (Oxford, 1954), pp. 75ff; Ehrenberg, *From Solon to Socrates* (London, 1968), pp. 230-8; E.M. Walker, *CAH*, vol. 4, p. 155; J.S. Morrison, 'The place of Protagoras in Athenian life', *CQ*, vol. 35 (1941), p. 11; K.J. Dover, 'Dekatos Autos', *JHS*, vol. 80 (1960), pp. 61-77; A.J. Podlecki, 'Pericles and Augustus', *CNV*, vol. 22, no. 2 (1978), pp. 55-6; and above all, Green, *Shadow of the Parthenon*, p. 20 whose blunt and pertinent remarks deserve quotation. Thus:

it is no answer to say what is quite true that Pericles was reelected annually by an assembly vote: a democracy which turns itself over to a guru, even though voluntarily and in due form, has abrogated its basic function.

Cf. pp. 26-7, esp. p. 27, Pericles as 'the high-minded moral bully'; cf. p. 74 to Ehrenberg's idealistic view in *Sophocles and Pericles* of the Periclean regime as united by a 'common belief in man's perfection and in the final goal of human harmony,' Green ironically asks, 'exemplified no doubt by the suppression of the Samian revolt'; Kagan, *Peloponnesian war* and *Archidamian war* (Ithaca, 1974), I find contradictory. Thus, while noting Pericles' regular re-election, submission to examination (*Peloponnesian*, p. 69) and helplessness in face of the peace party (*Archidamian war*, pp. 80-1, cf. p. 119) and suspicious of the term 'generalissimo' as applied to Pericles (*Archidamian war*, p. 56), he uses the latter term (*Archidamian war*, p. 79) to describe Pericles and argues (*Archidamian war*, p. 56) that Pericles could prevent a meeting of the assembly (Thuc. II. 22. 1) because of his *auctoritas* as opposed to *imperium*.

63. See Ehrenberg, *Sophocles and Pericles*, pp. 85 ff, citing D.L. Page, *Greek literary papyri* (London, Cambridge, Mass., 1950), no. 38; Plut. *Pericles* VII. 4; XI. 4; XV. 1; XXXI. 1; XXXIII; XXXIX; A.B. Breebaart, 'Plutarch

and the political development of Pericles', *Mnemosyne*, vol. 24, no. 3 (1971), pp. 260-72.

64. Thus Ehrenberg, *Sophocles and Pericles*, pp. 105ff; Ehrenberg, *From Solon to Socrates*, p. 230; Kagan, *Peloponnesian war*, p. 141; C.G. Thomas, 'Sophocles, Pericles and Creon', *CW*, vol. 69 (1976), pp. 120-1; Breebaart, 'Plutarch and the political development of Pericles', pp. 269-70; T.B.L. Webster, *Political interpretations in Greek literature* (Manchester, 1948), p. 51.

65. Morrison, 'The place of Protagoras in Athenian life', p. 12; Morrison, 'Pericles Monarchos', *JHS*, vol. 70 (1950), pp. 76-7. Though cf. A.W. Gomme, 'Pericles Monarchos — A reply', *JHS*, vol. 70 (1950), p. 77.

66. As illustrated particularly by G.F. Bender, 'Der Begriff des Staatsmannes bei Thukydides', Dissertation, Wurzburg, 1938. Cf. Lloyd-Jones, *Justice of Zeus*, p. 205, n 68; K. J. Dover, *Thucydides book VI* (Oxford, 1965), p. 49; V. Hunter, 'The composition of Thucydides' History. A new answer to the problem', *Historia*, vol. 26, no. 3 (1977), p. 284.

67. Those, in our view, too ready to accept Thucydides' idealised depiction include J.H. Finley, 'Review of Bender, *Der Begriff des Staatsmannes bei Thukydides*', *AJPh*, vol. 61 (1940), p. 249; H.D. Westlake, 'Hermocrates the Syracusan', *BRL*, vol. 41 (1958), pp. 239-68; cf. Westlake, 'Thucydides' narrative of the Sicilian Expedition', *PCA*, vol. 50 (1953), p. 27; Green, *Armada from Athens*, pp. 71-2. To counter the evidence for Hermocrates' tyrannical aspirations, moreover, scholars tend to indulge in unconvincing apologetics viewing Hermocrates as a 'Churchillian' democrat (*sic* Green, *Armada from Athens*, pp. 71-2) whose very individuality aroused Syracusan suspicion and who only out of desperation and inability to solve Syracuse's internal and external problems was forced to seize the despotate of Syracuse (*sic* Westlake, 'Thucydides' narrative of the Sicilian Expedition', p. 27; cf. Stroheker, *Dionysios I*, p. 34. Freeman, *History of Sicily*, vol. 3, p. 507, who writes: 'his tendency was to oligarchy; he might conceivably have been driven into tyranny'. Cf. Freeman, *Sicily: Phoenician, Greek and Roman* (London, 1892), p. 146; L. Pareti, *Sicilia antica* (Palermo, 1959), p. 154, who considers Hermocrates a representative of the conservative moderates, and Holm, *Geschichte*, vol. 2, p. 86, who sees Hermocrates as an aristocratic-type tyrant ('ein zweiter Gelon niemals ein Dionys geworden'). The problem with the interpretation which sees Hermocrates as a man forced by his consideration of Syracuse's perilous situation to resort to revolutionary activity is that this consideration seems to have underlain the motivation of every Syracusan tyrant including Dionysius I. Hence the dubious significance of the antithesis postulated by Holm between Dionysius and Hermocrates. Finally to Westlake's argument that Hermocrates' actions were determined by selfless concern for the Punic threat to Syracuse, we retort that Hermocrates' actions must to some extent have been instrumental in causing the Punic invasion of 407-406 BC, though Diodorus does not mention this factor in XIII. 79. 8 and 80. 1. Those more convinced by Diodorus than by Thucydides include T. Lenschau, *s.v.* 'Hermocrates', *RE*, vol. 8, col. 885; J. Bayet, *La Sicile grecque* (Paris, 1930),

p. 32; Stroheker, *Dionysios I*, pp. 35, 195, who suggests that Hermocrates' contact with Pharnabazus (Xen. *Hell.* I. 1. 31; III. iv. 13; Diod. Sic. XIII. 63. 2) fostered Hermocrates' despotic inclinations; and above all F. Grosso, 'Ermocrate di Siracusa', *Kokalos*, vol. 12 (1966), pp. 102-43. I followed by M. Sordi, 'Ermokrate di Siracusa: demagogo e tyranno Mancato', in *Scritti sul mondo antico in memoria di Fulvio Grosso* (Rome, 1980), pp. 595-60.

68. The association of the reform with Hermocrates is ignored by Plutarch, *Nicias*, XVI. 5 and Diodorus XIII. 4. 1.

69. The concrete reality of the Pansiceliot policy ascribed by Thucydides to Hermocrates at Gela in 424 BC, involving peaceful co-operation between the Siceliot cities and the avoidance of entanglements with mainland Greece which in some respects anticipated the fourth-century BC political concept of *Koine Eirene*, is equally questionable, given the increasing involvement of mainland Greece in Western affairs during the fifth century BC. Obviously within the context of the precise political situation in 424 BC, when Syracuse was more threatened than Athens, Hermocrates' advocacy of a policy of Pansiceliotism made perfect political sense. At a later period, under changed political circumstances, however, Hermocrates' policy was obviously bound to change. Hence we are not surprised to note Hermocrates' censure of the Siceliots for not aiding the Peloponnesians during the Archidamian War (Thuc. VI. 34. 8; cf. Westlake, 'Hermocrates the Syracusan', p. 244; Kagan, *Archidamian war*, pp. 267-8) as well as his attempted diplomatic manoeuvrings with Carthage (Thuc. VI. 34. 2) and concrete intervention on Sparta's side during the Decelean War (Thuc. VIII, 26. 1).

70. Cf. E. Bayer, 'Thukydides und Perikles', *WJA*, vol. 3 (1948), 55A, 3, pp. 1-57; J. Vogt, 'Das Bild des Perikles bei Thukydides', *HZ*, vol. 182 (1956), pp. 249-66. On the Athenian power-drive which largely accounts for the abandonment of Periclean moderation, see, J.H. Finley, *Thucydides*, pp. 143, 150-5; de Romilly, *Thucydides*, pp. 19ff.

71. Thucydides' condemnation of the manner of the direction of the Sicilian expedition rather than of the expedition itself (II. 65. 11) of course does not invalidate the claim of I. 144. 1 and II. 65. 7. On the significance of Thucydides' Cleon *vis-à-vis* the briefly alluded to Hyperbolus and Androcles (VIII. 73. 3 and 65. 2), see A. Andrewes, 'The Mytilene Debate', *Phoenix*, vol. 16 (1962), p. 75; J.B. Bury, *The ancient Greek historians* (London, 1909), pp. 122-3.

72. Modern scholarly consensus has generally followed Thucydides. Thus Finley, *Thucydides*, pp. 28, 93, 151, 156, 161f, 164-6, 187, 203f, 245f, 297, 305, 308; Finley, *Three essays on Thucydides* (Boston, 1967), pp. 154ff; Abbot, *Thucydides*, p. 56; B.X. De Wet, 'Periclean imperial policy and the Mytilenean debate', *AClass*, vol. 6 (1963), pp. 106-24; F. Wasserman, 'Post-Periclean democracy in action: The Mytilenean debate', *TAPhA*, vol. 87 (1956), pp. 27-41; V. Ehrenberg, 'Polypragmosyne: A study in Greek politics', *JHS*, vol. 67 (1946), pp. 46-67; A.B. West, 'Pericles' political heirs', *CPhil*, vol. 9 (1924), pp. 120-46, 201-28; Kagan, *Peloponnesian war*, pp. 105-6, 112, 168, 174, 339; Kagan, *Archidamian war*, pp. 199-200, 242, 319, 356-7; M.A. Fitzsimmons, 'Thucydides' history, science and power', *APSR*, vol. 37 (1975), pp. 380-7. At the same time, it is worth

noting that both Ehrenberg and Kagan do acknowledge continuity between the policies of Pericles and the demagogues (thus Ehrenberg, 'Polypragmosyne: A study in Greek politics', p. 51; Kagan, *Archidamian war*, pp. 359-61, 332). Similarly see Dickins, 'The true causes of the Peloponnesian War', pp. 238-48; M.H. Chambers, 'Thucydides and Pericles', *HSPhil*, vol. 62 (1957), pp. 79-91; A.W. Gomme, *More essays in Greek history and literature* (Oxford, 1962), pp. 92-111; H.T. Wade-Gery, *s.v.* 'Pericles', *OCD*, p. 904; Abbot, *Thucydides*, pp. 63ff; R. Meiggs, *The Athenian empire* (Oxford, 1972), p. 204. For the view that Thucydides himself acknowledged continuity between Periclean and post-Periclean Athens, see B.X. De Wet, 'The so-called defensive policy of Pericles', *AClass*, vol. 12 (1969), pp. 103-19.

73. See M.L. Lang, 'Cleon as the anti-Pericles', *CPhil*, vol. 67 (1972), pp. 159-69. On the essentially aristocratic nature of the Periclean state, see R. Sealey, 'The entry of Pericles into History', *Hermes*, vol. 84 (1956), pp. 234-47.

74. See especially J.H. Oliver, 'The praise of Periclean Athens as a mixed constitution', *RhM*, vol. 98 (1955), pp. 37-40. Cf. P. Walcot, 'The Funeral Speech. A study in values', *G and R*, vol. 20 (1973), pp. 111-21; M.H. Chambers, 'Thucydides and Pericles', p. 81.

75. Thus although Cicero favours the restoration of the tribune's power (*De Leg.* III. 26) and the people's power to make laws, elect magistrates, and serve as a final court of appeal (*De Leg.* III. 10-11), he emphatically states that democracy alone is the worst of the three constitutions (*De Rep.* I. 43-44).

76. Of course the idea pervades the early *Pro Roscio Amerino*. See R.E. Smith, *Cicero the statesman* (Cambridge, 1966), p. 29; cf. p. 4ff.

77. Thus Folcke, 'Dionysius', pp. 33-4, following Mazzarino, 'Tucidide e Filisto', p. 69.

78. Folcke, 'Dionysius', p. 33, though admitting that a military figure would furnish accurate military data and ignoring the likelihood of accurate figures from a Thucydidean like Philistus unconvincingly argues that the inflated figures probably derive from Philistus who would 'not hesitate to exaggerate the size of the enemy's force in order to make Dionysius' successful campaign look more impressive'.

79. See Folcke, 'Dionysius', p. 156.

80. Though Sicily was treated separately from the history of the Greek mainland by Ephorus, Books Sixteen and Twenty-eight discussing Dionysius I, Book Twelve the early tyrants, the war of 480 BC and probably Ducetius, and Book Twenty-nine, the period of Dionysius II, Dion and Timoleon (Plut. *Tim.* IV/F. 221), we should not deduce from this fact or from Diodorus' statement (V. 1. 4/T. 11) that Ephorus wrote κατὰ γένος history, that Ephorus' general practice was to write episodic history, particularly in his accounts of fifth and fourth century history. See R. Drews, 'Ephorus and history written κατὰ γένος', *AJPh*, vol. 84 (1963), pp. 244-55.

81. In this reconstruction I follow G.L. Barber, *The historian Ephorus* (Cambridge, 1935), pp. 41-8; Meister, 'Die Sizilische Geschichte', p. 4; and E. Schwartz, *s.v.* 'Ephoros', *RE* (1909), vol. 7, col. 5.

82. See pp. 45-6, 62.

83. See p. 76.

84. Followed by Aelian *VH* IV. 8 who substitutes a certain Helopides for Heloris. Cf. Plut. *Cat. Mai.* XXIV. 8 and *An. Seni.* 783d. where no context at all is provided. Cf. Procop. *Bell. Pers.* I. 24. 37 for Theodora's reproduction of the remark without specific mention being made of either Heloris or Dionysius, and Livy XXIV. 22. 8-9 where the events are described without reference to Heloris' quotation and again without a context being provided.

85. Cf. Folcke, 'Dionysius', pp. 186-7, who argues that Ephorus' and Theopompus' accounts of Dionysius' colonisation ventures derived from Philistus and were hence only succinctly considered.

86. See A.D. Momigliano, 'L'Europa come concetto politico presso Isocrate e gli Isocratei', *RFIC*, N.S. vol. 11 (1933), pp. 477-87.

87. Cf. praise in Diodorus XVI. 1. 4. 6 for Philip's possession of the combined qualities of *arete*, courage and greatness of soul — qualities hitherto individually held by Epaminondas, Sparta and Athens, on which see Momigliano, 'La storia di Eforo e le Elleniche di Teopompo', pp. 180-204, esp. 195ff.

88. See pp. 5, 7.

89. Cf. I.A.F. Bruce, 'Theopompus and classical Greek historiography', 96, who surprisingly maintains that the Sicilian excursus embraced Books XXXIX to XLIII.

90. Cf. Folcke, 'Dionysius', pp. 186-7.

91. Though cf. N.G.L. Hammond, 'The sources of Diodorus Siculus XVI', *CQ*, vol. 32 (1938), pp. 142-3. We might, of course, surmise that, given the existence of a Sicilian digression in the *Philippica*, a similar digression appeared in the *Hellenica*. Further, since as we shall see, a thematic link between Dionysius and Philip II associated with Theopompus' central notion of the disastrous political consequences of vice, does characterise the *Philippica*, it is certainly tempting to hazard the guess that a consideration of Dionysius' monarchy in its early years as a parallel to the main theme of the *Hellenica*, Lysander's monarchy, characterised the earlier work of Theopompus. The argument of H.D. Westlake ('The Sicilian Books of Theopompus' *Philippica*', *Historia*, vol. 2 (1953-4), p. 291) against the view that the *Hellenica* contained a Dionysian digression is, moreover, in our view particularly weak. For while it is true that Thucydides, whose history the *Hellenica* continued, only mentioned Sicilian affairs when they possessed direct relevance to the affairs of the Greek mainland, and Xenophon's *Hellenica*, which also continued Thucydides' history, barely touched on Sicilian affairs, we emphasise that Theopompus was not a Thucydidean or indeed a Xenophon and that Thucydides himself was quite capable of digressing into fields which scarcely related directly to the main line of argumentation pursued. However, notwithstanding these considerations, we stress that direct evidence to substantiate Hammond's guess is certainly wanting.

92. Though cf. Westlake, 'The Sicilian Books of Theopompus' *Philippica*', who argues that Diodorus' wording indicates specifically the beginning of Dionysius' tyranny and that a fifty-year period from that date makes perfectly good sense, if associated with the first rather than second and final expulsion of the younger Dionysius. Though dog-

matism on this point is to be eschewed, the general reference to an expulsion, in our view, suggests the final expulsion of the younger Dionysius and, following Hammond we favour the view that Diodorus' reference to the establishment of the tyranny of Dionysius constitutes in fact a reference to the establishment of Dionysius' empire in 392 BC.

93. To quote Westlake, 'The Sicilian Books of Theopompus' *Philippica*', p. 299: 'To Justin, the ignominious career of Dionysius II was the only noteworthy feature of Sicilian history of the middle of the fourth century B.C.'. Cf. Beloch, *Griechische Geschichte*, vol. 2, ii, p. 26, who believes that Trogus' source was Timaeus.

94. See above Chapter 1, n 24.

95. Cf. W.R. Roberts, 'Theopompus in the Greek Literary Critics', *CR*, vol. 20 (1908), pp. 118-22.

96. Thus A.D. Momigliano, 'Atene nel III secolo A.C. e la scoperta di Roma nelle storie di Timeo di Tauromenio', *RSIN*, vol. 71 (1959), p. 547: 'Il suo odio per il tiranno corrispondera a sentimenti ateniesi.' Cf. Timaeus' opposition to Alexander, condemnation of Callisthenes and praise of Demosthenes (Polyb. XII. 12b. 2/F. 155).

97. Hence Diodorus' caution (XXI. 17. 3/F. 124d) in accepting the veracity of the data found in the Agathoclean books.

98. Whence E. Schwartz's description of Timoleon ('Timaios Geschichtswerk', *Hermes*, vol. 34 (1899), p. 490) as 'Timaios Lieblingshelden'. The veracity of the Timoleon tradition was further lessened by Timoleon's own propaganda and by the negative characteristics of Plutarch's technique. See H.D. Westlake, *Timoleon and his relations with tyrants* (Manchester, 1952), p. 2. On the use of the Timaeus tradition in Plutarch and Nepos, see H.D. Westlake, 'The sources of Plutarch's Timoleon', *CQ*, vol. 32 (1938), pp. 65-74.

99. I follow Pearson's suggestion, *Greek historians of the west* (Scholars Press, Atlanta, Georgia, forthcoming) that Athenaeus' reference to Hegesander of Delphi probably was actually derived from Timaeus who is mentioned immediately following for two anecdotes describing flattery of the younger Dionysius.

100. For similar reasons as delineated in n. 99 Pearson, *Greek historians of the west* (forthcoming) ascribes this fragment to Timaeus who is cited in XII. 58, p. 541, b-c/F. 9, despite its attribution to Athanis (F. 1/Athen. III. 54, p. 98d).

101. Though T.S. Brown, *Timaeus of Tauromenium* (California, 1958), pp. 3, 6, dates Timaeus' initial departure from Sicily and arrival in Athens between 339 and 329 BC, scholarly consensus, basing itself upon Diod. Sic. XIX. 65; 72. 1; 102. 6; 20. 4, prefers a date between 317 and 310 BC. Thus Laqueur, *RE*, *s.v.* 'Timaios', cols. 1077-83; Momigliano, 'Atene nel III secolo A.C. e la scoperta di Roma nelle storie di Timeo di Tauromenio', p. 531; K.F. Meister, 'Das Exil des Timaios von Tauromenion', *Kokalos*, vol. 16 (1970), pp. 56-7; Jacoby, *FGH*, vol. 3b (Komm.), no. 556, p. 531; F.W. Walbank, 'Review of Brown's *Timaeus*', *EHR*, vol. 74 (1959), p. 333, emphasising Diodorus' association of the exile with Agathocles: φυγαδευθεὶς ὑπ' Ἀγαθοκλέους ἐκ τῆς Σικελίας.

102. While Brown, *Timaeus*, pp. 3, 6 and Meister, 'Das Exil von Timaios von Tauromenion', pp. 57-9, maintain that Timaeus did in fact

return, we follow Jacoby, *FGH*, vol. 3b (Komm.), no. 566, p. 532 and Walbank, *HCP*, vol. 2, p. 388 (cf. Walbank, *Polybius* (Los Angeles, 1972), p. 51, n 111) in rejecting this conclusion, noting in particular that the reference to a fifty-year period of exile referred to by Polybius XII, 25h. 1/F. 34, need not imply a return after fifty years and that the alleged bookishness of Timaeus is only comprehensible within the context of Timaeus' ending his days in Athens. One can, à la Meister, perhaps make too much of Polybius' use of a cardinal number and aorist tense, i.e., πεντήκοντα ἔτη διατρίψας as opposed to τὸ πεντηκοστὸν ἔτος διατρίβων. Similarly, Timaeus' claim to have seen Acragantine monuments personally (F. 26a/Diod. Sic. XIII. 82. 6) need not be taken at its face value.

103. Following De Sanctis (*Ricerche*, p. 51) we substitute ιζ for ζ in F. 29/Schol. Aesch. II. 10 and thus attribute the dream of the Himeraean woman and Timaeus' early discussion of Dionysius to Book XVI rather than to Book VI. That Timaeus' discussion of Dionysius extended to Book XXI is suggested by F. 32/Athen. VI, p. 250a on Damocles' flattery of Dionysius II, which is placed in Book XXII and accordingly suggests that the discussion of Sicilian history after Dionysius I's death began in Book XXII. Polybius' attribution of Hermocrates' speech at Gela and Timoleon's speech to Book XXI (XII. 25K. 2; 25. 7/F. 22. 31), thereby suggesting that Timoleon rather than Dionysius I was discussed in Book XXI and that the terminus of the Dionysian books must, therefore, be pushed back to Book XX at the least (thus Jacoby, *FGH*, vol. 3b (Komm.), 544) or even to Book XIX (Folcke, 'Dionysius', p. 55), is suspect either as an error of Polybius' (De Sanctis, *Ricerche*, p. 51) or of the excerptor (Walbank, *HCP*, vol. 2, p. 384), on the grounds that both speeches are unlikely to have appeared in the same book, Hermocrates' probably appearing in either Books XIII, XV or XVI and Timoleon's between Books XXII and XXVIII (cf. Athen. VI. 56., p. 250a; Athen. XI. 43. 471f/F32, 33) or more likely between XXII and XXXIII (cf. Diod. Sic. XXI. 17. 3/F. 124d). See De Sanctis, *Ricerche*, p. 51; K.J. Beloch, 'Die Ökonomie der Geschichte des Timalos', *NJCP*, vol. 27 (1881), p. 701.

104. Thus, Westlake, *Timoleon*, p. 5.

105. Clearly the MSS. reading ἀποθανόντος καθ' ἣν ἐγενήθη Διονύσιος should read καθ' ἣν τύραννος ἐγενήθη. Thus Brown, *Timaeus*, pp. 76-77; Pearson, *Greek historians of the west*.

106. Aristotle's Esau-like equating of red hair and roguish behaviour (οἱ πυρροὶ ἄγαν πανοῦργοι *Physiog.* VI. 812a) makes sense of Timaeus' reference to Dionysius' red hair. Possibly as Walbank suggests (*HCP*, vol. 2, p. 380), Polybius' derogatory reference to the effeminate tastes of Διονύσιος ὁ τύραννος (XII. 24. 2) as evidenced by the latter's interest in bed-hangings and woven work, derives from Timaeus and was associated with the elder Dionysius. Later references, without mentioning Timaeus' authority, to the dream occur in Tertullian (*De Anim.* 46) — possibly from Heracleides Ponticus as Jacoby, *FGH*, vol. 3b (Noten), p. 327, suggests. It also appears in *P. Ox.* 1012, frag. 9, col. I, again without reference to Timaeus as a source.

107. R. Vattuone, 'Su Timeo F. 29 *Jacoby*', *RSAnt*, vol. 11, nos. 1-2 (1981), pp. 139-45.

108. Thus compare in the fragment, the motifs of lust (πυρρός), physical robustness (μέγας), restrained violence (πυρρός; cf. κλοίος) with similar motifs in Justin XXII. I. 1-3, obviously derived from Timaeus (cf. F. 124c): 'Agathocles, Siciliae tyrannus, qui magnitudini prioris Dionysii successit, ad regni maiestatem ex humili et sordido genere perventit ... forma et corporis pulchritudine egregius, diu vitam stupri patientia exhibuit.'

109. Cf. F.W. Walbank, 'Polemic in Polybius', *JRS*, vol. 52 (1962), pp. 1-12 on the effect of past history on Polybius' grievances.

110. The claim of Tzetzes, *Chil.* X. 835 that envy accounted for Timaeus' criticism of Philistus is, for all its simplicity, not far from the truth.

111. On the other hand, given Timaeus' critical attitude to Plato (Diog. Laert. VIII. 54; Plut. *Nic.* I. 4/F. 14; T. 18) we can scarcely argue that Theopompus' hostility to Plato (Athen. XI. 118, p. 508c-d; Arr. *Epict. Diss.* II. 16. 5-6/F. 259, 275) would have hardly proved attractive to a historian like Timaeus, hostile to Plato's opponents, the Dionysii.

112. Convincingly deduced by K.F. Stroheker, 'Timaios und Philistos', *Satura. Früchte aus der antiken Welt O. Weinreich zum 13 März 1951 dargebrachte* (Baden-Baden, 1952), p. 147 and Stroheker, 'Platon und Dionysios', p. 240 from Athenaeus V. 40, p. 206e/F. 112 and Plut. *Pelop.* XXXIV. 1/556 F. 40b. The latter reference to tragedy is obviously more likely of Timaean than Philistan origin.

113. The former suggested by Vattuone, 'Su Timeo F. 29', p. 140; the latter by Sordi, 'Il fr. 29 Jacoby di Timeo e la lettura augustea di un passo di Filisto', pp. 534-9.

114. Despite Plutarch's precise statement (*Dion* XXXV. 6/F. 115) to the effect that the dictum that 'a tyrant should be dragged away by the legs' was not uttered by Philistus but by someone else, I am less convinced by Brown's argument (*Timaeus*, pp. 77-8) that blatant falsification of Philistus on Timaeus' part by interpolation of data stemming from Timonides of Leucas (Jacoby, *FGH*, vol. 3b, no. 561. F. 2, cf. vol. 2a, no. 70, F. 219/Plut. *Dion* XXXV. 3-5) to accord with Timaeus' own depiction of Philistus' degrading end is to be found in Timaeus' supposed attribution of this remark to Philistus in Diodorus XIV. 8. 5. Certainly since we know that elsewhere Diodorus attributed this remark to Megacles (XX. 78. 3), the likelihood that Diodorus' data in XIV. 8. 5 stems from error on the historian's part, must be seriously entertained.

115. Brown, *Timaeus*, pp. 71-90; accepted by H.D. Westlake in his review of the book in *CR*, vol. 9 (1959), p. 250; cf. the cautious scepticism of Walbank, 'Review of Brown's *Timaeus*', p. 333. The contrast is surely implicit in F. 105's equation of Euripides' death with Dionysius' rise and accompanying comment that Euripides was born on the day of the victory of Salamis. Thus the pre-Dionysius period was in Timaeus' eyes to be equated with the glorious days of Athens.

116. Despite our contention maintained below (p. 147) to the effect that the information on Acragas found in Diodorus ultimately derived from Philistus, the fact that the data was largely utilised by Timaeus into whose account it accordingly found its way can scarcely be gainsaid and may be deduced from the following phenomena: Timaeus' parallel

discussion of Acragantine affluence and of Acragas' predominant personality, Empedocles, in a corresponding part of the earlier historian's History (Diod. Sic. XIII. 83. 1; Diog. Laert. VIII. 51/F. 26a, 26b); parallel references to Acragantine strigils, flasks and racehorses quoted on the authority of Timaeus in Aelian and Diogenes Laertius (Aelian *VH* XII. 29/F. 26c; cf. Diod. Sic. XIII. 83. 3/F. 26a, Diog. Laert. VIII. 51/F. 26b, cf. Diod. Sic. XIII. 82. 7); and the fact that the other reference in Diodorus XIII to the wealth of Acragas, pertaining to the bull of Phalaris, is quoted on the authority of Timaeus (Diod. Sic. XIII. 90. 4-6/F. 28a). The view of E. Manni, 'Sileno in Diodoro?', *AAP*, Ser. IVa, vol. 18, no. 2 (1957-8), p. 87, that Philinus of Acragas via Silenus was Diodorus' source for the excursus is pure hypothesis.

117. That the excursus' emphasis upon the luxury of the Acragantines from youth upwards — the delicate clothing, flasks of silver and gold, wine cellar of Tellias, city's ornaments, the wedding of Tellias' daughter (XIII. 82-4) — is largely condemnatory may be deduced from the story of Antisthenes' son and the farmer (XIII. 84. 4; cf. F. 148/ Zenob. *Paroem.* I. 31 on the drunken youths of the house of the Trireme). Its clear association, moreover, with the Siceliot débâcle is well illustrated by passages external to the excursus and yet nevertheless intimately associated with it, which contrast earlier prosperity with present misfortunes, viz. the reference to the limitation of the bedding of the guards to one mattress, one cover, one sheepskin and two pillows (XIII. 84. 5); the observation that, in spite of the fact that the Acragantines were fleeing for their lives, they still thought of the riches which they were abandoning (XIII. 89. 1); the reference to the fact that the women and children were afraid of changing a pampered life for a strenuous journey and hardship (XIII. 89. 3), and the contrast between the ransacking of the buildings and the temples, and the city's former prosperity (XIII. 90. 3). Cf., however, Pearson's *Greek historians of the west* (forthcoming) who does not interpret the excursus in this manner.

118. Our argument that Books XIV and XV of Timaeus' history dealt with the two Punic invasions of Sicily is based: (a) upon the association of F. 23 and 24 (Athen. VII. 132, p. 327b; XIII. 54-55, p. 588b-589a) and their references to Hykkara in Book XIII with Thuc. VI. 62. 3-4, thereby suggesting that Book XIII discussed the great Athenian expedition to Sicily; and (b) upon the reference in Diod. Sic. XIII. 83. 2/F. 26a to the hospitality of Tellias of Acragas in Book XV.

119. See n 103.

120. On the chronology of Timaeus' history, see Beloch, 'Die Ökonomie der Geschichte des Timaios', pp. 697-706; H. Kothe, 'Zur Ökonomie der Historien des Timaios', *NJCP*, I, vol. 29 (1883), pp. 809-13; Schwartz, 'Timaios Geschichtswerk', pp. 481-93; Westlake, 'The sources of Plutarch's Timoleon', p. 67; De Sanctis, *Ricerche*, pp. 43ff; Walbank, *HCP*, vol. 2, p. 384. The relative meagreness of space allotted the Agathocles books has to be conceived of within the context of various factors: the historian's severance of all connections with Sicily after his exile; the unlikelihood of his return to his native land; given the possibility of such a return, the probable demise of the historian's friends and acquaintances, largely at the hands of Agathocles; Timaeus' likely

ignorance, in view of his exile, of geographical, political and military data pertaining to Sicily, whence Polybius' assault upon Timaeus (Polyb. XII. 3-4, 4b, c, d; 25d, e, f, g, h); and the historian's personal hatred for Agathocles which led him to minimise the significance of Agathocles' war against Carthage.

121. See Jacoby, *FGH*, vol. 3b (Komm.), no. 566. p. 537; Momigliano, 'Atene nel III secole A.C. e la scoperta di Roma nelle storie di Timeo di Tauromenio', p. 533; C.B. Wells, 'Review of Brown, *Timaeus of Tauromenium*', *AHR*, vol. 63 (1957-8), p. 1030; Walbank, *Polybius*, p. 52.

122. For Timaeus' popularity at Rome, see Varro *De Re Rustica* II. 5. 3; Cicero *Ad Attic.* VI. 1. 18; *Brut.* LXIII/F. 42b, T. 29, F. 138.

123. See Jacoby, *FGH*, vol. 3b (Komm.), no. 566, p. 526. For Greece, he followed the terminal point of Aratus' account (Polyb. I. 3. 2).

124. Against the view of P. Pedech, *Polybe. Histoires*, Livre XII (Paris, 1960), pp. xxxi-xxxiii, that Timaeus' popularity at Alexandria at the time of Polybius' visit (Polyb. XXXIV. 14. 6) induced Polybius' ire, see Walbank, *HCP*, vol. 2, pp. 388-9; Walbank, *Polybius*, p. 48. For a more charitable estimate of Polybius' motivation, based on Polyb. I. 14. 6; III. 26. 3-4; XII. 4a. b; 4b. 4c; 25d. 1; 12b; 25b, see M.A. Levi, 'La critica di Polibio a Timeo', *Miscellanea di studi Alessandrini in memoria di Augusto Rostagni* (Turin, 1963), pp. 195-202. Cf. also De Sanctis, *Ricerche*, p. 83. Though the extent to which personal subjective motivation underlies Polybius' attack upon Timaeus and others is well underlined by Walbank, 'Polemic in Polybius', pp. 1-12; Walbank, 'Three Notes on Polybius', *Miscellanea di studi Alessandrini in memoria Augusto Rostagni*, (Turin, 1963), p. 207; Jacoby, *FGH*, vol. 3b (Komm.), no. 566, pp. 526ff. See also A.H. McDonald's 'Review of Brown, *Timaeus of Tauromenium*', *JHS*, vol. 79 (1959), p. 188.

125. Cicero's adoption of Timaeus' viewpoint is comprehensible within the context of a probable change of heart during Caesar's autocracy and its aftermath — a phenomenon which is moreover suggested by the abandonment of Cicero's pro-monarchical stance in the *De Legibus.*

126. See E. Schwartz, *s.v.*, 'Amyntianos', *RE*, vol. 1 (1894), col. 2008.

127. To the same tradition belongs Dionysius' condemnation of Speusippus for his hedonism (Athen. VII. 279e; XII. 546d) which contrasts with Diodorus' account (XV. 74) of the tyrant's death through overeating and drinking. See A.P. McKinlay, 'The indulgent Dionysius', *TAPhA*, vol. 70 (1939), pp. 51-61.

128. For all his prejudice and bias as well as for his rhetorical tendencies (Polyb. XII. 25k, 26, 26a), superstitiousness (Polyb. XII. 24. 5), provincialism (Polyb. XII. 26b, 4-5), bookishness, personal ignorance of geography, politics and warfare (Polyb. XII. 3-4; 4b; 4c; 4d; 25d; 25e; 25f; 25g; 25h), Timaeus' stature within the context of Greek historiography is assured, if only because of his formulation of a precise chronological scheme and because of his polemicising role and geographical interests which were so closely emulated by Polybius. Thus, De Sanctis, *Ricerche*, p. 69:

Timeo, nonostante i suoi difetti deve essere considerato come uno dei massimi storichi antichi e uno di quelli che hanno recato il maggior contributo al progresso della storiografia. I suoi difetti d'altronde, se possono renderci antipatico il suo carattere personale, non oscurano sostanzialmente i suoi meriti di storiografo e quello inanzitutto di aver posto per primo le basi scientifiche alla storiografia del mondo occidentale.

Though for an opposite view, see Kothe, 'Zur Ökonomie der Historien des Timaios', pp. 813.

129. See Freeman, *History of Sicily*, vol. 4, p. 6ff; Beloch, *Griechische Geschichte*, vol. 3, p. 203; W. Huttle, *Verfassungsgeschichte von Syrakus* (Prague, 1929), p. 100; Stroheker, *Dionysios I*, pp. 149, 167, 238-9; Tod, *Greek historical inscriptions*, vol. 2, nos. 108, 133, 136.

3

Diodorus and Dionysius

I

Notwithstanding the comparatively recent attempt by scholars emanating from the University of Palermo to advance the claim of Silenus of Caleacte as Diodorus' chief source for his account of all Sicilian history, including, therefore, the narrative of Dionysius' reign,[1] modern *Quellenforschung* has tended to focus its attention upon those four obvious candidates whose work we have discussed in the previous chapter. Certainly, the likelihood of Diodorus' having recourse to all these authorities is suggested by that historian's clear references to the works of Philistus (Diod. Sic. XIII. 103. 3; XV. 89. 3; 94. 4; XIII. 91. 4; XIV. 8. 5/T. 11a, 11b, 11c [cf. 562 T. 2], 3, 4) and Timaeus (Diod. Sic. XIII. 54. 5; 60. 5; 80. 5; 109. 2; XIV. 54. 5; XIII. 108. 4; 85. 3; 90. 4-6; 82. 6; 83. 2/ F. 103, 104, 25, 107, 108, 106, 27, 28a, 26a) as well as to the specifically Sicilian testimonies of Ephorus (Diod. Sic. XIII. 54. 5; 60. 5; 80. 5; XIV. 54. 5/F. 201, 202, 203, 204) and Theopompus (Diod. Sic. XVI. 71. 3/F. 184) in his *Bibliotheke*. On the other hand, the fact that only Ephorus and Timaeus merit mention by Diodorus in the Dionysian or Sicilian sections of the thirteenth and fourteenth books has produced the prevailing opinion that the latter narrative as well as occasionally that of the fifteenth book stems directly either from Timaeus exclusively[2] or from Timaeus and Ephorus conjointly with the former undoubtedly exerting the decisive influence.[3] As a result, while Theopompus' candidacy as a source for the Sicilian data of the thirteenth and fourteenth books has, with one exception, been rejected,[4] and that authority has only been associated with the rather fragmentary Sicilian narrative of Diodorus' fifteenth book,[5] whatever modern scholars have discerned in Diodorus as emanating from Philistus has been essentially conceived of as data indirectly gleaned by Diodorus from Timaeus[6] whose narrative, we have seen, was certainly characterised by heavy reliance upon the Περὶ Διονυσίου of Philistus.[7]

Given then the importance which the fragments of Ephorus and Timaeus have assumed for source-critics investigating Diodorus' Dionysian narrative, before proceeding to evaluate the extent of influence exercised upon Diodorus by each of the sources favoured by modern source-critics individually, we do well to delineate two fundamental deficiencies which we feel have characterised argumentation based solely upon the Ephorus and Timaeus citations. First we note that the fragments have been utilised as evidence for much material whose links with Timaeus and Ephorus prove highly tenuous and that all that we can, in fact, deduce from such citations relates precisely to the immediate material to which they allude. Thus from the testimony of the fragments alone, we can only with confidence conclude that Timaeus' estimate of barbarian numbers (F. 103, 104, 25, 108/ Diod. Sic. XIII. 54. 5; 60. 5; 80. 5; XIV. 54. 5) was conservative *vis-à-vis* Ephorus (F. 201, 202, 203, 204) and that Timaeus wrote about the bronze statue of Apollo and Alexander (F. 106/Diod. Sic. XIII. 108. 4), Dexippus (F. 27/Diod. Sic. XIII. 85. 3), the bull of Phalaris (F. 28a/Diod. Sic. XIII. 90. 4-6) and aspects of Acragantine luxury (F. 26a/Diod. Sic. XIII. 82. 6; 83. 2). To assume, however, with Volquardsen and Schwartz on the basis of one reference by Timaeus to Dexippus (Diod. Sic. XIII. 85. 3/F. 27), that the other references to that individual (Diod. Sic. XIII. 87. 4-5; 88. 7; 93. 1, 4; 96. 1) must derive from Timaeus, or with Jacoby that two citations from Timaeus occurring in the Acragantine excursus (Diod. Sic. XIII. 82. 6; 83. 2/F. 26a) produce the corollary that the whole passage is to be associated with Timaeus' authority, is to indulge in what can only be described as patent guesswork. Moreover, once the attribution of the whole Acragantine excursus to Timaeus' authority has been eschewed, references to 200,000 Acragantine inhabitants (Diod. Sic. XIII. 90. 3) or to the wealthy Acragantine Tellias (Diod. Sic. XIII. 90. 2) cannot be automatically attributed to Timaeus' authority, merely by virtue of the fact that two random references to the same number of Acragantines and to Tellias — neither of which is directly associated with Timaeus' authority — occur in the excursus (Diod. Sic. XIII. 83. 2; 84. 3).

The tendency to guesswork on the basis of the Timaeus and

Ephorus citations reached its zenith with what undoubtedly constitutes the most detailed study of Diodorus' sources, that furnished by Richard Laqueur in his *RE* article on Timaeus[8] — an *oeuvre* whose significance can, above all, be gauged by the fact that its conclusions have been essentially accepted by the authoritative figure of Stroheker and, with reservations, by the modern *doyen* of ancient Greek historiography, Felix Jacoby.[9] Undoubtedly on general grounds, Laqueur's thesis holds obvious attractions. For one thing, ingeniously argued, it alone furnishes us with what is clearly the only study of Diodorus' sources to account for every nook and cranny of Diodorus' text in the minutest detail. Laqueur's argument that the more detailed local Sicilian data as opposed to the more superficial and general information supplied by Ephorus, stems from Timaeus and was incorporated to assuage Diodorus' own particular interest in the affairs of his homeland, moreover, might appear plausible given the fact that while Timaeus, the Western Greek historian, undoubtedly dealt with Western affairs in more detail than Ephorus, indeed devoted eight books to a period covered by Ephorus in two books, Diodorus, presumably as a patriotic Sicilian, did devote a proportionately large part of his *oeuvre* to Sicilian events, including the tyranny of Dionysius I. It is further highly unlikely that Ephorus, generally agreed by source-critics to be Diodorus' basic source for the affairs of the Greek mainland in the fifth and early fourth century BC, would have been totally ignored by Diodorus at the time that he was composing his history of the Greek West.

It is, however, at the point that we begin to explore the minutiae of Laqueur's argumentation that we realise the extent to which Laqueur's whole thesis is built upon a brilliantly composed substructure of guesswork. The very assumption that Diodorus' text incorporates a pot-pourri of extracts from Ephorus and Timaeus, presented according to the original scale of these authors, is open to question, since it is not confirmed by direct evidence[10] and is, in fact, contradicted by the fact that portions of the text said to derive from either of the two chosen authors are generally complementary to the texts supposedly deriving from the other.[11] Vocabulary identification with Timaeus or Ephorus on the basis of verbs like σαλεύω (Diod. Sic. XIII. 59. 7; XIV. 8. 3) or nouns like σκάφη (Diod. Sic. XIV. 50. 3; 59. 7) or of differing vocabulary or phraseology to describe the Italiots[12] are assumed as gospel on the basis of a couple of random references without proof being offered of their extensive use by Diodorus throughout

his text or of their exclusive employment in sections identified by
Laqueur with Timaeus and, more importantly, without any
attempt, on the one hand, to relate such vocabulary to definite
fragments of Timaeus and, on the other, to prove non-utilisation
by Ephorus of such vocabulary and phraseology in the latter's
fragments. Moreover, following Meister,[13] we do well to note how
certain words identified with Timaeus' authority by Diodorus
occur throughout Diodorus' history and hence are not to be associated exclusively with Diodorus' Western Greek data. For the
rest, we observe how Laqueur quite cavalierly and without confirmatory testimony from the fragments of Timaeus and Ephorus
either fabricates supposedly contradictory data in Diodorus'
text[14] which he ascribes to the authority of Ephorus and Timaeus
or extending the approach of Volquardsen and Schwartz by
purely subjective reasoning assumes, on the one hand, that
material repeated more than once can only have been discussed
by one source of Diodorus at a time,[15] while, on the other hand,
arguing in totally contradictory manner that twice-mentioned
data must indicate quite separate source-origins for each of these
quotations.[16]

Underlying such methodology, of course, lies the second
weakness which we feel characterises source criticism based
exclusively upon the evidence of the fragments cited by Diodorus,
namely the assumption that Diodorus was merely a scissors-and-
paste historian, unimaginatively and haphazardly combining
passages from his two sources without allowing his own personal
individual traits to colour his narrative — an evaluation whose
validity, we must emphasise, has increasingly been questioned
both within the context of Diodorus' *Bibliotheke* as a whole and
within that of the more specific Sicilian and Dionysian sections of
the work.[17] We initially note the simple and obvious fact that such
a modern technique is only possible with utilisation of books with
precise pagination and not with papyrus rolls.[18] Further, on general stylistic grounds J. Palm has demonstrated, by comparing
Diodorus' style with that of his sources, the considerable extent to
which Diodorus was capable of modernising his material and
effecting changes if necessary and thus unifying stylistically the
work[19] — a conclusion anticipated to some extent by M. Kunz
who already noted stylistic variations between the prefaces and
transitionary and summary passages linked to the prefaces, less
flattering to Diodorus than to the sources which he utilised,
revealing Diodorus' contribution to be somewhat dull, repetitious

and uninspiring.[20] The prefaces, moreover, by their sheer variety, illustrating the considerable range of source material undoubtedly utilised by Diodorus, including probably Ephorus, Timaeus, Polybius, Theopompus, Duris and Cratippus — all of whom wrote their own unique type of *prooemium* — suggest that Diodorus did not simply follow exclusively one or two sources at a time.[21] Above all, despite our doubts concerning any central Hellenistic philosophic influence — Stoic or possibly Epicurean — which might have been exerted upon Diodorus,[22] an undoubted central moral thesis does seem to permeate the *Bibliotheke*,[23] aimed at inspiring nobility and moral rectitude, unifying the narrative by the variety and quantity of the particular situations contained therein.[24] Thus we encounter throughout Diodorus' text an underlying emphasis upon the expediency of justice and virtue as illustrated by such qualities as piety, restraint, patience, clemency, mildness, pity, humility, courage, love of mankind and respect for *tyche*, the transgression of which, involving adherence to cruelty, arrogance, impiety, lawlessness, luxury and unreasonableness, creates *nemesis*, destruction arising from vice.[25] Obviously the fact that these *sententiae* occur throughout the *Bibliotheke* in passages where Diodorus cannot have used the same sources on every occasion negates the popular view of Diodorus as a slavish compiler, since Diodorus' very selectivity of material to correspond with the central thesis which he was trying to propagate reveals Diodorus as a historian with a clear-cut conception of the overall design of his work, to which he was obliged to subordinate his selection of source material. Moreover, as R. Drews has shown, Diodorus, in order to substantiate his central thesis was, in fact, quite prepared to extend the sentiments expressed by his sources, either by incorporating his own sentiments or those of lesser authorities, if he felt that the data enshrined in his sources over-reticent in supporting his central message.[26]

Turning from the general to the particular and from consideration of the *Bibliotheke* as a whole to that of the Sicilian and, more specifically, the Dionysian narrative, we immediately encounter a varied selection of source material as well as a certain amount of independence of thought on Diodorus' part. Thus in addition to the well known citations from Ephorus and Timaeus, we note one reference to the work of the shadowy Polycritus of Mende[27] (Diod. Sic. XIII. 83. 3/559. F. 3) which as we know from Aristotle (*Mirab. Auscul.* 112/F. 2), though composed before Timaeus' history, might well, in view of Diodorus' general catholicity of choice in source material, have been personally viewed by the Siceliot historian and its sentiments not simply incorporated into the text via Timaeus. That Diodorus, moreover, consulted a variety of sources in his Dionysian narrative is suggested by two references to the views of 'certain' sources (τινες), maintaining a higher figure of barbarian troop numbers than Timaeus (XIII. 109. 2) and a foundation date for Halaisa at the time of Himilcon's peace with Dionysius (XIV. 16. 4b). The former citation is particularly instructive since, in contrast to four other occasions, here alone Diodorus cites Timaeus' figures (F. 107) without mentioning those of Ephorus specifically, whence our conclusion that on this occasion Diodorus read other authorities than Ephorus.[28] That Diodorus read sources not specifically derived from and indeed later than Timaeus' is, finally, suggested by the passage describing the fate of the bull of Phalaris (Diod. Sic. XIII. 90. 4-6/F. 28a) which, while suggesting Diodorus' direct acquaintance with Timaeus also offers conclusive evidence to the effect that Diodorus read the historian who attacked Timaeus, probably Polybius, who certainly attacked Timaeus in this context (Polyb. XII. 25. 4/F. 28b),[29] was read by Diodorus[30] and certainly flourished after Timaeus.[31] Finally as testimony for Diodorus' independent presence within the Western narrative as a whole, we cite three facts. First we note the comparatively large allocation of space to Sicilian affairs, specifically to the first part of Dionysius' reign and the fact that three out of four major speeches in surviving portions of the *Bibliotheke* derive from the Sicilian narrative — perfectly understandable phenomena given Diodorus' Sicilian origin.[32] Secondly, we observe Dionysius' error in the preface to Book XIII (1. 3) in announcing that this book would end with the beginning of the Second Punic War of Dionysius — a statement contradicted so markedly by the fact that Book Thirteen, in fact, ends (114. 3) with the conclusion of the First Punic War against Dionysius, an error, moreover, which we may deduce from Diodorus' statement that he had completed what he intended, is likely to stem from Diodorus himself rather than from his sources.[33] Finally we note the undue importance attributed to Diodorus' birthplace, the somewhat insignificant Agyrium in Books IV (24; 80), XIV (9. 2-4; 78. 7; 95. 2-7; 96. 1) and XVI (82. 4; 83. 3), that city being viewed as the Sicilian city second in importance to Syracuse — a phenomenon, as Holm long ago observed, undoubtedly stemming from patriotic motivation on the part of the author of the *Bibliotheke* himself.[34]

To sum up our preliminary considerations: given the limitations of interpretation based upon the fragments alone, Diodorus' catholicity in his utilisation of his source material, the overall stylistic and, more importantly, thematic unity which characterises the *Bibliotheke* and the evidence which we have supplied of Diodorus' own individuality in his text, we suggest that it behoves us to abandon traditional methodology, based upon simple identification of the authors of the fragments with Diodorus' text, in favour of a broader approach which seeks particularly to discern likely content, thematic and structural influences of source material upon Diodorus' text within the context of the overall design and purpose of the *Bibliotheke*, assuming at the same time Diodorus' catholicity in his selection of sources.

II

Of all the claims which scholars have made with respect to the sources utilised by Diodorus in his Sicilian narrative, the least credence need be attributed to argumentation supporting Silenus' candidacy. On general grounds, the *Sicelica*'s brevity, as evidenced by its probable coverage in its third and final book of Sicilian history from the late fifth to the mid-third century, is unlikely to be reflected in the full narrative of Diodorus for the first two decades of Dionysius' reign.[35] Manni's counter argument,[36] moreover, advocating a less substantial role for Silenus in Diodorus' text and suggestion that Diodorus' text represents a conflation of the accounts of Silenus and Ephorus, the former supplying the basic chronological outline, supplemented by the latter's full and more detailed narrative, is, of course, as suspect on account of its subjectivity as Laqueur's precise division of the text into Ephorus and Timaeus-derived selections and it is surprising within this context to observe how Ephorus has been transformed from a source furnishing in Laqueur's reconstruction a basic chronological outline into a supplementary source, furnishing the detailed local data. Manni's attribution of a somewhat substantial narrative to Ephorus is, moreover, challenged by the very brevity which we have seen seems to have characterised Ephorus' perusal of Dionysius' reign — an account which, particularly for the early part of the tyrant's reign, contrasted sharply with Philistus' fuller narrative, which, accordingly, we shall argue below, is much more likely to have served as Diodorus' source for this particular period. As for Lauritano's more specific contention[37] that Diodorus' criticism of Timaeus for the earlier historian's treatment of Agathocles (Diod. Sic. XXI. 17. 3/F. 124d) and the bull of Phalaris (Diod. Sic. XIII. 90. 4-6/F. 28a) must derive from Silenus on the grounds that the latter historian was a contemporary of Hannibal (Nep. *Hannib.* XIII. 3) who very probably lived to 146 BC and therefore flourished after Timaeus, we suggest that such a hypothesis ignores, on the one hand, the possibility, suggested by more recent re-evaluation of the *Bibliotheke*, of Diodorus' ability to engage in critical comment alone, viewing the historian in traditional terms as a scissors-and-paste historian, and, on the other, the likelihood that Diodorus' criticism of Timaeus might well derive from Polybius — a source certainly consulted by Diodorus.[38] Finally, we follow Walbank in pointing out that Lauritano's theory overlooks or minimises the difficulties stemming from the fact that a contemporary of the Barcid Hannibal must have been about ninety years of age, if he had been alive to write about the capture of the bull of Phalaris, at the time of Scipio Aemilianus' destruction of Carthage.[39] At the very least, it is highly questionable whether Silenus, if he had attained nonagenarian status, would have possessed the intellectual vigour to compose at such an advanced age.

Ephorus, Theopompus, Timaeus and Philistus obviously merit closer consideration than Silenus as sources of Diodorus. The fact of their being cited by Diodorus, a historian whose recourse to source material, we have seen, was exceedingly catholic, in itself supports the likelihood that some influences from these sources were reflected in Diodorus' text. In the case of Ephorus more specifically, acceptance of the traditional viewpoint current certainly since Volquardsen that Ephorus was a decisive influence upon Diodorus' history of the Greek mainland for the fifth and early fourth centuries renders it exceedingly difficult for us to argue that Diodorus completely ignored Ephorus' account of Sicilian history, when he wrote his own account of Dionysius' reign. Further, Diodorus' reference to 150,000 Punic dead as a result of the plague of 396 BC (XIV. 76. 2) suggests that in this instance[40] Diodorus was following Ephorus' figures for barbarian troops of 300,000 as opposed to Timaeus' 130,000 (i.e., 100,000 + 30,000; Diod. Sic. XIV. 54. 5/70. F. 201). Similarly the reference in XIV. 62. 3 to 300,000 Punic infantry obviously is reflective of Diodorus' use of Ephorus.[41] Something moreover, of Ephorus' Isocratean positive attitude towards Dionysius (cf. Plut. *Dion* XXXVI. 2), scarcely negated by fragment 211 with its reference to the designs of Dionysius II and the Great King upon Greece, might well have penetrated Diodorus' Dionysian data which, we shall argue below, was essentially favourable towards Dionysius. Also one might be tempted to argue that the strong Panhellenic tone of Diodorus' narrative of the great Punic War of 398-396 BC derives to some extent, from the Isocratean historian Ephorus whose universalism within Sicilian context is clearly revealed by his exaggerated Punic numbers. Finally one might be tempted to argue that rhetorical influences from Ephorus infiltrated themselves into Theodorus' speech (Diod. Sic. XIV. 65-69) — though we shall argue below that its essential tenor seems ultimately reflective of Philistus.[42]

Despite, however, the likelihood that Diodorus consulted Ephorus' Dionysian narrative and that Ephorus-derived material is to be found in the Dionysian chapters of the *Bibliotheke*, a decisive influence in the main body of the text on the part of Ephorus is improbable. In the first place, though in Book XIV, in a couple of instances, Diodorus appears to have followed Ephorus' exaggerated figures for barbarian numbers, in Book XIII, on more numerous occasions, Diodorus seems to be adopting the more conservative estimate of Timaeus.[43] More importantly, Ephorus' attribution of equal emphasis to the post-392 BC period of Dionysius' tyranny as to the first two decades of his rule, is certainly not reflected in Diodorus' text which essentially focuses its attention upon the great Punic War of 398-396 BC and attributes very little importance to the later period of Dionysius' tyranny, virtually completely ignoring events after 386 BC. Moreover, the vivid depiction of the early part of Dionysius' reign, culminating in the description of the great war of 398-396 BC, undoubtedly stems from a contemporary of the events described who was, moreover, in a position to obtain historical material by virtue of his close proximity to the central field of action itself. Ephorus who, as we have seen, certainly did not utilise Philistus' account and cannot accordingly here be reproducing Philistus, can scarcely be described as a contemporary and he was certainly far from the central field of action. Even Isocrates, Ephorus' possible major source for much material on Dionysius, can hardly be said to have been placed in a crucially central position for the gathering of source material on the tyrant and his regime.

Finally, as we have seen, the period of intimacy between Isocrates and Dionysius essentially prevailed subsequently to Dionysius' great Punic War of 398-396 BC. Hence Ephorus could hardly have received detailed data on this war such as Diodorus' text contains from his mentor.

More attractive at first sight is the view first advanced by Schwartz[44] to the effect that the comparatively fragmentary treatment of Dionysius in Diodorus' fifteenth book stems from Ephorus, it being argued that with Philistus' detailed narrative as reproduced by Timaeus being abruptly terminated because of Philistus' exile, dated by Diodorus (XV. 7. 3/T. 5b) to 386 BC, but postdated by us to 384 BC, Diodorus was obliged to employ as his main source, at this point, the testimony of Ephorus, a historian whose material he had utilised for the narrative of the events of mainland Greece, and whose account was much briefer than Philistus'. Certainly Diodorus' account of Dionysius' Adriatic operations is exceedingly sketchy and lacks chronological precision (Diod. Sic. XV. 13. 1-4; 14. 1-4). Similarly succinct and chronologically imperfect is Diodorus' account of Dionysius' third encounter with Carthage (XV. 15-17, 24). We particularly note in this connection the curt dismissal of the course of hostilities with the comment πολλαὶ μὲν οὖν κατὰ μέρος ἐγίνοντο μάχαι (15.3). We might, moreover, be tempted to associate Diodorus' account of the Parian colonisation of Pharos (XV. 13. 4) with Ephorus, F. 89 (Steph. Byz. *s.v.* 'Φάρος'). It could further be argued that the reference to Dionysius as θαυμαστῶς ἀγωνισάμενος (XV. 15. 3) reflects a favourable source like Ephorus. Similarly, the positive depiction of Philistus and Leptines (XV. 7. 3/Jacoby, *FGH*, vol. 3b. 556. T. 5b) could be associated with Ephorus who we note praised Philistus and defended his honourable death (Plut. *Dion* XXXVI. 2/Jacoby, *FGH*, vol. 3b. 556. T. 9d = 566. F. 15.) against Timonides' gruesome account (Plut. *Dion* XXXV. 3/Jacoby, *FGH*, vol. 3b. 561. F. 3) which was accepted by Timaeus (Plut. *Dion* XXXV. 6/F. 115). The second and much briefer reference to Dionysius' flamboyant embassy to the Olympic games (XV. 7; cf. XIV. 109) might moreover be indicative of a source-change to a less detailed authority like Ephorus and the lack of reference to Lysias' attack on this occasion might well be conceived of as stemming from an Isocratean source such as Ephorus, obviously unfavourably inclined towards the extreme democratic faction led by Lysias, hostile to the Athenian pro-Dionysius element, probably headed by Isocrates, Ephorus'

119

mentor. The erroneous association of the early return of Philistus with that of Leptines (Diod. Sic. XV. 7. 4/T. 5b) and the absence of any reference to Philistus' secret marriage to Leptines' daughter (Plut. *Dion* XI. 4/T. 5c) certainly might suggest a source like Ephorus unacquainted with accurate information and far from the centre of political activity. Further, we have seen that Diodorus' neutral account of Leptines' death (Diod. Sic. XV. 17. 1) seems to have anteceded the development of the hostile tradition and, therefore, could have derived from Ephorus whom, we have seen, seems, as befitted a pupil of Isocrates, to have been somewhat favourably disposed towards the tyrant. Finally, it has been suggested[45] on the grounds that Dionysius accords Plato freedom of speech as a true philosopher and enters into conversation with him and that the φιλόσοφοι or φίλοι in what is regarded as a semi-critical or ironic stance, after their rescue of Plato, comment that a learned man ought to mix as little as possible and as amicably as possible with tyrants, that Diodorus' anecdote concerning Plato's enslavement at Dionysius' hands (XV. 7. 1) is, in fact, not in the least hostile towards Dionysius. Again the authority of Ephorus is conjured up, particularly if, like Sordi, we regard the sage advice given to Plato as a later Isocratean rebuttal to Speusippus' rebuke in Letter XXX of Isocrates for using Dionysius as an example to Philip II in 343 BC, the Isocratean historian arguing that at least his former master had the sense to deal with tyrants from afar.

At the same time, serious objections to Schwartz's view can be advanced. The favourable comment of Diodorus XV. 15. 3 could conceivably be attributed equally well to the two other sources whom we have seen were favourably disposed to Dionysius, Philistus and Theopompus. As we have seen, Philistus in particular was favourable to Leptines. More importantly, we question whether Ephorus' account of Dionysius' later years was as sketchy as Schwartz postulates. On the contrary, as we have demonstrated, Ephorus, as befitted a pupil of Isocrates, seems to have devoted an equal amount of space to Dionysius' later years as his earlier years and hence dealt with this later period in greater detail than Philistus or his reproducer, Timaeus. Accordingly Ephorus is unlikely to have exerted a decisive influence upon Diodorus who deals exceedingly sketchily with this period. We further note that no Panhellenic character of the type we should expect from Ephorus is discernible in the Sicilian chapter of Diodorus' fifteenth book. Isocrates himself and the pro-

Dionysian faction which he represented and probably headed, who obviously figured prominently in Ephorus' second Dionysian book, are not merely given no prominence: Isocrates is not even mentioned once. Further, we note that the hostile anecdotal data such as that pertaining to Dionysius' harsh treatment of Philoxenus (XV. 6) or that which attributed Dionysius' decision to exile Philistus to the tyrant's madness resulting from his literary failures (Diod. Sic. XV. 7. 3), obviously derives from a hostile source and since Ephorus does not seem to have been basically hostile to Dionysius, he is clearly not Diodorus' source for this account. In particular we reject Sordi's attempt to isolate the Plato anecdote from its obviously broader anti-Dionysius context recording the vicissitudes of the other literati at Dionysius' court, noting in addition that even if we were to interpret the Plato anecdote as Sordi does, the authority of that other Isocratean historian Theopompus, who we know was patently anti-Plato, could not be excluded. Further, we would have expected a universal historian like Ephorus to have set the events surrounding Plato's enslavement in a broader universal context of Spartan, Athenian and Aeginetan politics, as Plutarch (*Dion* V. 3) and Diogenes Laertius (III. 19) did. As for Sordi's thesis regarding the Diodorus narrative as Ephorus' response to Speusippus' Letter XXX, it is at the most a guess. Finally, we note that the statement that Dionysius ruled for thirty-eight years (Diod. Sic. XV. 73. 5) cannot derive from Ephorus who attributed forty-two years to the tyrant's rule (Polyb. XII. 4a. 3).

Our rejection of Ephorus as a decisive influence upon Diodorus in the Sicilian section of his fifteenth book leads us to consider Hammond's alternative view that Theopompus was Diodorus' source for this section.[46] The fact that Diodorus (XVI. 71. 3) refers to a specific part of the *Philippica*, the Sicilian excursus, certainly suggests Diodorus' direct acquaintance with the work. Moreover the setting of Dionysius' Adriatic scheme within a broad Western context, emphasis being placed upon Illyrian hostility to the Molossians and help to Dionysius in his projects against Delphi (XV. 13. 1-3) as well as upon the Parian colonisation of Pharos which preceded Dionysius' ventures in this area and war with the natives of the island (XV. 13. 4) might suggest Theopompus whose Sicilian excursus, we have seen, was placed within a broader Western excursus. Finally, Diodorus' account of Dionysius' death resulting from excessive eating and drinking might be regarded as a motif appropriate to Theopompus.[47] On the other hand, serious reservations preclude the likelihood of Theopompus' decisive influence upon Diodorus. First, as we have already seen the evidence of fragment 134 suggests that Theopompus criticised Dionysius not for his own hedonistic practices but for encouraging these in others. Secondly, we follow Meister in noting that the essentially pro-Plato stance encountered in Diodorus XV. 7 is unlikely to stem from Theopompus who we know was patently anti-Plato in outlook (Athen. XI. 118. p. 508c-d; Arrian *Epict. Diss.* II. 17. 5-6/F. 259, 275).[48] More importantly, Diodorus' recollection of the Sicilian excursus does not appear to have been of the most precise kind — a conclusion suggesting in turn a most superficial usage of Theopompus' work by Diodorus.[49] Thus we note how the facts that eight fragments from the Sicilian excursus are associated with Books Thirty-nine and Forty of the *Philippica* and that Diodorus (XVI. 71. 3/F. 184) declares that three books were devoted to the Sicilian excursus suggests that the excursus began not as Diodorus asserts in Book Forty-one but in Book Thirty-nine, continuing to Book Forty-one, or as Westlake suggests, perhaps even to the early part of Book Forty-two, the source of Diodorus' error being, as Westlake surmises,[50] that historian's confusion of the confines of the Sicilian excursus with those embracing the more general excursus on the Western Mediterranean which fragments 199 to 204 from Books Forty-three indicate ran from Books Forty-two to Forty-three. Diodorus' confusion with respect to the details of Theopompus' Sicilian excursus is, moreover, also evident from his comment that Theopompus covered a fifty-year period commencing with the beginning of the tyranny of the elder Dionysius and ending with the expulsion of the younger Dionysius in 343 BC — an obviously erroneous statement since the years 405-343 BC constitute, in fact, a sixty-two-year period, suggesting in turn that the chronological starting point of the excursus was 392 BC, a perfectly logical date, since it seems to have corresponded to a similar commencing point for Ephorus' second Dionysian book.

Since, moreover, Theopompus' Sicilian excursus began with the year 392 BC and we have no evidence that Theopompus discussed the rise and early career of Dionysius in his *Hellenica*, we may doubt whether Theopompus was of any use for the major part of Diodorus' account of Dionysius which was essentially concerned with the first two decades of the tyrant's rule. Further, the fact, as we have demonstrated, that Theopompus in the Sicilian excursus was less concerned with the elder Dionysius than with Dionysius II is likely to have rendered Theopompus' testimony unattractive to a historian, concentrating his attention upon Dionysius I. Also we have been unable to discern in Diodorus' text Theopompus' central thesis on the dissoluteness of the younger Dionysius, leading to political collapse, so obviously echoed in Justin's narrative (XXI. 1-3). As for Theopompus' criticism of Dionysius I in fragment 134 for encouraging dissoluteness in others, this too does not seem to be reflected in Diodorus' text either in the full earlier narrative of Books XIII and XIV or in the relatively sparse perusal of the fifteenth book. Finally we suggest that the meagre details of Diodorus' Sicilian narrative in his fifteenth book are hardly likely to reflect Theopompus' full treatment of Sicilian affairs during Dionysius' later years, to which the historian of Chios devoted no less than three full books.

III

The fact, as we have seen, that Diodorus cites Timaeus on numerous occasions seems to echo that historian's hostility in his consideration of Dionysius I in the *prooemium* to Book XIV (2. 2.) and, as we have also seen, quite clearly followed Timaeus' estimate of barbarian figures in Book XIII, indicates that obviously Diodorus read Timaeus' account of Dionysius' rule. Other argumentation, however, seeking to prove a more substantial influence from Timaeus and stipulating that local geographical and topographical detail, superstitious data, chronological scheme and hostility towards both Carthage and Dionysius were culled by Diodorus from Timaeus commands in our view less confidence.

Polybius' condemnation of Timaeus' tendency to write from a superstitious viewpoint (Polyb. XII. 24. 5/T. 19) by itself should not lead us to suppose that material in Diodorus describing Punic impiety and attendant divine displeasure which leads to Carthage's fall (XIII. 59. 1-2; 86. 1-3; 90. 1-3; 96. 5; 108. 4; XIV. 63. 1-2; 70. 4; 73. 5; 74. 3-4; 76; 77. 4; cf. XI. 89; XV. 24; 74; XVI. 79. 5; 80. 1, 6) automatically derives from Timaeus.[51] Moralising such as appears in these passages seems certainly to have been a feature of Ephorus' and Theopompus' histories,[52] whereas Philistus, we have seen, in his description of the omens which heralded the reign of Dionysius (Cic. *De Div.* I. 39; 73/F. 57a, 58) was certainly capable of presenting non-rational or supernatural data during the course of his narrative — a phenomenon not even uncharacteristic of Philistus' spiritual mentor, Thucydides.[53] Further, as we have seen, an overall moral design characterises the *Bibliotheke*, to which as Drews has shown, Diodorus' personal contribution was certainly not negligible.[54] The possibility that Diodorus himself is accordingly directly responsible for such moralising passages as we encounter in Diodorus' Dionysian narrative cannot be automatically gainsaid. The strong anti-Punic bias which marks these moralising passages, moreover, which obviously reflect Siceliot patriotic tendencies which we also encounter in passages which betray sympathy with Siceliot suffering (Diod. Sic. XIII. 55. 4; 57. 5; 58. 2; 90. 2; 111. 6; XIV. 51. 4) need not be automatically ascribed to Timaeus. On *a priori* grounds at least the patriotic Ephorus or Philistus, whose assessment of Dionysius, we have argued was distinctly positive, might well have been projectors of these sentiments. As for Schwartz's theory that the notices on the destruction of Selinus and Himera (Diod. Sic. XIII. 59. 4; 62. 4) two hundred and forty years after their foundation reflect Timaeus' chronological interests as well as that historian's patriotism,[55] we suggest that we have no grounds for not ascribing such patriotic tendencies to the equally patriotic Ephorus and Philistus; that we have no evidence that Timaeus' chronological scheme, associated with the priestesses of Argos, Athenian archons, Olympiads and Spartan kings, is reflected in the text; and that, as we shall see, Diodorus' chronological scheme appears more reflective of a Thucydidean like Philistus with his winter-summer arrangement than of Timaeus.[56] Finally, to the claim that Timaeus must have been Diodorus' source for precise local, geographical and topographical details[57] on the basis of the facts that Timaeus is often cited by Diodorus in connection with geographical details (XIII. 82. 6; 83. 2; 90. 4-5; 108. 4/F. 26a, 28a, 106), that many of these descriptions must derive from a third-century source[58] and that prominence is given to Tauromenium, Timaeus' birthplace (XIV. 59. 2; 88; 96. 4; XVI. 7. 1; 68. 7-8), we retort first with our previously expressed caveat regarding the limited use to which the fragments themselves should be subjected and secondly with the observation that, while much of the local detail might well derive from an authority who flourished before Timaeus, some of this material, particularly that dealing with the granting of Roman citizenship to the citizens of Halaisa and denial of kinship with the Herbitaeans (XIV. 16) might well stem from a source who flourished after Timaeus, possibly Polybius or whichever other source, we believe, may have challenged Timaeus' comments on the fate of the bull of Phalaris. Further, the prominence accorded Sicilian affairs by Diodorus, whence the allocation of a disproportionate amount of space as well as three out of four major speeches of the *Bibliotheke* to Sicilian history, leads us to conjecture that Diodorus was himself directly responsible for the inclusion of, at least, some of this geographical and topographical data. Consequently the statement on Halaisa might well have been included by Diodorus on the basis of the latter historian's own personal observation. We should add that, despite our caution in accepting Polybius' attack upon Timaeus for his bookishness and armchair historical approach (XII. 3-4; 4b, c, d; 25d, e, f, g, h) *in toto*, Timaeus' absence from Sicily for a fifty-year period (Polyb. XII. 25h, 1/F. 34) renders most improbable the view that Timaeus was Diodorus' chief and only source for directly gleaned geographical data. At the very least, such material was likely borrowed by Timaeus from Philistus. Finally as Holm pointed out long ago, Agyrium, a relatively insignificant Siceliot settlement is given even more prominence than Tauromenium in the *Bibliotheke* — a phenomenon obviously owing much to the fact that it was Diodorus' own birthplace (IV. 24; 80; XIV. 9. 2-4; 78. 7; 95. 2-7; 96. 1; XVI. 82. 4; 83. 3).[59]

IV

Obviously at the heart of any examination of the sources utilised by Diodorus in his Dionysian narrative lies the issue of the portrait provided by Diodorus of the tyrant himself. The overwhelming modern scholarly consensus[60] concludes that Diodorus' depiction of Dionysius is overtly hostile, deriving from the depiction of the foremost and indeed only hostile historical authority distinctly opposed to Dionysius, Timaeus, whom we, of course, know from Polybius, was notorious for his vitriolic personal assault upon characters in his history meriting his disapproval such as Demochares and Agathocles (Polyb. XII. 13-15/ F. 35b, 124b). This antipathy towards Dionysius, it is argued, assumes three forms. In the first place, there appear in the later sections of Book XIV and in the meagre portions of Books XV and XVI miscellaneous data, belonging perhaps to the hostile anecdotal tradition which deal with the following: Lysias' attack upon Dionysius at the Olympic games of 388 BC, the tyrant's assault upon the Rhegine Phyton, the victory of Dionysius at the Lenaean festival, the tyrant's plunder of Pyrgi, the relations of Dionysius with his literati, his victory over his betters, his overeating and resulting death, the references to Dionysius' tyranny as 'bound with fetters of steel' and the note on the end of the tyranny and restoration of liberty under Timoleon (XIV. 109; 112; XV. 6; 7; 14. 3; 74; XVI. 5. 4; 70. 2 (cf. Plut. *Dion* VII. 3; X. 3.) 82. 3-4). Of more substantial fare are the other two supposedly Timaeus-derived manifestations of hostility towards the tyrant: the bulk of the narrative of Books XIII and XIV and the verbal onslaught, launched upon the tyrant by the Syracusan knight Theodorus, which also appears in Book XIV (65-69).

In the depiction of Dionysius found in the narrative of the later sections of Book XIII and most of Book XIV it is argued that Dionysius, described significantly as tyrant ruling a tyranny[61] (XIII. 1. 3; 92. 7; 94. 3; 95. 6; 96. 2-4; 109. 1; 112. 3-4; XIV. 2. 2; 7. 1, 5-7; 8. 1, 3; 4. 5; 9. 1, 8; 10. 2-4; 14. 1; 18. 1; 40. 3; 44. 1, 5; 45. 1, 5; 47. 1; 54. 2; 100. 1; 102. 2; 103. 5; 109. 3; cf. in Theodorus' speech, XIV. 65. 3; 68. 4; 69. 1), at best an ignorant *grammateus* (XIII. 96. 4; cf. Demosth. XVIII. 127; XIX. 98), is portrayed as a selfish, egoistical, unscrupulous, unpatriotic, cunning military leader (XIII. 92. 2; 93. 2; 95. 6; XIV. 14. 6-8) who destroys Greek cities, murders, banishes and enslaves their inhabitants, ruthlessly transfers populations (XIV. 14. 1; 15. 2-4; 40. 1; 78. 5; 96. 4; 106. 3; 107. 2) and even enslaves his own Syracusan fellow-citizens (XIII. 91-96). As befits a ruler whose maintenance of power depends on force of arms, Dionysius has no real respect for democracy, liberty or constitutional government either at Syracuse or elsewhere (XIII. 91. 3; 96. 1; XIV. 7. 1-7; 8. 4; 45. 5-6; 70. 3) and he deliberately engenders a constant state of hostility with Carthage in order to ensure his permanent rule over Syracuse (XIII. 96. 2; 94. 1; XIV. 41. 1; 68; 75. 3). The tyrant's followers and supporters are either, on the one hand, slaves, aliens (XIV. 7. 4), mercenaries (XIII. 93. 2; 96. 1-2; XIV. 7. 5; 8. 4, 6; 9. 8; 67. 3; 78. 1-3), unscrupulous Spartans (XIV. 10. 3; 44. 2; 58. 1; 62. 1; 70. 1-3; cf. XV. 23. 5; 47. 7; 70. 1-3) or fellow tyrants (XIV. 14. 6-7; 15. 1-2; 78. 7), men as erratic, unscrupulous and unprincipled as Dionysius himself (XIV. 9. 9; 95. 6; XIII. 92. 5-7; 96. 1-2) or, on the other, the wrong-headed and ignorant *demos* which, used by the tyrant for the tyrant's own ends, is ultimately discarded by him once its usefulness has been exhausted (XIII. 91. 4-5; 92. 1, 3; 93. 3; 94. 1-2; XIV. 7. 6). The tyrant's opponents, on the other hand, are the *Chariestatoi*, the rich, the influential (XIII. 91. 4; 92. 3; 93. 3), or men of peace from the tyrant's own ranks, like Dionysius' own brother Leptines (XIV. 102. 2-3).

Finally there remains the speech of Theodorus (Diod. Sic. XIV. 65-69) in which scholarly consensus has discerned Timaeus' distaste for Dionysius' regime, Theodorus within this context accordingly constituting the historian's chief mouthpiece of hostility towards the tyrant.[62] The chief themes propounded in the speech are Dionysius' tyrannical schemes — murder, plunder, bribery and more particularly aggression directed against Naxos, Catana, Messana, Gela and Camarina and policy of maintaining a Punic foe in perpetual existence to distract the Siceliots from their subjection to Dionysius and loss of liberty; the nefarious character of the element constituting Dionysius' support; the preferability of Punic to Dionysian rule; and nostalgic reminiscences of the rule of Gelon contrasted with the reality of Dionysian oppression.

Of the three types of alleged hostility towards Dionysius, obviously the latter two categories are more important, since the first type is meagre, deriving from a section of Diodorus which is singularly sparse in data. It behoves us therefore to focus our attention essentially upon the material deriving from Books XIII and XIV of Diodorus, though initially the anecdotal data, particularly as reproduced in the Sicilian section of Book XV will merit our scrutiny.

V

In light of our earlier discussion of Philistus' approach to Dionysius' war with Rhegium, Diodorus' description of the sad fate accorded Phyton (Diod. Sic. XIV. 112) need not detain us unduly. Its data we have suggested are most likely to stem from Philistus and reflect the opposition of the historian and Leptines to Dionysius' policies in Magna Grecia. Turning our attention to the anecdotal data of Book XV and indeed to the narrative of Book XV as a whole, as little reason for attributing this material to Timaeus as to Ephorus and Theopompus, in our view, can be adduced.[63] For one thing, in the light of our previous discussion of Philistus' attitude to Dionysius' policy in Southern Italy, the seemingly hostile reference to Dionysius' plundering Pyrgi (XV. 14. 3) might well derive from Philistus. We further observe that Timaeus' criticism of Plato for plagiarism and other faults, not delineated, which the philosopher shared with Aristotle (*Diog. Laert.* VIII. 54; Plut. *Nic.* I. 4/F. 14; T. 18) renders unlikely the assumption that Timaeus' authority be attributed the favourable assessment of Plato which one encounters in Diodorus' description of the anecdote concerning Dionysius' enslavement of the philosopher (Diod. Sic. XV. 7. 1). Dionysius II's recall of the goodwill of the Syracusans towards his father which he as his father's successor, hoped to inherit (Diod. Sic. XV. 74. 5) and the description of Philistus and Leptines as 'men of great courage' who rendered numerous important services in Dionysius' war (Diod. Sic. XV. 7. 3/Jacoby, *FGH*, vol. 3b, 556, T. 5b) are, we maintain passages, moreover, whose sentiments are hardly compatible with a tyrant hater like Timaeus. Diodorus' notice pertaining to the magnificent funeral organised by Dionysius II for his father (Diod. Sic. XV. 74. 5), without a note of hostility such as was probably accorded this event by Timaeus (Athen. V. 40. p. 206e/566. F. 112; cf. Plut. *Pelop.* XXXIV. 1/556. F. 40b), we should add, also precludes Diodorus' use of Timaeus' history. Equally noteworthy, Diodorus' gossipy anecdote (Diod. Sic. XV. 74. 2) concerning Dionysius' drinking and eating bout following his victory at the Lenaean games obviously does not derive from Timaeus who viewed the tyrant's death within the context of court intrigues engineered by Dionysius' court physicians (Plut. *Dion* VI. 2/F. 109). Finally we note numerous examples of chronological imprecision to be encountered in these chapters which render the association of these passages with Timaeus, the master of chronography highly unlikely: the inaccurate placement of the events of the Olympics of 388 BC in 386 BC (XV. 7. 2; cf. XIV. 109. 1); the second notice pertaining to Dionysius' wall around Syracuse built in 401 BC (Diod. Sic. XIV. 18), incorporated completely out of context into the narrative of Dionysius' Northern Adriatic ventures, dated to 385 BC (Diod. Sic. XV. 13. 5); the confusing account of Dionysius' hostilities with Carthage in XV. 24 which, ascribed to the year 379-378 BC, suggests, on the one hand, that Diodorus' Third Punic War did not end as Diodorus XV. 17. 5 claims in 383 BC, and, on the other, on account of the reference to the plague and Libyan revolt, that it be linked to the war of 368-367 BC; and finally, in view of the fact that, two months after the Lenaean games, Dionysius concluded a treaty with Athens (Tod, *Greek historial inscriptions*, vol. 2, no. 136), the totally inaccurate association of Dionysius' death with these games (XV. 74).

VI

Turning our attention to the issue of the alleged hostility which is said to manifest itself in the narrative of Books XIII and XIV of Diodorus, we initially pass over Diodorus' reference to Dionysius as *grammateus*, and acknowledge the likelihood that Dionysius occupied a perfectly responsible position as secretary to the generals. More important given our earlier conclusion that Philistus' Περὶ Διονυσίου constituted a work concerned objectively with power politics, discussing military and political history exclusively — and that from a Thucydidean and Machiavellian stance — we question whether details regarding Dionysius' political and military aims and accomplishments such as source critics, from Volquardsen onwards, regarded as hostile in character, were, in fact, eliminated from Philistus *oeuvre*. What is to be emphasised is the fact that no moral stricture towards Dionysius' actions such as one would expect from Timaeus and, as we have seen, one certainly discerns directed against the Punic foe, accompanies Diodorus' narrative, while the reader should in turn be cautioned to resist the temptation to assume for Diodorus a moral stance of condemnation, when confronted with data unpalatable to his own moral sensitivity. Thus we have no reason not to assume that the details of deaths, destruction and banishment to be found in the narrative's description of Dionysius' campaign against Siceliots, Italiots and Sicilian native elements, or the description of the mercenary support of the tyrant, were not of interest to Philistus and included in the history written by an individual who was, after all, in Nepos' words 'hominem amicum non magis tyranno quam tyrannidi' (*Dion* III. 2/T. 5d) — a man, in addition whose work was read by two military campaigners, Alexander the Great (Plut. *Alex.* VIII. 3/T. 22) and Quintus Cicero (Cic. *Ad Quint. Fratr.* II. 11. 4/T. 17a) at a time, we have seen, when monarchical absolutism as a political and intellectual phenomenon was attracting increasing interest and even absorbing the attention of Marcus Tullius Cicero himself. Nor should we fail to emphasise in this connection that Philistus' spiritual mentor, Thucydides, did not allow his appraisal of the Athenian

Empire as a tyranny to obscure his admiration for Pericles — a figure who, in Thucydides' words (II. 63. 2), did not hesitate to voice similarly negative sentiments about his native city's imperialistic ventures. Further, we cannot doubt that Philistus in his analysis of the sources of Dionysius' power, would have been unquestionably only too aware of the importance of the perpetual maintenance of the Punic foe for Dionysius' competent control of Sicilian affairs — a factor which he is accordingly unlikely to have omitted from his consideration of Dionysius' rule in the Περὶ Διονυσίου.

As for Diodorus' assessment of the internal Syracusan position, we note that the contempt of the text towards the *demos* which falls victim to the tyrant's machinations and is unable to formulate decisive resistance to Dionysius, would also fundamentally accord with the point of view of Philistus whose main interest was, after all, not the democratic liberty prevalent at Syracuse but the problem of the attainment and maintenance of power and the *arche* of Dionysius, just as Thucydides' chief interest was the Periclean 'monarchy' rather than the Periclean democracy. We may add that extensive references in the text allude both to Dionysius' concern where possible with respecting constitutional and democratic format — certainly in the period immediately preceding the great Punic War of 398-396 BC (Diod. Sic. XIV. 45. 2; 61. 3; 64. 3-4; 96. 2) — and to the fact that the greatest potential of the *demos* is realised only in conjunction with the tyrant's guiding hand (Diod. Sic. XIV. 41. 4; 42. 1; 44. 3; 45. 1-2; 46. 1; 47. 2) — precisely the sentiments one expects from a Thucydidean like Philistus for whom, on the basis of the obviously Philistus-derived passages in Diodorus (Diod. Sic. XIV. 18; 41-44) on Dionysius' preparations for war in 398 BC, we suggest Dionysius assumed a role not unlike that pertaining to Pericles or Hermocrates in Thucydides' history. We should add that the fact that Philistus was most probably a member of the *Chariestatoi* should not lead us to surmise an unwillingness on the historian's part to criticise that element of the Syracusan and Gelan citizen body and presume that the description of the attack on the *Chariestatoi* must derive from Timaeus. Philistus' spiritual mentor, Thucydides, had, after all, been quite willing to support Pericles, in spite of the latter's opposition to the historian's presumed kinsman, the Philaïd Cimon, and direct evidence of the Syracusan historian's stance is seen, above all, in Philistus' willingness to pay the fine, when Dionysius attacked the Syracusan generals (Diod. Sic. XIII. 91. 4/T. 3), an occasion when the historian worked against both the democratic and oligarchic elements in favour of Dionysius.

In sum, when Volquardsen and other source-critics argue that Diodorus portrays Dionysius as a ruthless tyrant, citing as examples the tyrant's contempt for liberty and democratic rule, his attack upon Naxos and Catana and utilisation of the Punic threat, the unscrupulous supporters of the tyrant, the banishment and death accorded the tyrant's victims, the opposition of the 'best' men, the deception of the multitude and the citation regarding the fetters of steel, and proceed to identify this information with Timaeus, they overlook the simple fact that the same evidence would fit just as logically and probably more so into the scheme of a Philistus, intimately involved with and intrigued, both on a practical and intellectual level, by the vicissitudes of power politics at Syracuse during the reign of Dionysius.

A further weakness in the methodology of Volquardsen and the scholars who developed his approach is to be encountered in the process of selectivity which marks their research. To base their reconstruction upon isolated references in Diodorus which they regard as representative of the Timaeus approach leads them to ignore the existence of an equally important part of the narrative which portrays Dionysius in extremely positive terms as an outstanding political and military leader, epitomising Siceliot patriotic aspirations in the face of Punic aggression and barbarity.[64] The solution offered by Laqueur, Folcke and those of similar mind, to the effect that these passages were found by Timaeus in Philistus' account, tends in our view to underestimate the effectiveness of Timaeus' onslaught upon Philistus. Volquardsen's retort, on the other hand, that the favourable and patriotic depiction also reflects the view of Timaeus, it being argued that Timaeus' nationalistic sentiments overcame his hostility to the Syracusan despot, might appear to gain plausibility from Polybius' statement (XII. 26b. 4/F. 94) regarding Timaeus' aim to glorify Sicily at the expense of the rest of Greece. Yet even Polybius' evidence fails to indicate any association in Timaeus' mind between Dionysius as despot and Dionysius as defender of Western Hellas. No evidence exists at all to indicate with any degree of certainty that Timaeus pictured Dionysius as defender of Western Hellas. Indeed this argument appears to be a figment of the imagination of Volquardsen and his colleagues. The patriotic depiction, moreover, though possibly derived to some extent from Ephorus, in view of the fullness of the description of the early period of Dionysius' reign and the undoubted Philistus-derived account of the preparations for war in 398 BC, is much more likely to have stemmed from Philistus who, as we have seen, sought to justify tyranny as a form of government and seems to have based his argument upon Dionysius' position as defender of Western Hellas against Punic aggression.

We further note how Diodorus confirms Polybius' claim that Timaeus was extremely biased against Agathocles (Diod. Sic. XXI. 17. 3; Polyb. VIII. 12. 12; XII. 15/F. 124d, a, b) and adds that the Timaeus books on Agathocles are consequently to be disbelieved. It follows that considerable discretion must be assumed on the part of Diodorus in his selection of source material and it is logical to assume that suspicion of the Agathocles books would have been reflected in Diodorus' attitude to those books in which Timaeus covered the reign of Dionysius, as we have seen in a pretty biased and hostile manner. Consequently, even if we were to argue in accordance with scholarly consensus that Diodorus' text is hostile to Dionysius, we may question whether this hostility derives from Timaeus. However, the fact that we have been attempting to demonstrate that Diodorus is not actually hostile to Dionysius suggests that Diodorus' caution with respect to Timaeus' jaundiced approach to Dionysius prevented the historian's acceptance of Timaeus' hostile viewpoint.

Diodorus' reference to Dionysius as tyrant and to his oligarchic opponents as *Chariestatoi* cannot be regarded as exclusive evidence for Timaeus or indeed for the existence of a particularly hostile source. While it is true that the term *tyrant* already possessed elements of an evil connotation by Solon's time, this was by no means totally the case and the possessor of tyranny was still in an essentially enviable position. Hence both Pindar (*Pyth.* III. 85) and Isocrates (*Evag.* 40) could use the term in favourable addresses to Hieron and Evagoras. It was only as a result of the Platonic judgement of tyranny that the word began to assume any likeness to the modern meaning and a late source would certainly use the word in a Platonic or Aristotelian pejorative sense. Yet the fact that Isocrates employed the word in a favourable address to Evagoras is indicative of the fact that by the mid-fourth century, the word could still be employed without a tone of philosophic disapproval and undoubtedly the possibility that such a use characterised the two Isocratic historians who wrote about Dionysius, Ephorus and Theopompus, whence its appearance in Diodorus, cannot be automatically excluded. In the case of Philistus whose position *vis-à-vis* tyrants and reference to tyrants might certainly parallel those of Pindar and Isocrates, there is no doubt that the word tyrant would be perfectly appropriate; for we have seen that Philistus appears to have approved of tyranny as an institution. On the other hand, even if we accept that the word possesses in Diodorus a hostile connotation, given our acceptance of the view that Diodorus employed a wide range of source material and allowed his own distinctive presence to infiltrate into his *oeuvre*, we must ask whether use of the word tyrant could not have derived from any post-Platonic authority rather than inevitably from Timaeus or whether Diodorus himself did not utilise the word on his own initiative, without simply copying his source's use of the word.

Similarly, the reference to the oligarchic opponents of Dionysius as *Chariestatoi* need not reveal favour towards this element and opposition to Dionysius on the part of Diodorus' text, since *Chariestatoi* was a term which could be used to describe those who were either aristocrats by virtue of character-refinement or by consideration of birth. Hence οἱ χαριέστατοι appears, for example, in Isocrates (*Panath.* 8) and Aristotle (*Metaphys.* 1060a, 26) to signify men of taste, while in the *Nicomachean Ethics* (1095b, 16) the contrast is provided, οἱ πολλοὶ καὶ οἱ φορτικώτατοι. Consequently since Philistus' chief concern in the Περὶ Διονυσίου was to provide an Antiphon-type sophistic examination of the essence of absolute power as manifested by the career of Dionysius rather than to depict Dionysius as a man of taste — notwithstanding the appeal which Dionysius' intellectual interests must have undoubtedly exerted upon the Syracusan historian — the depiction of Dionysius' opponents in Diodorus as men of taste, if this indeed be the manner in which we interpret Diodorus' references, might well be conceived of as having been derived from Philistus for whom the aristocratically derived euphemism constituted no embarrassment. On the other hand, if we argue that the term *Chariestatoi* in Diodorus denotes simply the old aristocratic class opposed to Dionysius, who were aligned against the masses who supported Dionysius, this reference again can be associated with Philistus, who by virtue of his own intimate involvement in the events of 406-405 BC knew only too well that Dionysius rose to power by championing the *demos* against the oligarchs. Furthermore, the possibility that Ephorus and Theopompus, who were after all not essentially hostile to

Dionysius, used the word in this neutral sense cannot on *a priori* grounds be denied. Finally, even if the orthodox view, which maintains that Diodorus' text derives from Timaeus, is accepted, the possibility that Timaeus might have ultimately drawn the word *Chariestatoi* from Philistus — a historian, we emphasise, upon whom Timaeus was deeply dependent — and hence not used the word in a hostile sense, cannot be excluded from our consideration.

VII

There remains the alleged Timaeus-derived hostility towards Dionysius, discerned in the speech of Theodorus. That the sentiments of the speech are hostile to Dionysius, of course, cannot be denied. More questionable in our view is the assumption that the hostility is reflective of an anti-Dionysius viewpoint on the part of Diodorus or his source.

In the first place, since we have seen that Philistus' Περὶ Διονυσίου was no mere eulogy, that it was chiefly concerned with the issue of power politics as manifested in Dionysius' regime, and that Philistus was linked with that Machiavellian historian *par excellence*, Thucydides, who was quite prepared to indict his central phenomenon of interest, the Periclean regime, of harbouring tyrannical designs, Theodorus' castigation of the Syracusan tyranny is not unlikely to have appeared originally in the pages of Philistus' history. Clearly Philistus' interest in the power structure of the Syracusan tyranny would not have blinded that historian to the fact that Dionysius deliberately kept alive the Punic threat to secure his own position within Syracuse and he would not have felt any embarrassment at the fact that Theodorus referred to this. Similarly the tyrant's treachery at Gela and Camarina, the enslavement of Catana and Naxos, the plundering of temples, the somewhat morally dubious clientele of Dionysius, the exile and death meted out to the tyrant's opponents — all this material was in no way unpalatable to a historian concentrating his attention upon power-politics as manifested in the tyranny of Dionysius.

More noteworthy, albeit generally ignored by scholarly consensus,[65] is what we perceive as a considerable degree of objectivity permeating the speech — an objectivity which distinguishes decisively between the speculative and factual elements voiced by

Theodorus and renders the automatic attribution of the speech to the highly subjectively hostile Timaeus less likely than one might initially suspect.[66] Thus observing how, while in the speech Dionysius is said to have fled Motya, earlier in the narrative, he is said to have left because he was widely separated from the allied cities and food supplies were scarce (Diod. Sic. XIV. 66. 2; 55. 5), we conclude that Theodorus' text omits motives which would justify Dionysius' action and in so doing places Dionysius in an exceedingly poor light. A similar example of factual mis-representation on Theodorus' part marks the contrast between Theodorus' statement that, immediately after the battle at Catana with Magon's fleet, a storm arose and the narrative's contention that this storm arose later, after the arrival of Himilcon (Diod. Sic. XIV. 68. 6; 61. 4). Obviously, the later occurrence of the storm renders doubtful the alleged strategic advantage attributed to Dionysius by Theodorus. Yet Theodorus appears deliberately to have obscured the chronological positioning of the storm in order to emphasise that Dionysius had a chance to prevail over Carthage, and in order to paint Dionysius in the blackest of colours. A third example of deliberate fabrication of data on Theodorus' part to suit his own purpose of arousing discontent against Dionysius is implicit in the contrast between Theodorus' statement that Dionysius treacherously avoided attacking the enemy who had arrived at Panormus after a stormy passage and the earlier statement of the narrative that the loss of Motya resulted from the fact that at the time Dionysius was before Segesta (Diod. Sic. XIV. 68. 5; 55. 4). In all these cases, we are obliged to conclude that we are dealing with information derived from a responsible source, committed to distinguishing between perceived factual truth and inaccurate distortionist data. mouthed by Theodorus at a time when uncertainty and speculation with respect to Dionysius' actions was bound to prevail — speculation which, we might add, could indeed be utilised advantageously by the representative of the Syracusan knights in his efforts to undermine the tyrant's power. Such objectivity we emphasise is hardly likely to have characterised Timaeus' *oeuvre*, given the undoubted intense and biased opposition to Dionysius manifested by the latter historian and Timaeus' probable omission of even the slightest amount of data unfavourable to the tyrant's opponent, and hence is much more likely to have characterised the pages of the much more objective Philistus. A similar type of objectivity, more likely manifested by Philistus than by Timaeus, which distinguishes between veracity of fact and Theodorus' distortion, is, moreover, discernible in the contrast between the deliberate attribution of the destruction of Messana to Dionysius in Theodorus' speech and the omission of such a sentiment in the narrative (Diod. Sic. XIV. 68. 5; 61. 2), and by Theodorus' more manifest emphasis upon Dionysius' treachery to Gela and Camarina than that betrayed by the narrative (Diod. Sic. XIV. 68. 2; XIII. 111. 5).

Accordingly we conclude that far more objectivity than traditionally attributed to the speech of Theodorus manifests itself in the text, whence the speech's automatic attribution to Timaeus is to be eschewed. Indeed, to proceed a step further, we maintain that the fact that the text admits that Theodorus fabricates spurious data and distorts for his own ends descriptions of events suggests not only that the source of Diodorus cannot simply have utilised the speech to propagate his own hostile sentiments towards the tyrant but that he is, in fact, unlikely to have sympathised with the hostile stance adopted by Theodorus.

Our conclusion that the speech of Theodorus reproduced the views of a historian who was distinctly unsympathetic to Theodorus is confirmed by significant evidence, indicating that Theodorus' views are hardly consistent with Syracusan traditional and popular sentiment. The corollary is that Theodorus is portrayed as an impractical statesman whose political ineptitude is illustrative of weaknesses inherent in the camp of the opposition to Dionysius.

Thus Theodorus declares that the Carthaginians, if victorious, would impose tribute, whereas Dionysius takes property and plunders temples (Diod. Sic. XIV. 65. 2). Yet the narrative of Books XIII and XIV[67] reveals clearly that the Siceliots hated the Carthaginians for their violence and devotes extensive reference to Carthaginian brutality — a fact to which archaeological evidence of destruction lends confirmatory testimony. The narrative, at no point, suggests that Carthage would merely impose tribute. On the contrary, we are clearly told that the Syracusans and other Siceliots and indeed non-Siceliots joined Dionysius because of a wish to inflict vengeance upon the Carthaginians for outrages committed against them, more specifically the destruction of Selinus, Himera, Acragas, Gela and Camarina (Diod. Sic. XIV. 45. 5; 46. 2-5; 48. 1; 51. 4; 52. 1-2; 53. 1).

Theodorus argues that Dionysius gave the property taken from the private owners to the slaves through whom he ruled.

Syracusan territory is in the hands of those who increased Dionysius' power (Diod. Sic. XIV. 65. 2-3). Theodorus' words imply that Dionysius' support is essentially based upon the loyalty of slaves and those of slave mentality. It certainly appears that, according to Theodorus, the majority of the Syracusans were crushed beneath an unbearably heavy yoke which they were eager to cast off at the first favourable opportunity. This picture contrasts noticeably with that given in the narrative of the popular Dionysius, launching a crusade for the survival of Hellenic civilisation in the West. While it is true that the text states that the Syracusans ultimately hoped to assert their freedom and were eager to lessen the weight of Dionysius' yoke, there is no suggestion that Dionysius' rule was devoid of all leniency. Dionysius gained co-operation in his venture by creating patriotic zeal and by mixing with the populace. The declaration of war is taken by the Syracusans as a whole. The Siceliots are in a position to desert, if they so desire. Further, Dionysius' rewards are given to citizens as well as slaves and mercenaries. Finally the very fact that Theodorus is in a position to attack Dionysius in the assembly contradicts his own statement to the effect that Dionysius depended purely upon the support of slaves, and mercenaries (Diod. Sic. XIV. 45. 2; 61. 3; 96. 2; 7. 5; 9. 6; 65. 2-3). Certainly even if we accept the hypothesis that the speech represents the personal viewpoint of Timaeus, we should have to conclude that Timaeus was willing to acknowledge that the situation as described by Theodorus did not accord with the facts. Indeed the ease with which the text notes that Dionysius was able to win over the Syracusans fully confirms the fact that Theodorus, far from being a realist, espousing sensible policies, was a man δοκῶν εἶναι πρακτικός (Diod. Sic. XIV. 70. 3; 64. 5).

This is confirmed by a final point. Theodorus' references to the enslavement of Catane and Naxos can only be viewed within the context of an idealistic Pansiceliotism of the type associated with Hermocrates, and as such is hardly likely to have appealed to Syracusan popular opinion under the Dioclean democracy and Dionysius' regime (Diod. Sic. XIV. 66. 4; 68. 3). In view of the ancient hostility of Syracuse and the Ionian states, Theodorus again hardly emerges as a practical politician.

Thus we claim that Theodorus' speech can hardly be regarded as a vehicle whereby a hostile source like Theodorus expressed his disapproval of the regime of Dionysius. The source of its inclusion in Diodorus' text, in our view, is threefold. First, the alleged hostile description of the Dionysian tyranny constitutes data likely utilised by a source such as Philistus whose interest was focused upon *realpolitik* as manifested by the Syracusan despotate. Secondly, variations between data supplied by the speech and those found in the narrative reveal Diodorus' source to have been a good deal more objective than generally assumed, whence the automatic attribution of the speech to Timaeus deserves a strong caveat. Finally, on the basis of these variations of information, we suggest that the speech in actual fact does not present a singularly edifying picture of Theodorus. In the first place, Theodorus is depicted as either distorting the facts or at the very least, if we adopt a more charitable stance towards him, of being in ignorance of the reality. Secondly, the Syracusan knight is painted as a particularly impractical politician, hardly capable of arousing the Syracusans against Dionysius on the basis of real and relevant issues.

Our view that the speech of Theodorus was included in Diodorus for sound historiographical reasons, is challenged by Bachof's claim that its inclusion derives from Timaeus' interests in rhetorical exercises. Bachof adds the argument that the speech is to be regarded as a manifestation of Timaeus' patriotric feelings. In support of his thesis, he produces two pieces of evidence. First he notes that three out of four of the major speeches found in the *Bibliotheke* of Diodorus deal with Sicilian affairs. Indeed the only major speech which occurs in a non-Sicilian context is Endius' speech. Secondly, Bachof argues that Polybius' statement about Timaeus' use of speeches for patriotic and rhetorical purposes (Polyb. XII. 25k, 26, 26a, 26b/T. 19. F. 22. 94) would support his contention that the speech is representative of Timaeus' rhetorical and patriotic tendencies.

Polybius' statement certainly indicates that Timaeus employed speeches less for their importance at elucidating the text and as a source of accuracy of fact than as a vehicle for glorifying Sicily and her great men and indulging in feats of verbosity. Yet the problems which we face are, can the speech of Theodorus be regarded as patriotic in sentiment and was it the practice of Diodorus to include speeches merely for the sake of rhetorical effect?

Certainly, on any level, the speech's sentiments can hardly be interpreted as patriotic, while for Timaeus there is little in the speech that can be considered edifying. While it certainly constitutes a call to action for the Syracusans to resist Dionysius, it at the same time emphasises the effectiveness of Dionysius' despotate and the tyrant's ability to succeed in nefarious policies towards the Syracusans, Siceliots as a whole and Carthage. It portrays the great conspiracy of the Syracusan despot. Theodorus' subsequent failure hardly lends credence to the view that the speech is representative of Syracusan or Siceliot patriotic awareness.

More important is the fact that we have sought to demonstrate, that the speech is distinctly aimed at portraying the dishonesty and incompetence of the leader of Syracusan resistance to the tyrant and the unrealistic nature of the policies which he advocated.

Finally it is clear that it was not the practice of Diodorus to include speeches for reasons of rhetorical effect. The historian's own statements make this quite clear. Endius' speech was included for its succinctness and Laconianism. Moreover, Diodorus argues against the use of tedious rhetorical exercises of speech. He adds that only when the subject matter is great and a speech worthy of memory is a historian justified in including speeches (Diod. Sic. XIII. 52. 2; XX. 1-2).

It is unfortunate that Diodorus' assertions about his own personal intellectual integrity have simply been ignored by scholars of the Volquardsen *genre*. Their refusal to admit that Diodorus' caution in regard to the amount given by Timaeus of Agathocles is likely to have affected his appraisal of Timaeus' books on Dionysius has already been noted. Similarly Diodorus' statement that he has no interest in mere verbal gymnastics has received little serious consideration. Diodorus is explicit: the subject matter determines whether a speech be included or not. Therefore the implication is that the speech of Theodorus is not a figment of the imagination of Timaeus, or indeed, of any other source, incorporated purely to stress Siceliot patriotism by a show of rhetoric. The fact that Diodorus rarely included speeches in the course of his history would appear to confirm the sincerity of his intentions and indicate that he was not simply repeating stock formulae, current since Thucydides.[68]

It is thus clear that the importance of the subject matter was the determining factor in Diodorus' decision concerning the inclusion of speeches. As a Sicilian himself and a historian, devoting considerable effort to the Sicilian narrative — a fact to which the mere length of the text testifies — Diodorus no doubt considered the speech of Theodorus significant enough for inclusion. This is confirmed by the very fact that three out of the four major speeches in the *Bibliotheke* are placed within a Sicilian context. However the Sicilian flavour of the speech is hardly decisive in view of the absence of true patriotic content in it and the fact that the speech's inclusion seems to have been determined largely by the desire to underline the deficiencies which characterised the Syracusan opposition to Dionysius.

Finally Bachof argued that Theodorus' favourable reference to Gelon was representative of the Timaeus tradition whose purpose was to contrast the moderate rule of Gelon with the despotism of Dionysius,[69] the result of which was the contrast in Diodorus, though not in other sources, between the *basileus* Gelon and the *tyrannos* Dionysius.[70]

To Bachof's argument, we must respond that although Timaeus certainly seems to have presented Gelon as a liberator (Schol. Pind. *Pyth.* II. 2; Polyb. XII. 26. 1/F. 20, 94) and might well have depicted the earlier Syracusan tyrant as a noble ruler in contrast to the absolutism of the Dionysii and Agathocles, it cannot be proved that such a view originates with Timaeus, is solely to be associated with that historian and therefore does not derive in Diodorus' text from another source. If on the one hand we argue that the favourable reference to Gelon derives from a source hostile to Dionysius, the possibility that another authority was a source of the remark cannot be entirely discounted in view of the fact that Diodorus used many sources for his narrative — even though we have shown that the only overtly hostile historical source to Dionysius in antiquity before Diodorus appears to have been Timaeus. Moreover since modern scholars — Holm, Freeman, Palm and Drews in particular[71] — have claimed to discern evidence of Diodorus' own personal hand in the text, the possibility must be entertained that the remark about Gelon derives from Diodorus himself who could have obtained this information from a variety of sources, both written and oral. To cite Oldfather,[72] 'Diodorus as a native Sicilian would not let the opportunity escape him of magnifying the exploits of his fellow countrymen' — exploits, we may add, which the hostile tradition might well have magnified and rendered available to Diodorus. On the other hand, since we have seen that the seemingly hostile material about Dionysius in Diodorus' text, need not, in fact, be conceived of as reflecting a hostile source and can be identified with a favourable authority like Philistus, we could equally well argue that the remark about Gelon derives from a source like

Philistus who would not have been embarrassed to include such a comment in his account, in spite of his pronounced sympathy towards Dionysius.[73]

VIII

Admittedly, most of the argumentation submitted above is negative and polemical in nature, its purpose being to disprove the commonly held theory that Diodorus' narrative of Dionysius' reign in Books XIII and XIV of the *Bibliotheke* derives from Timaeus. It remains for us, therefore, to submit confirmatory data for the hypothesis heretofore presented to the effect that Philistus rather than Timaeus was Diodorus' chief source.

We initially note that Philistus is certainly cited by Diodorus on numerous occasions both as a historian and as a figure of political importance under Dionysius, specifically responsible for supporting the tyrant during the revolution which first brought Dionysius to power and for later saving the tyrant's skin during the counter-revolution which wellnigh obliterated the tyranny (XIII. 103. 3; XV. 89. 3; 94. 4; XIII. 91. 4; XIV. 8. 5/T. 11a, b, c, 3. 4).[74] It should further be pointed out against Volquardsen[75] that the fact that Diodorus used and cited Apollodorus (I. 5. 1; XIII. 103. 5) is not sufficient evidence to prove that Diodorus did not see Philistus' history or that the citation regarding the dates which marked the terminus of the works of Thucydides and Philistus (XII. 37; XIII. 103. 3) are not derived from Diodorus' personal knowledge of these two writers' works. Volquardsen further argued that as Diodorus' notice on the date which marked the close of the first part of Philistus' work appears in the narrative of the Peloponnesian War and not in the narrative of Sicilian history (XIII. 103. 3), therefore Diodorus did not read Philistus. The untenability of this argument is apparent when it is appreciated that Diodorus rounds off the affairs of 406 BC with this fact together with the death of Sophocles and the possible death of Euripides. Thus Diodorus' mention of the termination of Philistus' work occurs in a perfectly logical position and the fact that it does not appear in the Sicilian sections cannot be regarded as decisive evidence against the possibility of direct use of Philistus by Diodorus. Finally in this context, Laqueur[76] argued that since Plutarch (*Dion* XXXV. 6/Jacoby, *FGH*, vol. 3b. 566. F. 115; 556. F. 59) reported that Timaeus and not Philistus recorded

that at the time of the Hoplite revolt of 403 BC Philistus advised
Dionysius to be cast out and dragged by the leg rather than run
away from the tyranny, and Diodorus (XIV. 8. 5/T. 4) attributed
this advice to Philistus; therefore Diodorus was following
Timaeus. To this we retort that, at the very least, this evidence
merely indicates Diodorus' choosing to follow Timaeus on this
point alone. However, it should also be noted that, though,
according to Plutarch, Philistus denied making this remark himself, he never denied placing this statement in another person's
mouth in his history. It is certainly consistent with Philistus' attitude. Consequently Diodorus might be himself in error in his
transmission of the data of Philistus — a fact certainly suggested
by the reference later in Book XX. 78. 3, where Megacles,
Dionysius' brother-in-law is attributed this advice and where
Diodorus is likely to be voicing a viewpoint which he found in
Philistus' history. Finally, I attribute no significance to the reference to tyranny as a fair winding-sheet (XIV. 8. 5), even though
the same phrase is encountered in Aelian (*VH* IV. 8) who elsewhere cites Timaeus (*VH* XII. 29/F. 26c), since the phrase is
already known to Isocrates (*Archid.* 44-5) and hence could easily
have been found in Philistus, Ephorus or Theopompus.

The likelihood that Diodorus utilised Philistus' Περὶ Διονυσίου
is further suggested by the fact that while Timaeus' history proved
to be the most popular Western history in the second century BC,
by the first century BC, Philistus' works seem to have challenged
its supremacy — a phenomenon, we have suggested particularly
stemming from the new respectability accorded monarchism in
the late first century BC but also due probably to the renewed
interest in Atticism during the same period. Hence we encounter
references to Philistus in Cicero (*Ad Quint. Fratr.* II, 11. 4; *De Orat.*
II. 57; *Brut.* 66; *De Div.* I. 39; 73/T. 17a, b, 21, F. 57a, 58),
Dionysius of Halicarnassus (*Ad Pomp.* IV/T. 16b) and Cornelius
Nepos (*Dion* III. 2/T. 5d) as well as in Diodorus.

Turning to the more concrete relationship which we suggest
can be established between Diodorus' text and Philistus' *oeuvre*,
we observe an absence of digression in the Dionysian narrative
which immediately accords with the testimony of T. 20b (Theon
Progymn. II. p. 80, 27). More significantly we note that a clear
break in presentation of material occurs in Diodorus XIII. 91. 1,
where the conflict between Carthage and the Siceliots is transformed into the narrative of Dionysius' rise. This phenomenon
accords with the division between Philistus' two chief *corpora* —

the Περὶ Σικελίας and the Περὶ Διονυσίου (Diod. Sic. XIII. 103. 3; XV. 89. 3; Cic. *Ad Quint. Fratr.* II. 11. 4/T. 11, 17a). Further, we maintain that it is hardly a coincidence that Diodorus' narrative for the last twenty years of Dionysius' reign is exceedingly sparse — precisely the period during which Philistus was in exile and for which he probably possessed little data with which to work, when he composed his Περὶ Διονυσίου. Timaeus, on the other hand, as we have seen, devoted six books to Dionysius, two more than Philistus, and it does seem significant that the hostile and gossipy material which clearly appeared in Timaeus' history and must have filled the additional two books, hardly appears at all in Diodorus' text and then only briefly in the latter portions of Book XIV and in scattered notices in Book XV. Moreover what we do encounter there, as we have seen, can hardly be attributed with confidence to Timaeus.

To venture beyond our negative conclusions to the effect that the sparse description of the last two decades of Dionysius' rule found in Diodorus' fifteenth book is unlikely to derive from Timaeus and is reflective of the phenomenon of Philistus' exile is, however, in our view, hazardous, both because of our afore-mentioned argumentation negating the claims of Ephorus, Theopompus and Timaeus and because solid reasons can be adduced for dissociating Philistus' authorship from most of the Sicilian narrative of Diodorus' fifteenth book. Certainly Diodorus' praise of Dionysius as θαυμαστῶς ἀγωνισάμενος (XV. 15. 3) and of Leptines for his courage, heroism and distinction in inflicting many deaths on the Carthaginians (XV. 17. 1) — the latter passage recalling Philistus' praise for Leptines' daughters (Plut. *Tim.* XV. 10/F. 60) — as well as the account of the goodwill shown towards Dionysius I (Diod. Sic. XV. 74. 5) which contrasts with the account of court intrigue to be encountered in Timaeus (Plut. *Dion* VI. 2/F. 109) and of Dionysius' funeral, which recalls Philistus' positive account (Theon *Progymn.* II. 68/F. 28; cf. Plut. *Pelop.* XXXIV. 1/F. 40b), undoubtedly conjures up the authority of Philistus. Conversely, however, we have suggested that personal dissatisfaction with Dionysius' Italian policy manifested itself in Philistus' descriptions of the post-396 BC period, whence the infiltration of hostile data into Diodorus' text. Consequently the favourable notices concerning the Carthaginians in the depiction of the Third and possibly Fourth Punic Wars (XV. 15. 3; 16. 2, 3; 17. 5; 24) might well derive from Philistus. We might also be tempted to ascribe the chronological imprecision of XV.

24 already noted to Philistus who was, of course, in exile at the time of these events and consequently lacked direct access to full information. At the same time, we duly observe that the anecdotal data in the fifteenth book pertaining to Dionysius' relations with the literati at his court (Diod. Sic. XV. 6-7) and of his carousing following his victory at the Lenaean games (XV. 74. 2) can hardly be ascribed to Philistus for three reasons: the facts that Philistus' history anteceded the flowering of the anecdotal tradition; that the anecdotal tradition's hostile character was non-Sicilian, being associated with Athens and its distinguished refugee, Timaeus; and that the pro-Plato biased account of Dionysius' enslavement of the philosopher (Diod. Sic. XV. 7. 1) can hardly have derived from Plato's arch-rival at the court of the younger Dionysius. For the rest, we note that Philistus, who obviously dealt with Dionysius' great wall around Syracuse and whose account, we shall suggest, was reproduced by Diodorus XIV. 18, is unlikely to have been Diodorus' source for the superficial, repetitious and inaccurately dated material of XV. 13. 5, while the obviously unsubtle motivation ascribed to Dionysius' Northern Adriatic expansionist policies, to the effect that the tyrant hoped to gain control of the Ionian Gulf and a safe route to Epirus in order to attack Epirus and sack Delphi (Diod. Sic. XV. 13. 1) can hardly be associated confidently with the authority of a historian who was, we have seen, deeply involved in these schemes.[77] Finally we question whether Philistus, an active operator in the Northern Adriatic schemes, would have been oblivious of the contradiction between Dionysius' alleged design of attacking Epirus and the restoration of Alcetas (Diod. Sic. XV. 13. 2).[78]

To return to the bulk of Diodorus' Dionysian data in Books XIII and XIV, the friends who advised Dionysius not to fight a land battle in XIV. 61. 2 probably included Philistus. This information, accordingly, might well echo Philistus' account. More significantly, the notice in XIII. 96. 4 on the establishment and long duration of Dionysius' tyranny obviously directly echoes Philistus' sentiments. Clearly an opponent of Dionysius like Timaeus would have had no inclination to emphasise the greatness of Dionysius' achievement in creating from such humble beginnings and single-handedly the 'greatest and longest tyranny', centred around the 'greatest city of the Greek World'. On the contrary, to Timaeus, this phenomenon would have been regarded as a cause of Syracusan and Siceliot shame. The depiction of Dionysius' seizure of power, moreover, undoubtedly in essence reproduces Philistus. In the first place, Philistus' prominent role in paying the fines imposed upon Dionysius by his opponents is obviously likely to have been mentioned by Philistus (Diod. Sic. XIII. 91. 4/No. 556. T. 3a). Secondly, Dionysius' attack upon the nonsensical laws (Diod. Sic. XIII. 91. 3) accords well with the sentiments of a historian like Philistus, as we have seen deeply inculcated with the tenets of sophistic argumentation pertaining to the superiority of φύσις to νόμος.[79] Thirdly, given as we have seen, Thucydides' high praise of Pisistratus and Philistus' emulation of Thucydidean ideology, the notice on Dionysius' imitation of Pisistratus (Diod. Sic. XIII. 95) might well echo Philistus' sentiments. Finally, Diodorus' obliviousness of the tradition emanating from Plato (*Ep.* VIII. 353b) and followed by Aristotle (*Polit.* 1306a) and Plutarch (*Dion* III. 2) to the effect that Hipparinus was Dionysius' colleague in 405 BC indicates that Diodorus XIII. 95. 1 was not following the Platonic tradition, undoubtedly accepted by Timaeus, but rather the more ancient and indeed more reliable account of Philistus which attributed to Dionysius the sole generalship.[80]

An association of Philistus and Diodorus is, of course, suggested by fragment 28 of Philistus (Theon *Progymn.* II. 68. 17 sp) which refers to the preparations of Dionysius for the great Punic War of 398-396 BC, its content clearly corresponding to the data which we encounter in Diodorus XIV. 41-44 — a fact even acknowledged by source-critics attributing the bulk of Diodorus' text to Timaeus.[81] Echoes, moreover, of the political ideals enshrined in this narrative pertaining to the broad social support enjoyed to Dionysius' tyranny are discernible in other passages of Diodorus. Thus the vivid description of the building of the walls of Epipolae (XIV. 18) with its depiction of Dionysius as the organiser *par excellence*, encouraging the people to work by fostering a co-operative spirit, recalls the similar depiction found in the account of Dionysius' preparations in 399 BC (XIV. 41. 3-6; 42. 1-2; 45. 1).[82] Similarly, the notice in XIV. 73. 1, on the universal zeal of the Syracusans in attacking the boats and docks and upon Dionysius' free circulation among his men, again recalls the earlier depictions and consequently also seemingly reflects Philistus' account. Finally, although owing to the process of conflation[83] of Philistus' narrative on Diodorus' part, details from Philistus' account of the siege of Motya were overlooked by Diodorus, such as pertained to the construction of wooden rollers

Diodorus and Dionysius

and overt encouragement on Dionysius' part of his men, recalling
earlier passages already noted (thus Polyaen. V. 2. 6), in essence
we are again confronted in Diod. Sic. XIV. 44-53. 3) with an
obviously positive Philistus-derived account, emphasising the co-
operative nature of Dionysius' imperialistic ventures.

We are further tempted to surmise that Philistus' view of
Dionysius as a figure blessed by fortune (F. 58/Cic. *De Div.* I. 73)
underlies the five references in Diodorus' text to Dionysius'
miraculous escapes: after the defeat of Hermocrates in 408 BC
(XIII. 75. 9); after the Gela campaign in 405 BC (XIII. 112. 6); in
404 BC, when blockaded on the island (XIV. 9); before the
Rhegine and Messanian attack (XIV. 40. 4-7) and during the
storm following the confrontation with the Crotoniates (XIV. 100.
5).

In three cases, Diodorus' text is conspicuous by its omission of
data deriving from the hostile tradition. First, while in Diodorus'
account of the mercenary revolt, we are simply informed that
Dionysius gave the rebels Leontini (Diod. Sic. XIV. 78. 1),
Polyaenus (V. 2. 1), no doubt reflecting a hostile source, probably
Timaeus, provides negative details about Dionysius' begging in a
grovelling manner for his life in attire of a distinctly modest type.
Secondly, Diodorus' depiction of Dionysius' marriage alliances
(Diod. Sic. XIV. 44. 3-8), which we have already attributed to
Philistus, is marked by total omission of data encountered in the
later anecdotal, largely Timaean and consequently negative ver-
sion. Thus Diodorus makes no mention of the Rhegine offer to
Dionysius of the daughter of the public executioner (Strabo VI. 1.
6) — only doing so in XIV. 107. 3 where, as we have seen,
Philistus' disenchantment of Dionysius might well be echoed; of
the prior refusal of Plato's friend Aristides to give Dionysius his
daughter (Plut. *Tim.* VI); and of the fact that Locri was ruined by
the marriage alliance with Dionysius (Arist. *Polit.* V. 1307a, 38).[84]
Finally, as we have seen, Diodorus' description of Leptines' death
at Cronium (XV. 17. 1), though distinctly pro-Leptines and somewhat critical of Dionysius, antedates the fully fledged hostility of
the anecdotal tradition such as one encounters in Aelian (*VH*
XIII. 45) and Plutarch (*De Alex. Fort.* II. 5. 338a). It is also noteworthy that other examples of anecdotal data recording serious
differences between Dionysius and Leptines pertaining to
Dionysius' jealous relegation of his brother to Himera (Aen. Tact.
X. 21), Leptines' tactical error in allowing the Carthaginians to
move camp during the Third Punic War (Polyaen. VI. 16. 1) and

Leptines' willingness to burn his property for patriotic reasons (Frontin. *Strateg.* II. 5. 11) are unrecorded by Diodorus.

As we should expect, of course, from Diodorus' use of Philistus or indeed of any other of the sources whose claim as Diodorus' authority has been advanced by source critics, Diodorus' text is certainly centred around Syracuse, its internal and foreign policy and above all its predominant personality, Dionysius. More noteworthy, however, is the fact that accompanying this concentration of interest upon Syracuse, we observe a minimal attribution of importance to the internal affairs of other Siceliot cities, except within a Syracusan context — a phenomenon which is encountered not merely in the Dionysian sections of Diodorus' narrative but more significantly in the narrative describing developments preceding Dionysius' rise to power, where information regarding Siceliot resistance to Carthage divorced from a Syracusan context is singularly sparse. Thus, apart from an isolated and mysterious reference to a pro-Punic party at Selinus headed by a certain Empedion (XIII. 59. 3) and an equally enigmatic reference to the pity of certain Greeks in the service of Carthage whose national origins are not clearly delineated,[85] for Selinuntine sufferings (XIII. 58. 1), the only substantial insights[86] provided into the internal affairs of Siceliot cities other than Syracuse occur at points where Syracusan military forces, led alternatively by Diocles, Daphnaeus and Dionysius, enter the scene: at Himera where an assembly decides on evacuation (XIII. 61. 2-6); at Gela, where we are treated to a digression on the statue of the river Gela and to an exceedingly vivid description of the battle of Gela[87] (XIII. 108. 4-5; 109-110); and, above all, at Acragas, where we are provided with an even more vivid description of the assembly and its preliminaries (XIII. 87) as well as of Acragantine affluence (XIII. 81. 4-84). Consequently we suggest that all the above data, including the description of the statue of the river Gela and Acragantine wealth — an excursus incidentally whose content we can gather from Diodorus XIII. 81. 4-5 and 89.1 is not as isolated, as one might originally suspect, from the rest of Diodorus' text — which is associated by Diodorus with Timaeus' authority, constitute material Syracusan in origin, gathered by a Syracusan contemporary source either deriving from the Syracusan militia relieving the Siceliot cities or from a source in direct contact with such a Syracusan source.[88] All this information we accordingly suggest either derived originally from Philistus directly who, in view of his being of military age, might well have been personally serving in the Syracusan militia, or indirectly from the same historian who, in view of the political and military position which he occupied at Syracuse, could have easily gleaned this information from the Syracusan military source who originally had access to it. We should add that the data regarding the dispute between Segesta and Selinus (Diod. Sic. XIII. 43. 1-3), in view of the longstanding duration of the conflict, it having indeed provoked Athenian intervention six years earlier, can hardly be regarded for our purposes as detailed, local, non-Syracusan Sicilian information of the type only likely to have been culled from a non-Syracusan Siceliot source. Moreover, as we shall see, Diodorus' source was well acquainted with Punic data. Details regarding the conflict, which were voiced by the Segestan embassy at Carthage, might accordingly have been gleaned from Punic-derived information.

It is further possible that not merely non-availability of evidence but a real desire to suppress non-Syracusan Siceliot evidence on the part of Philistus, to highlight the role of Dionysius and magnify the tyrant's achievements, accounts for the sparseness of data pertaining to the internal affairs of Siceliot cities other than Syracuse which we encounter in Diodorus. This is suggested by two further facts: that little interest and consequently confusing data regarding the Siceliot League headed by Syracuse is provided by Diodorus;[89] and that only at the point of its disintegration does Diodorus emphasise the League's existence, highlighting in the process the negative aspects of Campanian, Italiot, Lacedaemonian and Syracusan treachery (Diod. Sic. XIII. 88. 5, 7; 91. 2).

What is, moreover, particularly surprising in this context is the considerable amount of detail provided by Diodorus for Punic affairs, contrasting markedly with the sparse testimony for Siceliot, as opposed to purely Syracusan, affairs and including detailed descriptions of the deliberations of the Punic Senate (XIII. 43. 5-6; 80. 2) as well as of the Punic populace as a whole, pertaining to the desirability or lack thereof of waging war with the Siceliots (XIII. 43. 4); precise statistics of Punic military forces, seemingly reasonable and accurate as far as those identified with the authority of Timaeus are concerned (XIII. 44. 6; 54. 1, 4-5; 80. 2-5; XIV. 54. 5-6; 62. 2; 95. 1); a vivid and detailed description of activity within the Punic camp during the course of Punic-Siceliot hostilities 410-396 BC (XIII. 58. 1; 62. 5; 86. 1-3; 88. 2-3; XIV. 62. 1-4; 76. 3);[90] precise directives and commands of Carthaginian leaders (XIII. 59. 3; 62. 5; 86. 3; XIV. 55. 1); personal, intimate thoughts of Carthaginian generals (XIII. 88. 3; XIV. 56. 1; 58. 3); a quite unique reference to the wine and oil trade between Acragas and Carthage (XIII. 81. 4-5);[91] a note on the personal, aesthetic interests of Himilcon (XIII. 90. 3-4); and, above all, a lengthy and highly informative description of the crisis which developed in Africa following the destruction of Himilcon's fleet — an excursus set entirely within a Punic context, containing no reference to Syracusan and Siceliot affairs at all (XIV. 76-77).[92] Since Diodorus does not explicitly refer to his use of a Punic source and since from his citations of the authorities which he consulted we can gather that he relied exclusively upon Greek sources for his narrative of Greek history, it is unlikely that Diodorus utilised for this detailed account of Punic affairs a Punic source, even in a Greek translation, if such a source existed. Since, moreover, Theopompus who certainly wrote extensively about the West, including Carthage, does not appear to have covered the early part of Dionysius' reign in his *Hellenica* and was, as we have seen, not utilised for this reason extensively by Diodorus and since no other historian consulted by Diodorus shared Philistus' intimacy with Dionysius and Syracusan governmental affairs, as befitted one of Dionysius' φίλοι, and we discover Philistus on one occasion perusing a letter from Dion to Carthage (Plut. *Dion* XIV. 4/T. 6a) — evidence perhaps of Philistus' diplomatic role and familiarity with the minutiae of foreign policy at the Syracusan court — Philistus is clearly the most likely source for the detailed Punic material which we encounter in Diodorus' thirteenth and fourteenth books.

Further, as we have already noted in connection with our discussion of the political theory of Philistus, the positive tone towards Dionysius' achievement in Diodorus begins to recede in the narrative of Dionysius' Italian War with the Rhegine bloc, whence the hostile Phyton anecdote (Diod. Sic. XIV. 112) and equally negative anecdote about the Rhegine offer to Dionysius of the public executioner's daughter (XIV. 107. 2-3) whose absence, we have seen, is conspicuous in its earlier and chronologically more precise context (XIV. 44). Thereafter, moreover, little interest is shown in the war with Carthage of 392 BC, while in the sketchy depiction of Dionysius' Third Punic War, as well as a more positive approach being shown Carthage, Leptines' bravery is stressed at the expense of Dionysius (Diod. Sic. XV. 17. 1) — though we stress that open hostility of the type which characterises other and presumably later treatments of this episode is noticeably absent from Diodorus' account. All these phenomena, we have argued, might well be reflective of Philistus' opposition to Dionysius' policies following his great Punic War of 398-396 BC and more specifically of the tyrant's war in South Italy, criticism, we add, which cost Philistus his position as confidant and counsellor of Dionysius and provoked his exile — though, as we have seen, our ascription of data in Diodorus, dated to the period following Philistus' exile of 384 BC and including, therefore, Diodorus' description of Dionysius' Third Punic War, to Philistus or any other source can hardly be assumed with any degree of confidence.

There remains the issue of whether Diodorus' text contains any material which can be construed of as Thucydidean in character and hence ascribed to Philistus who, as we have seen, was regarded in classical antiquity as the historian most resembling Thucydides. Obviously, the philological and stylistic unity of the *Bibliotheke*, so convincingly demonstrated by Palm, precludes any serious investigation on our part into possible Thucydidean stylistic characteristics in Diodorus' Dionysian narrative. With argumentation pertaining to likely influences of Thucydidean thematic data upon Diodorus, we are probably on firmer ground. For one thing the description of sea-battles in XIV. 60. 3 and 62. 2 recall Thucydides' battles in confined spaces like the battle in the great harbour of Syracuse. Similar treatment of women can also be traced in Thucydides and Diodorus' narrative of Book XIII and XIV. Thus, just as in Thucydides, women appear as brave defenders of besieged cities and contributors to the civic effort (I. 90. 3; II. 78. 3; V. 82. 6) and even as missile throwers (II. 4. 2; III. 74. 1), so too in Diodorus women are defenders (XIII. 55. 4-5; 108. 6, 8; XIV. 52. 1) distinguished for hurling stones at the enemy (XIII. 56. 7).[93] Similarly, in both historians, women lament (Thuc. II. 34. 4; Diod. Sic. XIII. 56. 6; XIV. 52. 1) and endure ultimate hardship, including slavery (Diod. Sic. XIII. 57. 3-5; 58. 1-2; 62. 4; 89. 3; Thuc. I. 89. 3; 103. 3; II. 6. 4; cf. 72. 2; 78. 3; 14. 1; 27. 1; III. 36. 2; 68. 3; IV. 48. 4; 123. 4; V. 3. 4; 32. 1; 116. 4; VII. 29. 4; 68. 2; VIII. 74. 3). Finally, on one occasion, similar comment on the unusual quality of women's assumptions of the role of defence is made by the two writers, Thucydides remarking that the women at Corcyra by throwing tiles acted παρὰ φύσιν (Thuc. III. 74. 1), Diodorus observing τὴν αἰδῶ καὶ τὴν ἐπὶ τῆς εἰρήνης αἰσχύνην παρ'οὐδὲν ἡγούμεναι (Diod. Sic. XIII. 55. 4).

More significantly, we follow Hejnic in noting that Diodorus' chronological scheme from both Greek and Sicilian portions of his narrative, involving a dating system by summers and winters identical to Thucydides', ends at Book XV at the chronological terminal point of Philistus' Περὶ Διονυσίου.[94] Further, we should expect that a disciple of Thucydides — a historian, after all, who was deeply influenced by medical developments of the age of the sophists, who did not hesitate to incorporate into his analysis of political behaviour and causation of war medical terminology, and who supplied a detailed analysis of the great plague which struck Athens in the early years of the Peloponnesian War (Thuc. II. 49-50) and even felled Pericles — should include in his history a detailed description of a plague at some point in the narrative, since on numerous occasions in the course of the hostilities between Dionysius and Carthage, according to Diodorus, plague actually struck the Punic host with disastrous consequences (XIII. 86. 2; 114. 2; XIV. 70. 4-71; XV. 24. 2; 73. 1). Thus given the especially detailed presentation of Dionysius' great Punic War of 398-396 BC in Diodorus, as we have seen undoubtedly deriving ultimately from the pen of Philistus, the detailed description of the plague of 396 BC (XIV. 70. 4-71) comes as no surprise and is likely as Volquardsen long ago suggested, to have derived from Philistus' Περὶ Διονυσίου.[95] Further, suggestive of an ultimate Thucydidean derivation of Diodorus' plague is the fact that the key symptoms of the two plagues are identical: the contagiousness of the disease, the rash, fever and period of crisis.[96] The differences in the two accounts, moreover, according to R. Littman, are of relatively little importance. Thus the back-pains are diagnostically insignificant and the five-to-six days crisis-period of Diodorus, as opposed to Thucydides' seven-to-nine days, to be expected, particularly if both plagues are to be identified as smallpox. The additional Thucydidean symptoms — prostration, vomiting, thirst, progressive attacks on head and extremities — moreover, are to be expected from a more detailed analysis than a Diodorean summary, while the smog-factor from the Syracusan marshes inducing catarrh constitutes an obvious relevant local detail, to be expected from a local Syracusan source like Philistus, utilising Thucydidean medical knowledge, devoid of slavish imitation. It is also perhaps significant that this analysis of the plague is placed in the context of Punic moral, political and social collapse, paralleling perhaps Thucydides' similar placement of the Athenian plague within the context of Athenian moral, political and social collapse.[97] We should finally not be surprised to observe that far more detail is accorded this plague than Diodorus' description of the plague at Athens (XII. 45. 2) which scholarly consensus probably correctly associates with Ephorus' testimony, whose narrative of the Peloponnesian War was obviously less full than Thucydides' and whose interest in medical data is undoubtedly likely to have been less marked.

With respect to the question whether we can discern in Diodorus' text any echo of Thucydidean political ideology which could derive from the Thucydidean Philistus, we reiterate our former observation to the effect that a Thucydidean-derived political system wherein a popular *princeps*-type monarch rules with the assistance of an oligarchy of *novi homines* and a *demos* with distinct but limited political and constitutional powers, does seem to be favoured in Diodorus' description of the preliminaries of the Great War of 398-396 BC — a passage which we have seen is associated by most scholars ultimately at least with Philistus' authority. The rationale for the viewpoint adopted by the text is, moreover, easily discernible within the context of the patriotic tone and sympathy which it manifests towards the Syracusan *demos* and other Siceliots,[98] albeit significantly tempered by a realisation of weaknesses inherent in that body,[99] necessitating in turn the firm directive hand of the despot to promote ideals towards which the Syracusans specifically, and Siceliots as a whole, aspire.[100] As we have seen, such rationalisation certainly befits a Thucydidean-like Philistus. For the rest, as we have also seen, Diodorus, throughout his text, most certainly depicts Dionysius as an effective and popular, though despotic, figure, ruling, we add, in true Thucydidean style with oligarchic support despite his initial opposition to the old oligarchy, whence the description, noted by Sartori, of Dionysius as *dynast* and his government as *dynasty*.[101] Further as befits a historian echoing a Thucydidean-like Philistus, Diodorus concentrates his attention in the bulk of the Sicilian narrative of Books XIII and XIV upon political and military affairs, eschewing gossipy and personal anecdotes such as Timaeus obviously included in his history, except where such data possessed clear political relevance, as in the case of the tyrant's double marriage (Diod. Sic. XIV. 44. 4-8), illustrating as we have suggested in Philistus' eyes, the grandeur and political skill of the tyrant's schemes in 398 BC and the firm social oligarchic structure underlying the tyrant's rule, or in the case of Dionysius' hostility to Phyton (Diod. Sic. XIV. 112),

Philistus' opposition to Dionysius' South Italian policy. Both examples might indeed be compared to Thucydides' digression on Alcibiades' vices (Thuc. VI. 15) which in Thucydides' eyes merited discussion by virtue of its relevance to the ultimate fate of the Sicilian expedition. Finally, we suggest that echoes of a Philistus Thucydides-derived concept of imperialistic limitation might possibly be discerned both in the text's opposition to Dionysius' Italian policy and more significantly perhaps in Diodorus' description of the *hybris* accompanying Carthaginian imperialistic ventures, creating in turn well-earned *nemesis* for the Punic state. Certainly, while as we have seen, little if any moral censure characterises Diodorus' description of Dionysius in the bulk of the Sicilian narrative of Books XIII and XIV, hostility towards Dionysius only making its appearance in the description of Dionysius' Italian War, a distinct moral condemnation of Carthage is prevalent throughout the text. Thus the Punic foe is condemned for cowardice (XIII. 88. 2), for victories won purely on the basis of numerical superiority (XIII. 54. 1-2; 55. 2, 5, 8; 56. 1, 5, 8; 59. 7; 60. 3, 6; 80. 2-5), for brutality (XIII. 57. 2-3; 58. 1-2; 59. 4; 62. 3-4; 111. 4; XIV. 76. 2; 77. 1), for lust for material wealth (XIII. 57. 3-4; 62. 4, 6; 89. 1; 90. 3-5; 108. 3) and accretion of empire (XIII. 79. 8; 80. 1), for attacking defenceless women and children (XIII. 58. 2) and for impiety manifested towards Greek shrines and temples (XIII. 57. 3; 59. 2; 62. 3-4; 86. 1-4; 90. 1-2; XIV. 76. 2). For these misdemeanours and transgressions which constitute a challenge to *tyche* (XIII. 86. 2-3; XIV. 46. 4; 76. 1-2, 4), she suffers both just retribution from the Siceliots (XIV. 45. 5; 46. 2-3; 48. 1; 51. 4; 52. 1-5; 53. 1, 3) and punishment from the gods who support the Siceliots for the justice of their cause (XIV. 63. 1-3; 70. 4; 73. 5; 74. 3-4; 76. 1, 4; 77. 4; 77. 5). Since we have suggested that Philistus is the likely authority from whom Diodorus derived his substantial Punic data, these moralising passages which condemn Carthage, we feel, are more likely to derive from Philistus than from Timaeus who, as we have seen, has generally been favoured as their original source. It should be added that even though, as we have seen, Timaeus obviously employed Philistus' account, his actual reproduction of this aspect of Philistus' historical thought is unlikely, since it was Timaeus' concern to emphasise Dionysius' immorality rather than Carthage's and as we have seen, Volquardsen's assumption that Dionysius was a necessary evil, an instrument of divine vengeance in Timaeus' eyes, is a figment of that scholar's imagination. That

Philistus should have, moreover, entertained such sentiments seems particularly significant, bearing in mind the fact that Thucydides, for all his rationality, held similar views on war and imperialism, especially as applied to Athens, whence that historian's chief reason for composing his history of the Peloponnesian War to underline not Herodotean glory but, on the contrary, the brutality of war as illustrated particularly by such comparatively unimportant events as the Corcyraean civil war (Thuc. III. 82-4), the destruction of Plataea (Thuc. III. 52-68), the Athenian proposals with respect to Mytilene (Thuc. III. 36-51), the harsh treatment of Melos (Thuc. V. 84-116), the fate of the Athenian generals sent to Sicily (Thuc. IV. 65) and the destruction of Boeotian Mycalessus (Thuc. VII. 29). Indeed it is within this context not inappropriate to note that Clement of Alexandria in his *Stromata* (VI. 8. 9/F. 67) discerned a distinct association of hybristic philosophy on the part of Philistus and Thucydides, the very wording of Thucydides being reproduced by Philistus.[102] To carry the parallel, moreover, closer, one might be tempted to argue that the *hybris* of Himilcon, which epitomises the *hybris* of the Punic State, parallels Thucydides' depiction of the *hybris* of that most violent of Athens' sons, Cleon (Thuc. III. 36. 3; cf. IV. 39. 3; 17; III. 45. 4), whose challenge to fortune and resultant fall epitomises and foreshadows the collapse and failure of Athens itself.[103] Finally, given our suggestion that Diodorus' account of Dionysius' war against Rhegium and possibly the tyrant's third war against Carthage derives from Philistus, it would appear from the notices pertaining to Phyton's virtues and Dionysius' *hybris* for taking vengeance fit for tragedy (Diod. Sic. XIV. 112) and upon the deities' siding with the barbarians at Cronium (Diod. Sic. XV. 16. 3) and absence of hybristic motivation for the plague affecting the Punic force dated to 379-378 BC (Diod. Sic. XV. 73), that Philistus' Thucydidean-derived hybristic philosophy, until now reserved for Carthage, was, at this point, turned against Dionysius.

IX

It remains for us to determine why Diodorus relied so heavily upon the authority of Philistus, given the broad consultation of source material which characterised Diodorus and the overall thematic as well as stylistic unity which we have discerned in the

Bibliotheke. There were, we should initially note in the light of our earlier investigation, solid reasons why the histories of Ephorus, Theopompus and Timaeus would have been less appealing to Diodorus than Philistus' Περὶ Διονυσίου. As a Sicilian, as we have seen, Diodorus betrayed a particular interest in Sicilian history, including Dionysius' reign, which he could hardly have dealt with in the relatively superficial manner of an Ephorus, particularly for the earlier period, marked by Sicilian success against Carthage, so graphically described by Philistus and, to a large extent, reproduced by Timaeus. As for Ephorus' second Dionysian book, since, as we have seen, it probably stressed Dionysius' role within the context of universal Greek history, rather than that of Sicily, it would perhaps have been on such grounds less appealing to Diodorus, the Sicilian nationalist. Theopompus' testimony, on the other hand, is unlikely to have exercised a significant influence on Diodorus for two reasons. First, we have no evidence that Theopompus covered the early part of Dionysius' reign prior to 392 BC at all in his *Hellenica* and secondly, Theopompus' coverage of the post-392 BC period in the *Philippica* was highly idiosyncratic, providing more data on the younger Dionysius than on the latter's father. Finally, there remains Timaeus' history of Dionysius which might appear to us initially to have proved more attractive to the historian of Agyrium. In the first place we might be induced to argue that since Timaeus obviously utilised Philistus' history, albeit in a highly distorted manner, much local Sicilian patriotic data, particularly relating to Dionysius' great war against Carthage in 398-396 BC, could have been gleaned by Diodorus from Timaeus' account to enhance his own Sicilian patriotic aspirations. Against such reasoning we have expressed doubt as to whether in fact Timaeus would have accepted any aspect of Philistus' favourable stance towards Dionysius. On the contrary, deliberate distortion of Philistus seems to have marked Timaeus' history. More important, however, it could be conjectured that Timaeus' negative portrait of Dionysius as a tragedy bringing death and destruction to Sicily might appear to validate Diodorus' statement of intent in his *prooemium* to Book XIV to the effect that it was the historian's purpose to denounce in this book the Thirty Tyrants (XIV. 2. 1) and Dionysius I (XIV. 2. 2) — an individual who, in Diodorus' words, probably echoing Timaeus, 'although the most fortunate of such rulers, was constantly plotted against while alive, was compelled by fear to wear an iron corselet under his tunic and has bequeathed since his death his own life as an example to all ages of the maledictions of men' (translation by C.H. Oldfather, Loeb Classical Library 1954) illustrating more-over the adage 'that wicked men leave to posterity an undying image of their whole life; for the life which has preceded death becomes far worse throughout all time for the evil memory that it enjoys' (XIV. 1. 3). What is, of course, surprising, is that the picture of Dionysius delineated in the *prooemium* is not en-countered in the bulk of Diodorus' Dionysian narrative which contains little censure of the tyrant prior to the account of the Phyton episode (Diod. Sic. XIV. 112) and is totally devoid of data pertaining to the tyrant's fear of cabals and plots devised against his person such as we encounter in Plutarch (*De Alex. Fort.* II. p. 338b; *Dion* III. 3; IX. 3-5; *De Garrul.* p. 508f) and Cicero (*Tusc.* V. 20. 57) — testimony undoubtedly reflective of the anecdotal tra-dition whose origins we have traced to Dionysius' own lifetime.

Why then, we must ask, did Diodorus not essentially follow Timaeus' evaluation of Dionysius in the bulk of his narrative and why did he prefer Philistus' account to the extent of contradicting his own statement of intent in the *prooemium* of Book XIV? We suggest that three considerations influenced Diodorus' ultimate choice of Philistus as his chief source for Dionysius' reign. First, as we have already observed, Diodorus' suspicion of Timaeus' bias towards Agathocles (Diod. Sic. XXI. 17. 3/F. 124d) is likely to have been paralleled by identical suspicion on Diodorus' part towards that historian's treatment of Dionysius — an estimate which Diodorus is accordingly unlikely to have incorporated into his own account of the tyrant in the Dionysian chapters of the *Bibliotheke*. Secondly, the revival of popularity enjoyed by Philistus in the latter part of the first century BC, as testified to by the references to the historian and his works by Diodorus, Cornelius Nepos, Dionysius of Halicarnassus and Cicero and the major source for this rediscovery of Philistus, the new allure exerted by despotism and one-man rule both in a theoretical and practical sense — a re-evaluation, we stress, which appears to have won the adherence of even so staunch a republican as Cicero — rendered Diodorus' dependence upon Philistus' history and the ideology of despotism contained therein most probable. Finally, we suggest — and perhaps this was the decisive fact influencing Diodorus' choice of Philistus — that the central moral thesis of the Dionysian chapters pertaining to Carthaginian *hybris* and resulting *nemesis*, which we have ascribed to Philistus rather than Timaeus' authority, was appealing to Diodorus since it accorded with the latter historian's own central thesis regarding the success which accompanies the pursuance of justice and virtue, and the destruction which violation of such moral principles entails. In Philistus' description of the events culminating in the destruction of the Punic host in 396 BC, containing such overt manifestations of Punic arrogance, cowardice, brutality, greed and impiety which received their just deserts, it would thus appear that Diodorus discovered more than ample testimony to substantiate the central moral thesis which he was attempting to disseminate throughout his *Bibliotheke* — material which he accordingly incorporated into his work, even though, in the process, substantiation of the sentiments pertaining to Dionysius of the *prooemium* of Book XIV was patently ignored, just as we have seen Diodorus' statement in the *prooemium* to Book XIII on the chronological limits of the data presented in the latter book was similarly contradicted by the concrete chronological limitation ultimately imposed by Diodorus upon that book.[104]

Notes

1. Thus R. Lauritano, 'Sileno in Diodoro', *Kokalos*, vol. 2 (1956), pp. 206-16; Manni, 'Sileno in Diodoro?', pp. 81-8; Manni, 'Recenti studi sulla Sicilia Antica', *Kokalos*, vol. 7 (1961), p. 37; Manni, 'Ancora a proposito di Sileno-Diodoro', *Kokalos*, vol. 16 (1970), pp. 74-8.

2. Originally entertained by C. Volquardsen, 'Untersuchungen über die Quellen der griechischen und sicilischen Geschichte bei Diodorus, XI-XVI', Dissertation, Kiel, 1868.

3. Thus E. Bachof, 'Timaios als Quelle für Diodor XIV 54-78', *NJCP*, Abt. 1, vol. 25 (1879), pp. 161-3; Bachof, 'Timaios als Quelle Diodors für die Reden des dreizehnten und vierzehnten Buches', *NJCP*, Abt. 1, vol. 30 (1884), pp. 445-78, E. Schwartz, *s.v.*, 'Diodoros', *RE* (1905), vol. 5a, cols. 685-86; R. Laqueur, *s.v.*, 'Timaios', *RE*, Ser. 2 (1936), vol. 6a, cols. 1076-1203; Jacoby, *FGH*, vol. 3b (Komm. Text), no. 566, pp. 529, 541; Beloch, *Griechische Geschichte*, vol. 2b, p. 26; vol. 3b, p. 47; C. Wachsmuth, *Uber das Geschichtswerk des Sikelioten Diodoros* (Leipzig, 1892), vol. 2, p. 10; Barber, *The historian Ephorus*, pp. 160-9; De Sanctis, *Ricerche*, p. 37; Stroheker, *Dionysios I*, pp. 11-31, esp. pp. 17-18, reproducing essentially 'Timaios und Philistos', pp. 139-61; Sartori, 'Sulla δυναστεία di Dionisio il vecchio nell'opera Diodorea', pp. 3-66; Sartori, 'Review of Stroheker, *Dionysius I*', *Athenaeum*, vol. 37 (1959), pp. 209-10; A.G. Woodhead, *The Greeks in the west* (London, 1962), p. 88; Berve, *Die Tyrannis*, vol. 2, p. 637; P.E. Arias, *Dionigi il vecchio* (Catania, 1942), pp. 3-4; Meister, 'Die Sizilische Geschichte', pp. 3, 74ff; R. Lauritano, 'Sileno

in Diodoro', pp. 206-18; M. Sordi, 'I rapporti fra Dionigi I e Cartagine fra la pace del 405/4 e quello del 392/1', *Aevum*, vol. 54, no. 1 (1980), pp. 23-34.

4. Folcke, 'Dionysius', pp. 35-6, whose conclusion we reject for (a) his incorrect assumption, in our view, of hostility towards Dionysius in F. 134 (see pp. 22-3); (b) the likelihood that Dionysius II rather than Dionysius I was the focal point of Theopompus' hostility (see p. 78); (c) our view that Diodorus' fourteenth book is essentially not hostile to Dionysius (see pp. 125-41); and (d) Folcke's acceptance of Photius' conjecture that Theopompus was hostile to Philistus as fact (F. 25/Phot. *Bibl.* 176, p. 120b, 30).

5. Thus Hammond, 'The sources of Diodorus Siculus XVI', p. 142; Westlake, 'The sicilian books of Theopompus' *Philippica*', p. 288.

6. Already assumed by E. Bumbury, *Dictionary of Greek and Roman mythology* (London, 1849), vol. 3, p. 297. Argued in detail by R. Laquer, *s.v.*, 'Philistos', *RE*, vol. 19b, col. 2419, and Folcke, 'Dionysius', pp. 79ff and followed by numerous authorities, *viz.* De Sanctis, *Ricerche*, pp. 37ff; Stroheker, *Dionysios I*, p. 26; Jacoby, *FGH*, vol. 3b (Komm.), no. 556, p. 501; Beloch, *Griechische Geschichte*, vol. 2b, p. 26; vol. 3b, p. 42; Meyer, *Geschichte des Altertums*, vol. 5, 4. 65; Zoepffel, 'Untersuchungen', p. 7; Meister, 'Die Sizilische Geschichte', pp. 3, 75, 84, 87-8; H. Meier-Welcker, *Dionysios I, Tyrann von Syrakus* (Göttingen, Zurich, Frankfurt, 1971), p. 9; R. Lauritano, 'Ricerche su Filisto', *Kokalos*, vol. 3 (1957), pp. 98-122; M.I. Finley, *Ancient Sicily*, p. 75; J.K. Davies, *Democracy and classical Greece* (Glasgow, 1978), p. 203; cf. M. Kunz, 'Zur Beurteilung der Prooemien in Diodors historischen Bibliotek', Dissertation, Zurich, 1935, who on p. 17 speaks of 'irgendeinem Sizilischen Autor' for the Sicilian portion of XI-XV without specifically mentioning Philistus; cf. pp. 13 and 17 where she accepts Timaeus for parts of Books IV and V, XVIII and XX.

7. Arguments for a more direct use of Philistus by Diodorus have only been proposed by S. Hejnic, 'Das Geschichtswerk des Philistos von Sizilien als Diodors Quelle', *Studia antiqua A. Salac septuagenerio oblata* (Prague, 1955), pp. 31-5; and L.J. Sanders, 'Diodorus Siculus and Dionysius I of Syracuse', *Historia*, vol. 30, no. 4 (1981), pp. 394-411. G.W. Botsford and C.A. Robinson, Jr, *Hellenic history* (New York, 1956), p. 281, without detailed discussion, state that Diodorus' sources included Philistus. Somewhat vague is J.B. Bury's statement, ('Dionysius I of Syracuse', p. 108), that the description of Sicilian events in Diodorus XII-XV stems from the Syracusan Philistus and also from the works of Ephorus and Timaeus.

8. Laqueur, *s.v.*, 'Timaios', *RE*, Ser. 2, vol. 6a, cols. 1076-1203.

9. Jacoby, *FGH*, vol. 3b (Komm.), p. 529; Stroheker, *Dionysios I*, p. 15. Also noteworthy is the emulation of the very approach of Laqueur by Meister, 'Die Sizilische Geschichte', pp. 76ff.

10. See the highly pertinent comments of T.S. Brown, 'Timaeus and Diodorus' eleventh book', *AJPh*, vol. 73 (1952), pp. 340-1. The only scholar who has attempted an inevitably tedious yet detailed line-by-line refutation of part of Laqueur's thesis pertaining to Books XI and XIII is L. Pearson, 'Ephorus and Timaeus in Diodorus: Laqueur's thesis rejected', *Historia*, vol. 33 (1984), pp. 1-20.

11. As examples of complementary data needlessly and, from the point of view of the logic of the text, detrimentally wrenched apart by Laqueur, we note initially Hannibal's landing at Lilybaeum (Diod. Sic. XIII. 54. 2; 54. 4) which, far from representing a needless duplication, deals with the landing itself, on the one hand, and the subsequent pitching of tent, on the other. Similarly Diod. Sic. XIV. 18 and 41. 1-2, while both concerned with Dionysius' preparations for war in 396 BC, deal with totally different material: the construction of Epipolae, on the one hand, and the development of weaponry, on the other. Similar criticism can be applied to Laqueur's failure to distinguish between the construction of ships and the ships themselves, between the gathering of the craftsmen and Dionysius' methods to effect their zeal, between the gathering of the skilled mechanics and the catapult which they created and between the decision to enrol soldiers and the details of the enrolment itself (Diod. Sic. XIV. 41. 3; 42. 2; cf. XIV. 43. 4; 44. 1). Similarly in opposition to Laqueur we note how Diod. Sic. XIV. 46. 5 and 47. 1, far from representing a duplication of data pertaining to the dispatch of messengers and one single messenger, actually distinguish between Dionysius' plan to send messengers and the actual dispatch of one envoy. Further *contra* Laqueur, we observe how the two notices pertaining to Himilcon's one hundred ships (Diod. Sic. XIV. 50. 1; 50. 2) distinguish between the manning and sailing of the craft. Of similar dubious validity, we maintain, is Laqueur's distinction between Diocles the constitutional reformer (Diod. Sic. XIII. 33. 2-3) and Diocles the legislator (XIII. 34. 6); Laqueur's assumption that the description of the capture of Selinus (Diod. Sic. XIII. 58. 1-2) should be shorn from the main narrative; that two victories, as opposed to one, have been erroneously given the Carthaginians because of utilisation of two separate sources in Diod. Sic. XIII. 59. 9-60; and that the details about Hermocrates' career (Diod. Sic. XIII. 63; 75) represent a conflation of Ephorus' unfavourable account and Timaeus' favourable narrative. Cf. also Laqueur's arguments centred around Hannibal's and Himilcon's towers of XIII. 85. 3b-5 and the far-fetched distinction effected between the beginning of the siege of Acragas and the offer of peace terms (Diod. Sic. XIII. 85. 1-2); between the plague and the destruction of monuments (Diod. Sic. XIII. 86. 1-3) and between the alleged responsibilities of the Syracusans, on the one hand, and the Acragantine generals, on the other, in allowing the barbarians to escape (XIII. 87). Similarly misdirected, we maintain, is Laqueur's interpretation of Diod. Sic. XIII. 88 as a conflation of two accounts, emphasising, on the one hand, the loss of the supply fleet and, on the other, the excessive consumption of corn since the loss of the Syracusan fleet added to the hunger. In XIII. 91. 3, *contra* Laqueur, we note that Dionysius actually gives advice, *viz.* distrust the oligarchs and replace the generals. Despite Polybius' notice (XII. 4a) regarding a two-year discrepancy with respect to the differing evidence for the establishment of Dionysius' tyranny, Laqueur's attempt to view Diodorus' text as a conflation of two accounts, the one (Timaeus) dating its establishment to the period of the Acragantine crisis of 405 BC, the other (Ephorus) dating it to 403 BC within the context of Spartan aid under Aristus, the Lacedaemonian commands little confidence. For besides attributing to Ephorus and

Diodorus and Dionysius

Timaeus information in a purely arbitrary manner and forcing, in our view, Diodorus' use of the participle συνκατασκευάζοντες, thereby denying the likelihood of a gradual establishment of Dionysius' tyranny during the years 405-403 BC, Diodorus' text, in the very portion which, according to Laqueur, derived from Ephorus, states that the Lacedaemonians on the surface aimed to *restore* this liberty (προσποιούμενοι καταλύειν τὴν δυναστείαν: Diod. Sic. XIV. 10. 2; 10. 3). Nor can great confidence be attributed Laqueur's division between local (Timaeus) and universal (Ephorus) data in Diod. Sic. XIV. 14-16 and 44-5; for we are not merely conscious of Laqueur's arbitrariness in assuming that Timaeus' obsession with Herbitaeans, Henna and Helaisa would render him oblivious of Naxos, Catana, Leontini and Sicels but we are also aware that by attributing Southern Italian interests to Ephorus and the great war with Carthage to Timaeus, he may be said to convert equally arbitrarily Timaeus into a universalist and Ephorus into a local historian. Similarly cavalier is Laqueur's distinction between two separate accounts of street- as opposed to wall-fighting, on sea- as opposed to land-battles (Diod. Sic. XIV. 52-53; 56-57); the conclusion that the note on Messanian indecision (Diod. Sic. XIV. 56. 3-6) must be out of context and have occurred before the Punic arrival; and the assumption that the apparent contradiction between the notice on the penetration of the harbour and Dionysius' subsequent concentration of forces to prevent such penetration stems from a conflation of separate source material rather than from error on Diodorus' part (XIV. 50. 3). Similarly we must ask whether Diodorus' description of Himilcon only at one point as admiral (Diod. Sic. XIV. 50. 1; cf. 49. 1 and 54. 5) does not stem from Diodorus' own vagueness or tendency to err. Final examples of Laqueur's arbitrariness occur in Diod. Sic. XIV. 61. 1b-3a (Timaeus) as opposed to 1a-3b (Ephorus) where contrary theses of Siceliot desertion *vis-à-vis* offensive action are postulated, in total oblivion of the fact that desertion only follows Dionysius' failure to meet rebel demands; in Diod. Sic. XIV. 63. 3a and 3b where separate causes of divine wrath are quite arbitrarily discerned; and in Diod. Sic. XIV. 72-76 and 100-103 where the narratives of the destruction of the Punic Camp and the campaign in Southern Italy are divorced decisively from one another.

12. I.e., as οἱ κατ' Ἰταλίαν (ἐκ, ἀπὸ Ἰταλίας) Ἕλληνες or as Ἰταλιῶται (thus cf. Diod. Sic. XIII. 109. 1; 110. 5 with 190. 5 and 110. 2-4). Other arguments in the Dionysian narrative pertain to the similarity of ῥαδίως κατεπονοῦντο (Diod. Sic. XIII. 55. 7) and ῥδίως ἠλαττοῦντο (Diod. Sic. XIII. 55. 8), τοῖς ἐφ'ἡγεμονίας τεταγμένοις and τῶν ἐφ'ἡγεμονίας τεταγμένων (Diod. Sic. XIV. 7. 4; XIII. 88. 8), μεταβάλλεσθαι τοῖς μεταβαλλομένοις and τοὺς μεταβαλλομένους (Diod. Sic. XIV. 8. 3; XIII. 88. 2), ἀνακῦψαι ταῖς ἐλπίσιν and ἀνέκυψαν αἱ ἐλπίδες (Diod. Sic. XIV. 9. 3; XIII. 88. 6) and ἔρημον or ἐρήμου τῶν ἀμυνομένων (Diod. Sic. XIV. 61. 2b; XIII. 61. 2; XIV. 57. 1). Cf. Meister, 'Die Sizilische Geschichte', pp. 85 and 89 on κύριοι τῶν ὅπλων ὄντες or ἦσαν (XIV. 7. 6; 64. 4; 67. 2); τῶν δ'ἵππῶν οἱ πλεῖστοι συνκατεκαύθησαν ταῖς σκηναῖς or τῶν δὲ ἐγκαταληφθέντων σωμάτων ἃ μὲν τοῖς οἰκίαις συνκατέκαιον and πολλοὶ μὲν ἐν στεναῖς ταῖς διόδοις ἀποληφθέντες ζῶντες κατεκαύθησαν (XIV. 54. 3; XIII. 57. 2; XX. 65. 2).

13. Meister, 'Die Sizilische Geschichte', pp. 17, 171.

14. As demonstrated in n 11 above.
15. Thus in Book XIII; Campanians (Diod. Sic. XIII. 44. 1-2; 55. 7; 62. 5; 85. 4; 88. 2-5); cf. Meister, 'Die Sizilische Geschichte', p. 79; Diocles' aid (Diod. Sic. XIII. 44. 4; 54. 3; 56. 1; 59. 1-3; 59. 9; 61. 3; 61. 6); Dexippus (Diod. Sic. XIII. 85. 3; 87. 4-5; 88. 7; 93. 1; 93. 4; 96. 1); Tellias (Diod. Sic. XIII. 90. 2; 83. 1-3; 84. 1); bravery of Siceliot women and children (Diod. Sic. XIII. 55. 4-5; 56. 6-7; 57. 3-5; 58. 1-2; 62. 4; 89. 3; 108. 6; 108. 8); Punic plague (Diod. Sic. XIII. 86. 1-3a; 114. 2b); Hannibal's hatred for Himera (Diod. Sic. XIII. 43. 5; 59. 5-6); the two Punic Camps (Diod. Sic. XIII. 54. 6; 59. 6). Similarly in Book XIV we note the Knights' revolt (Diod. Sic. XIV. 7. 6; cf. XIII. 112. 3-4); the flight of the Knights to Aetna (Diod. Sic. XIV. 8. 1; 9. 6-8; cf. XIII. 113. 3); autonomous Sicels (Diod. Sic. XIV. 7. 6; 58. 1a; 75. 6-7; 78. 7; cf. XIII. 114. 1); Philistus (Diod. Sic. XIV. 8. 5, cf. XIII. 91. 4); Libyan plague (Diod. Sic. XIV. 41. 1; 45. 3; 47. 2b-3; cf. XIII. 114. 2b; the mole at Motya (Diod. Sic. XIV. 49. 3; 51. 1; 53. 1-3); theme of the bravery of women and children (Diod. Sic. XIV. 52. 1, cf. XIII. 55. 4-5; 56. 6; 57. 3-5; 58. 1-2; 62. 4; 89. 3; 108. 6; 108. 8); the cruel tyrant Dionysius who plunders temples (Diod. Sic. XIV. 40. 3; 45. 5; 46. 2-3; XV. 13. 1-5; 14. 3-4); Elymi (Diod. Sic. XIV. 55. 4; 54. 2); Halyciae (Diod. Sic. XIV. 48. 4; 54. 2; 55. 7a); Sicans (Diod. Sic. XIV. 48. 4; 55. 6-7a); Agyris and Tauromenium (Diod. Sic. XIV. 9. 2; 78. 7; 95. 2-7; 96. 1; 59. 2; 87. 5; 88; 96. 4). Cf. Meister, 'Die Sizilische Geschichte', pp. 85, 101 on the triple references to the exiles on Aetna (XIII. 113. 3; XIV. 9. 8; 14. 2) and to the construction of walls and ships (XIV. 18; 42; XV. 13. 5).
16. As delineated in the examples cited in n 11 above.
17. The traditionalists include: De Sanctis, *Ricerche*, pp. 77, 83; A.D. Momigliano, *s.v.*, 'Diodoro', *Enciclopedia Italiana* (1949), vol. 12, pp. 924-5; Wachsmuth, *Diodoros*, vol. 2, p. 3; Westlake, 'The Sicilian Books of Theopompus' *Philippica*', p. 300; A.W. Gomme, 'The end of the City State', *Essays in Greek history and literature* (Oxford, 1937), p. 247; Meister, 'Die Sizilische Geschichte', p. 1. More specifically for Books XVIII, XIX and XX see F. Bizière, 'Comment travaillait Diodore de Sicile', *REG*, vol. 87 (1974), pp. 369-71. For Book XVI, see A.D. Momigliano, 'Le fonti della storia greca et Macedone nel libro XVI di Diodoro', *RIL*, vol. 45 (1932), pp. 523-43 and Hammond, 'The sources of Diodorus Siculus XVI' (1937), pp. 79-91 and (1938), pp. 137-51. Though cf. P. Treves, 'Per la critica e l'analisi del libro XVI di Diodoro', *ASNP*, ser. 2, vol. 6 (1937), pp. 255-79.
18. Thus Pearson, 'Ephorus and Timaeus: Laqueur's thesis rejected', p. 19.
19. J. Palm, *Über Sprache und Stil des Diodorus von Sizilien* (Lund, 1955).
20. Kunz, 'Zur Beurteilung der Prooemium', pp. 39-40.
21. Thus Kunz, 'Zur Beurteilung der Prooemium', pp. 38, 74, 79-80, 87. Though for Ephorus alone as a source, see R. Laqueur, 'Die Prooemien. Die Disposition', *Hermes*, vol. 46 (1911), pp. 161-206, 321-54; cf. Barber, *The historian ephorus*, pp. 68-74.
22. For the influence of Stoicism, see G. Busolt, 'Diodors Verhältnis zum Stoizismus', *NJCP*, Abt. 1, vol. 35, no. 1 (1889), pp. 297-315; Wachsmuth, vol. 2, *Diodoros*, p. 18; B. Farrington, *Diodorus Siculus, universal historian* (Swansea, 1937) (Reprinted in Farrington, *Head and hand in*

ancient Greece (London (1947), pp. 55-85); M. Pavan, 'La teoresi storica di Diodoro Siculo', *RAL*, vol. 16 (1961), pp. 19-52, 117-51. Though see also the sensible reservations of A.D. Nock, 'Poseidonius', *JRS*, vol. 49 (1959), p. 5, who regards Diodorus as the 'small man with pretensions and with a tinge of stoicism', scarcely indebted to Poseidonius in the Book I *prooemium.* Similarly we follow R. Drews, 'Historiographical objectives and procedures of Diodorus Siculus', Dissertation, Johns Hopkins University, Baltimore, 1960, pp. 10ff, 132 in noting how little the interrelationship of events in a philosophic as opposed to purely moral sense interested Diodorus and the general insignificance from a Stoic point of view of the terminal date of Diodorus' history of 60 BC. Ultimately, of course, the lack of sufficient evidence, because of the fragmentary nature of Diodorus' text, to effect agreement with Polybius or Poseidonius prevents a decisive conclusion on this matter. On likely Epicurean influence, see Busolt, 'Diodors Veerhältnis zum Stoizismus', pp. 305-6.

23. Thus Busolt, 'Diodors Verhältnis zum Stoizismus', p. 314:

> er war kein wirklicher Philosoph, sondern ein frommer dog-matischer Moralist ... trotz der im Geiste der Stoa gehaltenen Einleitung ist Diodors Weltgeschichte keineswegs von einer wahrhaft philosophischen Auffassung durchdrungen und getragen.

24. A point not appreciated by Bury, The ancient Greek historians, p. 236, but clearly delineated by Drews, 'Historiographical objectives', pp. 22ff, and Drews, 'Diodorus and his sources', *AJPh*, vol. 83 (1962), pp. 383-92.

25. Diodorus' belief in *Nemesis*, X. 16. 2; XX. 13. 3; XXVII. 6. 2; XXXIV-V. 28. 2; the expediency of justice and virtue *vis-à-vis* the inexpediency of vice, IX. 18. 1; X. 12; 23. 1; XIV. 2. 1; *prooemium* to Book XV; XVIII. 47. 3; the *tyche* which subordinates and humbles man, XVII. 38. 6; XVIII. 59. 5-6; XXV. 5. 2; XXVII. 1. 2; XXXI. 3. 1; 3. 3; 4. 1; XXXI. 12; motif of restraint, I. 77. 10; V. 31. 5; XVIII. 67; clemency, XXI. 14. 3; mildness, I. 93. 4; V. 29. 6; XXXI. 3. 3; XXXIV-V. 2. 33; pity, XVII. 38. 4-7; humility, XXXIII. 8. 1; love of mankind, XXXI. 3. 1-3. The ethical types who adhere to these dictates include Zeus who possesses *eusebeia, epieikeia, philanthropia* and all *aretai* (III. 61. 4-5; V. 71. 3; 71. 6); Aeolus who has *eusebeia, philanthropia* and *dikaiosyne* (V. 7. 7); Jason with *epieikeia* and *megalopsychia* (IV. 53. 1-3); Castor, Polydeuces and Admetus with *eusebeia* and *dikaiosyne* (IV. 53. 1-3; VI. 6. 1, 8. 1); Aeneas with *eusebeia* to the gods (VII. 4. 1-4) and Sesostris with *epieikeia* and *eusebeia* (I. 55. 10-12). Similarly we note these qualities in the Egyptian kings and Cyrus (I. 70-1; IX. 24); the *epieikeia* of Battus of Cyrene and all the *aretai* of Pittacus of Mytilene (VIII. 30. 1; IX. 11. 1-2); the *homilia* and *arete* of Aristeides (XI. 46. 4); the *philanthropia* and *epieikeia* of Theron (X. 28. 3; XI. 53. 2); Pythagoras' *sophrosyne*, patience, courage and aversion to luxury (X. 3. 3; 7. 1; 9. 3-4, 9); Gelon's *epieikeia, philanthropia*, ability to bear good fortune *anthropinōs* and dislike of pomp and luxury (XI. 26. 1-4; 67. 2; 38. 2); Dion's *epieikeia* and Timoleon's *aretai* (XVI. 20. 6; XVI. 65. 2); Epaminondas' *epieikeia, megalopsychia, arete, andreia* and *philanthropia* (XV. 88. 1-4; 57. 1; 39. 2-3); Philip's *arete, eusebeia* and *philanthropia* (XVI. 1. 4, 6; 60. 4; 64. 2-3; 38. 1-2; 8. 2); Alexander's *philan-*

thropia, epieikeia, arete, megalopsychia and regard for *tyche* and the gods
(XVII. 2. 2; 4. 1-3; 16. 3-4; 37. 3-6; 38. 3-7; 40. 1; 69. 4, 5, 9; 72. 1; 73. 1, 4;
74. 4; 76. 1; 84. 1; 86. 3; 89. 3; 89. 6; 93. 4; 95. 1; 97. 3; 100. 1; 104. 1, 4;
106. 2; 116. 4); Eumenes' *philanthropia* and insight into the workings of
tyche (XVIII. 40. 4; 41. 6; 42. 1; 60. 1); Ptolemy I's *philanthropia* and *epieikeia*
(XVIII. 14. 1; 33. 3; XIX. 55. 5; 56. 1); Hamilcar Barca's and Hannibal's
humaneness and respect for *tyche* (XXV. 3; XXIV. 13. 1; XXVI. 14. 1; 16. 1);
Scipio Africanus' good fortune tempered by an ability to accept *tyche
anthropinōs* (XXVII. 6. 2); Aemilius Paullus' *epieikeia, philanthropia* and
respect for *tyche* (XXX. 23. 1-2); Scipio Aemilianus' respect for *tyche* and
possession of *aretai* (XXXII. 23; 24; XXXI. 26. 5-27. 1); Philopoemen's
aretai (XXIX. 18. 1); the *epieikeia, philanthropia* and avoidance of *tryphe* of
Arsaces of Parthia (XXXIII. 18. 1); Alexander Zabinas' *aretai* (XXXIV-V.
22); Caesar's *epieikeia* (XXXII. 27. 3); and the *epieikeia, philanthropia* and
dikaiosyne of Rome (XXX. 23. 2; XXXII. 4-5; XXXIII. 26. 2; XXXIV-V. 33. 5).
Conversely we note at the other extreme those traits of characters which
do not conform to Diodorus' ethical ideal: the debauchery of Sardana-
pallus (II. 23); Pausanias' *tryphe* (XI. 44. 5); the defiance and impudence of
Tyndarides (XI. 86. 4); Cambyses' inability to bear good fortune *anthropinōs* (X. 14. 2); the *asebeia* and *paranomia* of Philomelus and the Phocians
(XVI. 56. 4; 56. 8; 57. 3; 61. 1; 64. 1); the *paranomia* of Cleon, Chares and
the Persian Bagoas (XII. 55. 8; XV. 95. 3; XVI. 47. 4); the *paranomia* and
tryphe of Harpalus (XVII. 108. 4-6); Antiochus III's *asebeia* (XXVIII. 3. 1;
XXIX. 1; 15. 1); the *asebeia* and arrogance of Philip V (XXVIII. 2; 3. 1; 5; 7.
1; 9. 1); the vices, including *paranomia* and *pleonexia* of Andriscus (XXXII.
9a); the vices of Ptolemy Physcon (XXXIII. 12; 23; XXXIV-V. 14. 1) and
Demetrius I (XXXIII. 4. 1; 9. 1); the *paranomia* and *misanthropia* of the Jews
(XL. 2-3; XXXIV-V. 1. 1-5); Marius' *pleonexia*, cruelty and refual to heed
tyche (XXXVIII-IX. 6); and finally the *tryphe* affecting Ninyas of Assyria,
Cleonymus of Sparta and the city of Tarentum, Antander, brother of
Agathocles, Hieronymus of Syracuse, Ptolemy Philopater, Prusias, Alexander Balas, Antiochus Cyzicenus, the Etruscans, Sybarites and Rome
after the Punic Wars (II. 21. 1-2; XX. 104. 3-4; XX. 16. 1; XXVI. 15. 1; XXX.
17. 1; XXXI. 15. 1; XXXIII. 3; XXXIV-V. 34; V. 40. 4; VIII. 18. 1; XXXVII. 3.
2. Examples of characters reaping negative treatment following unethical
behaviour (cf. Philip II's success following *eusebeia* (XVI. 1. 4; 38. 2; 60. 4;
64. 3) include Tantalus (IV. 74. 2); the Sybarites (X. 23. 1); Cleophon (XIII.
53. 2); the Carthaginians (XIV. 46. 4; 76. 1; XIX. 103. 5); Agathocles (XX.
30. 1; 101. 1-4); the huntsman who failed to dedicate a boar's head to
Artemis (IV. 22. 4); Himilcon (XIV. 63. 1); Bura and Helike (XV. 48-49);
Philomelus and the Phocians (XVI. 24; 31. 4); the Argive demogogues
(XV. 58. 4); Marius and Cinna (XXXVIII-IX. 6. 1); the mocker who is pro-
scribed (XXXVIII-IX. 19. 1); Perilaus the contriver of the bull of Phalaris
(IX. 18. 1); Olympias (XIX. 11. 6-7); slave owners (XXXIV-V. 2. 1-48).
Finally we note how ethical ideas permeate some speeches and letters:
tyche in Nicolaus' speech (XIII. 20. 5; 21. 2, 4-5; 24. 5; 27. 6); *epieikeia* and
euergesia in Seleucus I's letter to his son, the future Antiochus I (XXI. 21);
epieikeia, euergesia, nemesis and *tyche* in Scipio's speech (XXVII. 13-18).

26. See especially Drews, 'Diodorus and his sources', pp. 383-92; cf.
Drews, 'Historiographical objectives', pp. 84-6 comparing Diod. Sic.

XXXI. 35 with Polybius XXXII. 15. 13-14 and Diod. Sic. XXXI. 18a with Polyb. XXXI. 9. 4 where Diodorus elaborates upon his source's data by distinctly associating Prusias' sacrilege with the dysentery experienced by his soldiers and Antiochus IV's plunder of the temple of Tabae with the King's subsequent death. Of course, in the past, a few lone voices have championed Diodorus' individuality. Thus Mrs. G. Grote, citing her husband in *The personal life of George Grote* (London, 1873), p. 49; Holm, *Geschichte Siziliens*, vol. 2, p. 340; Freeman, *History of Sicily*, vol. 3, pp. 607, 610. More recently a more charitable view of Diodorus can be found in R.K. Sinclair, 'Diodorus Siculus and the writing of history', *PACA*, vol. 6 (1963), p. 36; S. Usher, 'Some observations on Greek historical narrative', *AJPh*, vol. 81 (1960), p. 362; and above all C.R. Rubincam, 'Ephorus Fragment 76 and Diodorus on the Cypriot War', *Phoenix*, vol. 28, no. 1 (1974), pp. 123-43; C.R. Rubincam, 'A note on Oxyrhynchus Papyrus 1610', *Phoenix*, vol. 30, no. 4 (1976), pp. 357-66; cf. the same writer's review of A. Burton, *Diodorus Siculus, book I: A commentary* (Leiden, 1972) in *C Phil*, vol. 72, no. 1 (1977), pp. 66-8; J.M. Bigwood, 'Diodorus and Ctesias', *Phoenix*, vol. 34 (1980), pp. 195-207.

27. Since Muller the MSS. reading of Diodorus, Πολύκλιτος or Πολύκλειτος has been amended. Thus Pearson, *The Greek historians of the west* (forthcoming).

28. Though cf. Meister, 'Die Sizilische Geschichte', p. 83 who surprisingly suspects that τινες implies Ephorus.

29. A third later reference comes from the scholion on Pindar *Pyth.* I. 185/F 28c. For a defence of Timaeus' account, see Brown, *Timaeus of Tauromenium*, p. 55.

30. See n 26 above.

31. Holm, *Geschichte Siziliens*, vol. 2, p. 342; E. Schwartz, *s.v.*, 'Diodoros', *RE*, vol. 5a, col. 685-6. Though F.W. Walbank, 'The bull of Phalaris', *CR*, vol. 59 (1945), pp. 39-42, noting Polybius' omission of Scipio's role in sending the bull back to Acragas, the implication being that it had not taken place yet, suggests that Diodorus only drew upon general recollections. Meister, 'Die Sizilische Geschichte', p. 82 seems to ignore the possibility of Diodorus' use of a late source simply on the flimsy basis of the fact that Greek historians tended to follow citations of sources with whom they disagreed with their own data.

32. The non-Sicilian speech is Endius' (Diod. Sic. XIII. 52. 3-8). The Sicilian speeches include Theodorus' (Diod. Sic. XIV. 65-69), Nicolaus' (XIII. 20-27) and Gylippus' (XIII. 28. 2-32).

33. See Laqueur, 'Die Prooemien Die Disposition', p. 281.

34. Holm, *Geschichte Siziliens*, vol. 2, p. 371.

35. Thus Manni, 'Ancora a proposito di Sileno-Diodoro', p. 74; Meister, 'Die Sizilische Geschichte', p. 75.

36. Manni, 'Ancora a proposito di Sileno-Diodoro', pp. 74-8.

37. Lauritano, 'Sileno in Diodoro', pp. 206-16.

38. See n 26 above.

39. F.W. Walbank, 'The historians of Greek Sicily', *Kokalos*, 14/15 (1968/9), p. 488.

40. Cf. the 80,000 Carthaginians (Diod. Sic. XIII. 60. 3), obviously reflective of Timaeus' figures.

41. Holm, *Geschichte Siziliens*, vol. 2, p. 340; Bachof, 'Timaeus als Quelle für Diodor XIV, 54-78', p. 161; Meister, 'Die Sizilische Geschichte', pp. 4, 76, 91.

42. See pp. 139-41.

43. Thus the 80,000 barbarians (Diod. Sic. XIII. 60. 3) and 40,000 (XIII. 59. 6) approximate to Timaeus' 100,000 (Diod. Sic. XIII. 54. 5/F. 103) as opposed to the 200,000 of Ephorus. Similarly the 40,000 Libyans (Diod. Sic. XIII. 85. 1) and over 40,000 other troops accompanying the Iberians and Campanians (Diod. Sic. XIII. 87. 1-2) approximate to the 120,000 of Timaeus (Diod. Sic. XIII. 80. 5/F. 25).

44. Schwartz, *s.v.*, 'Diodoros', *RE*, vol. 5a, col. 681. Accepted by Laqueur, *s.v.*, 'Timaios', *RE*, col. 1148, who nevertheless also accepts the possibility of intrusions from Timaeus. The same view is adopted with reserve by Barber, *The historian Ephorus*, pp. 168-9 and by Meister, 'Die Sizilische Geschichte', pp. 100-4, who at the same time, obviously influenced essentially by Laqueur's reconstruction, accepts the possibility of minimal influence from Timaeus. Diodorus' account of Dionysius' enslavement of Plato (XV. 7. 1) is identified by Sordi, 'Dionigi I e Platone', pp. 2015ff with Ephorus.

45. Thus Sordi, 'Dionigi I e Platone', pp. 2015ff.

46. Hammond, 'The sources of Diodorus Siculus XVI' (1938), p. 142, followed by Stroheker, *Dionysios I*, p. 14.

47. Hammond, 'The sources of Diodorus Siculus XVI' (1938), p. 144.

48. Meister, 'Die Sizilische Geschichte', p. 101. Though we reject the likelihood that Theopompus exerted a decisive influence upon the Sicilian data of Diodorus' fifteenth book, much of Meister's argumentation we find defective. Thus to Meister's contention that, since Diodorus did not use Theopompus for his account of Philip II, who was after all the central figure of the *Philippica*, therefore he did make use of the data enshrined in the Sicilian excursus, we respond that it is surely not inconceivable that Diodorus merely consulted one section of a work which was, after all, of immense and rambling proportions and accordingly lent itself to a process of selectivity on the part of the researcher. Might not, we ask, the Sicilian excursus have occupied a status similar to that attained by the distinguished or notorious Chapters Fifteen and Sixteen on Christianity in Gibbon's *Decline and fall of the Roman empire*? To Meister's argument (followed by Folcke, 'Dionysius', p. 191) that the objectivity of Diodorus XV. 15. 3-4 is unlikely to derive from Theopompus since F. 134 indicates that Theopompus attacked Dionysius, we retort that this fragment attacks not the tyrant's arbitrary power but his promotion of vice and that in line with acceptance of Meister's reasoning, we might utilise the description of Dionysius' crisis with his literati as evidence of Theopompus' hostility. Finally to Meister's argument that the favourable estimate of Philistus in XV. 7. 3 is unlikely to stem from Theopompus, who hated Dionysius, we respond that we know nothing at all about Theopompus' view of Philistus and that our investigation above has revealed that Theopompus, for all his disfavour towards Dionysius II, was not hostile to Dionysius I.

49. We emphasise, in view of our contention that Diodorus' employment of source material was exceedingly catholic, that we do not main-

tain, as Meister does, that Diodorus never viewed Theopompus' excursus personally and that his information about Theopompus derived from a chronographer.

50. Westlake, 'The Sicilian Books of Theopompus' *Philippica*', p. 290. Cf. Chapter 2, n 89.

51. F. 106/Diod. Sic. XIII. 108, equating the day of Alexander's capture of Tyre with the day of the Punic capture of the bronze statue of Apollo subsequently sent to Tyre, might reinforce this argument's validity. Folcke, 'Dionysius', pp. 123, 130-1, sees Timaeus' emphasis upon the deity's role in destroying Carthage as reflective of Timaeus' desire to obscure Dionysius' native role in defeating the Carthaginians.

52. For Ephorus' moralising see Strabo VII. 3. 9/F. 42. Also see Diod. Sic. XVI. 1. 4, 6 where Diodorus is also probably following Ephorus. For Theopompus' moralising see Chapter 1, n 24.

53. See Chapter 2, p. 61 and Chapter 2, n 46.

54. See notes 25 and 26 above.

55. Elaborated upon on the basis of chronological details of Diod. Sic. XIV. 91. 1; 108. 2; III. 1; XIV. 15. 1; 105. 1; by Meister, 'Die Sizilische Geschichte', pp. 82-3, 86, 99.

56. Following S. Hejnic, 'Das Geschichtswerk des Philistos von Sizilien als Diodors Quelle', pp. 31-5. At the same time Philistus might have dated events also by Olympiads (F. 2/Steph. Byz. *s.v.* 'Δύμη'), a method which he also shared with Thucydides (III. 8; V. 49).

57. Including Diod. Sic. XI. 76. 3; 89. 1; XIII. 35. 2; 54. 3; 81. 4-84; 86. 2; 113. 3; XIV. 7. 1-5; 16. 1-4; 18; 48. 2; 53. 4; 62. 3; 63. 1; 95. 2; 105. 2; 111. 1; XVI. 70. 6; 83. 2; 90. 1.

58. These include the chapters on Diocles' legislation, the note on the Syracusan calendar, the observation that Agathocles was jealous of Gelon's grave and the statement on the citizens of Halaisa (Diod. Sic. XIII. 35. 3; XVI. 70. 6; XI. 38. 5; XIV. 16. 4).

59. Holm, *Geschichte Siziliens*, vol. 2, p. 371; followed by Meister, 'Die Sizilische Geschichte', p. 2.

60. Cited in n 2 and 3 above.

61. The significance of Diodorus' use of the words *tyrannos* or *tyrannis* has been emphasised by F. Sartori, 'Sulla δυναστεία di Dionisio il vecchio nell'opera Diodorea', pp. 3-66, who, besides viewing the words as deriving from the hostile Timaeus, contrasts them with Diodorus' use of the words dynast and dynasty to describe Dionysius and his rule in a constitutional or illegal manner, emphasising the *arche*'s diplomatic or territorial aspect. Thus X. 4. XIII. 96. 4; 112. 1; XIV. 2. 2; 10. 2; 107. 2; XV. 15. 1-2; 16. 2; 23. 5; 73. 5; XVI. 16. 3.

62. Bachof, 'Timaeus als Quelle Diodors für die Reden des dreizehnten und vierzehnten Buches', pp. 445-78; Meyer, *Geschichte des Altertums*, vol. 5, pp. 111-12; Stroheker, *Dionysios I*, pp. 17, 78; Berve, *Die Tyrannis*, vol. 2, p. 641; Folcke, 'Dionysius', pp. 57, 125-9, who sees the speech as a deliberate reply on Timaeus' part to Philistus' pro-Dionysius' viewpoint; Meister, 'Die Sizilische Geschichte', p. 93, 'ein erbitterter Tyrannenhass macht sich hier Luft — Die Rede ist demnach reinster Timaios.'; Vattuone, 'Su Timeo F. 29', p. 140.

63. A view championed by Volquardsen, 'Untersuchungen', pp. 103ff, alone.

64. Numerous examples of the tyrant's political ability are provided. Thus *vis-à-vis* Rhegium (XIV. 100, 107. 4-5); the Syracusan rebels (XIV. 9. 5), Aeimnestus and the Ennaeans (XIV. 14. 6-7), the Libyan plague of 397 BC (XIV. 41. 1), Messana (XIV. 78. 5), Locrian marriage alliance (XIV. 44), Punic plague (XIV. 74), acceptance of Pisistratean model (XIII. 95. 6), and Philistus' advice (XIV. 8. 5-6); politically motivated harshness against Leptines (XIV. 102) and the cavalry rebels (XIII. 113. 3) contrasted with politically motivated leniency to rebels (XIV. 9. 5), Italiots (XIV. 105. 3-5), and Syracusans (XIV. 7. 5; 45. 5; 70. 3). Examples of military and tactical sagacity include the tyrant's speed to crush the cavalry revolt (XIII. 112. 5), his building of Ortygia (XIV. 7. 1), his military preparations for war (XIV. 41-43) and personal bravery during hostilities conducted against the Siceli of Tauromenium (XIV. 88. 3-5) and Rhegium (XIV. 100. 5). The tyrant's patriotic aspirations found in XIII. 92. 5-6; XIV. 41. 2; 44. 3; 45. 4; and generally in XIV. 41-46.

65. Bachof, 'Timaeus als Quelle Diodors für die Reden des dreizehnten und vierzehnten Buches', pp. 445-78, though noting the differences between speech and narrative, regards them as insignificant and hence attributes the speech to the ultimate authority of Timaeus.

66. Thus the thematic parallels often noted between speech and narrative assume in our view less significance, i.e. destruction of Messana in XIV. 68. 5 and 56; Dionysius' policy of distracting the Siceliots from the real issue in XIV. 68. 4 and 41. 1; unwillingness of Dionysius to destroy the Punic army in XIV. 68. 1 and 75. 3 and in XIII. 112. 1 and XIV. 7. 1; slavery of Catana and Naxos in XIV. 66. 4; 68. 3; 14-15; treachery over Gela and Camarina in XIII. 111. 5 and XIV. 68. 2; treaty in XIII. 114. 1 and XIV. 68. 2; Dionysius as public clerk in XIV. 66. 5 and XIII. 96. 4; Dionysius' plunder of temples in XIV. 65. 2; 67. 4; 69. 2.

67. See p. 153.

68. On speeches in post-Thucydidean historiography, see the remarks of F.W. Walbank, 'Speeches in Greek Historians', *The third J.L. Myres memorial lecture* (Oxford, N.D.), pp. 4-5. De Sanctis, *Ricerche*, p. 40, significantly believes that Thucydidean-style speeches were included in Philistus' history. Cf. E. Manni, 'Da Ippi a Diodoro', *Kokalos*, vol. 3 (1957), p. 136, who considers Philistus a historian rather than an orator.

69. Thus, Diod. Sic. XIV. 66. 3 echoes XIII. 22. 4; XI. 25. 5; 26. 6.

70. Gelon as *basileus* in Diod. Sic. XI. 38. 2; 38. 7; cf. Gelon as *tyrannos* in Herodotus, VII. 157; 163; Aristot. *Polit.* V. 2. 6; 9. 23. 35 (1302b, 1315b); Aelian, *VH*, XIII. 37; Justin, XXIII. 4. 4).

71. See pp. 113-14.

72. C.H. Oldfather, *Diodorus*, Loeb Classical Library (London, 1946), vol. 4, p. 187.

73. The fact that Diod. Sic. XI. 22. 5 and XIII. 59. 5 provide a figure of 150,000 Punic dead at Himera and that Theodorus inflates this figure to 300,000 dead (XIV. 67. 1) as do the Syracusan masses seeking to elect Dionysius *strategos autokrator* (XIII. 94. 5) does suggest that Diodorus' source admits that the higher figures result from rhetorical inflationary

tendencies. Consequently again it might appear that Diodorus' source is not particularly favourable to Theodorus, even though, in XIV. 67. 1, on the surface a highly favourable reference to Gelon is suggested. Cf., however, Diod. Sic. XI. 20. 2 where again the figure of 150,000 is provided. It is accordingly possible that the higher figures derive, as is generally the case, from Ephorus, and the lower from Timaeus or Philistus who were, of course, generally more conservative. Consequently, perhaps not too much should be read into these figures.

74. Whence I fail to appreciate the relevance of Folcke's argument ('Dionysius', p. 155) that Philistus' rare appearance in Diodorus results from Timaeus' deliberate suppression of the earlier historian's public role.

75. Volquardsen, 'Untersuchungen', p. 9.

76. Laqueur, *s.v.*, 'Philistos', *RE* (1938), vol. 19, col. 2410. See also Brown, *Timaeus of Tauromenium*, p. 78; Sordi, 'I rapporti fra Dionigi e Cartagine fra le pace del 405/4 e quello del 392/1', pp. 24ff.

77. Contradicted by Diod. Sic. XIV. 57. 2-3 where we read that Dionysius sent gold and ivory statues to Delphi and Olympia, a passage illustrating manifestly the weakness of the Dionysian data of Book XV.

78. Thus A.G. Woodhead, 'The Adriatic empire of Dionysius', p. 504.

79. See Folcke, 'Dionysius', pp. 80-1, 157, pertinently citing Grote, *History of Greece*, vol. 10, p. 195, comparing Dionysius' attack on the oligarchs with Critias' assault on Theramenes. At the same time Folcke, 'Dionysius', pp. 100, 126, in seemingly contradictory manner, argues that Philistus' portrait of Dionysius constituted a eulogy on Dionysius' rule as purveyor of justice, to which Theodorus' attack on Dionysius as the epitome of injustice (XIV. 65. 3) constituted a response.

80. See Chapter 1, pp. 24-5.

81. See n 6 above. Though surprisingly Laqueur, *s.v.* 'Timaios', *RE*, ser. 2, vol. 6a, col. 1127, sees here the usual fusion of Ephorus and Timaeus and Pearson, *Greek historians of the west* (forthcoming) associates Dionysius' feasts (Diod. Sic. XIV. 45. 1) with Timaeus' authority owing to the latter's interest in Antisthenes' feasts (Diod. Sic. XIII. 84. 1).

82. Thus also Stroheker, *Dionysios I*, p. 63; Folcke, 'Dionysius', p. 105; though cf. Meister, 'Die Sizilische Geschichte', p. 86, who ascribes this to the 'local' Timaeus.

83. Another example of loss of Philistus' material as a result of Diodorus' process of abridgement occurs in XIV. 55. 1, describing the Punic passage to Sicily which, while essentially agreeing with Frontinus, *Strateg.* I. 1. 2 and Polyaen. V. 10. 2, omits mention of Himilcon's raising of the ships' lights which were shielded in front to render the enemy unaware of the Punic approach — a passage in Polyaenus which recalls Philistus' phrase 'at night they would raise up shielded lamps' (thus Pollux X. 116/F. 7 probably from Book II of the Περὶ Διονυσίου and not from Book II of the Περὶ Σικελίας as Pollux states. Though cf. Folcke, 'Dionysius', p. 118, who attributes this passage to Book I of the Περὶ Διονυσίου and regards Diodorus' evidence as a reproduction of Timaeus).

84. Less hostile variations are also omitted by Diodorus, i.e. pertaining to Dionysius' equal treatment of his wives (Plut. *Dion* III. 2) and to the

tyrant's taking one wife at a time on his sojourns, leaving the other at home (Aelian *VH* XIII. 10).

85. Since Diodorus in Book XIII refers to Siceliot Greeks as either σύμμαχοι of the Syracusans (XIII. 55. 3; 59. 9) or as Σικελιῶται (XIII. 35. 3; 55. 1; 61. 1; 63. 5; 80. 4; 91. 2; 109. 4; 110. 4; 110. 6; 113. 4) and only uses the term Ἕλληνες upon two occasions to indicate the sorry state or abstract 'position of the Greeks' (XIII. 57. 1; 88. 5), the Greeks who pitied are unlikely to have been Siceliots. These Greeks, moreover, are unlikely to have belonged to the σύμμαχοι ἀπὸ Σικελίας who were sent home after the capture of Himera (XIII. 62. 5) since the latter were more probably the Sicels and Sicans who indeed joined Carthage (Diod. Sic. XIII. 59. 6). Since, moreover, the Greeks of Southern Italy are referred to as Ἰταλιῶται or as Ἕλληνες ἀπό or ἐξ Ἰταλίας (XIII. 109. 1; 110. 5; 109. 5; 110. 2-4), the Greeks who pitied are unlikely to have been Italiots. This suggests, in turn, that the Greeks who pitied derived from the mainland, possibly from Athens directly, given the close relationship which traditionally existed between Athens and Carthage (see especially M. Treu, 'Athen und Karthago und die Thukydidesche Darstellung', *Historia*, vol. 3 (1954-5), pp. 41-57; Stroheker, 'Athen und Karthago', pp. 163-71), though more probably they came from survivors of the Athenian expedition for whose existence some evidence exists. Thus Thucydides (VII. 85. 4) certainly mentions that some Athenian survivors escaped, while non-Athenians, non-Siceliots and non-Italiots were freed after seventy days (Thuc. VII. 87. 3). Other captives ameliorated their lot by virtue of their superior education and acceptance of careers as teachers or as reciters of choruses (Diod. Sic. XIII. 33. 1; Zenob. IV. 17; Plut. *Nic.* XXIX. 2-3). For the view that some in the quarries survived and were ransomed (*contra* Diod. Sic. XIII. 33. 1; Plut. *Nic.* XXIX. 1) on the basis of Xen. *Hell.* I. 2. 13-14; Thuc. VII. 87; 82. 2; Lysias XX. 24-25; Andocides III. 30; Demosth. XX. 41-42, see D.H. Kelly, 'What happened to the Athenians captured in Sicily?', *CR*, vol. 20 (1970), pp. 127-31. Probably this element was enrolled at a late point, after the great Punic enrolment of Diod. Sic. XIII. 44. 1, 5-6, whence their omission by Diodorus. It might have taken its cue from the Campanians who had previously been in the service of Athens and had been wandering around Sicily until Carthage made use of them (Diod. Sic. XIII. 44. 1-2).

86. The descriptions of Siceliot resistance tends to be repetitious and stereotyped with constant recourse to motifs of Siceliot fortitude, especially of women and children, and Punic barbarity, especially relating to defilement of temples and tombs, and rapaciousness (Diod. Sic. XIII. 56. 7-58; 62; 90; 108. 2, 4; 111. 2-5).

87. See particularly D. Adamesteanu, 'Osservazione sulla battaglia di Gela del 405 a.C.', *Kokalos*, vol. 2 (1956), pp. 142-57; G. Uggeri, 'La battaglia di Gela del 405 a.C. secondo Diodoro e le resultanze topografiche', *SIFC*, vol. 39 (1967), pp. 252-9; Uggeri, 'Problemi di topografia geloa', *MDAI* (Rom. Abt.), vol. 75 (1968), pp. 54-63; Meister, 'Die Sizilische Geschichte', p. 83; Folcke, 'Dionysius', p. 89.

88. The lack of reference to the *Telemones* of the temple of Olympian Zeus at Acragas (on which see M. Guido, *Sicily, an archaeological guide* (London, 1967), pp. 124-5 and P. Griffo, 'Note sul tempio di Zeus

Olimpico di Agrigento,' in 'ΑΠΑΡΧΑΙ: *Nuove ricerche e studi sulla Magna Graecia e la Sicilia antica in onore di Paulo Enrico Arias* (Pisa, 1982), pp. 253-70) is noteworthy.

89. The confusion is twofold, relating, on the one hand, to the formation of the League and, on the other, to its constituent elements. Thus, to illustrate the former point, we note initially how, whereas the comment that the Selinuntines expected the arrival of Syracusans and other allies (Diod. Sic. XIII. 55. 3) implies a prior formation of a Siceliot League headed by Syracuse, the notice regarding the Selinuntine despatch for help to Syracuse, Acragas and Gela (Diod. Sic. XIII. 56. 1-2) seems to negate this information. The vicissitudes affecting the League subsequent to the destruction of Himera, moreover, are obscurely delineated. Hence Syracuse acts completely alone in censoring Carthage (Diod. Sic. XIII. 79. 8) and fighting the Punic navy (Diod. Sic. XIII. 80. 6), whereas the notice on Syracuse's negotiations with Italiots and Lacedaemonians and *continuous* dispatch of emissaries to Sicilian cities (ἀπέστελλον) to arouse the masses to fight for their common freedom suggests the continued existence of the League (Diod. Sic. XIII. 81. 2). Subsequently while Συρακόσιοι and significantly not Συρακόσιοι καὶ οἱ σύμμαχοι fear for the future of Acragas and decide to send that city aid, the arrival of Italiots, Messanians Geloans, Camarineans and troops ἐκ τῆς μεσογείου is not regarded as an *addition* to the alliance (Diod. Sic. XIII. 86. 4-5). The allies, moreover, are not mentioned in XIII. 87. 1 where the Punic advance-force of Iberians and Campanians only fights with Syracusans (Diod. Sic. XIII. 87. 1). Obviously the allies were involved in the fighting, since Dexippus was accused of treachery. Yet his treachery only merits mention subsequently to the battle (Diod. Sic. XIII. 87. 5). Similar omission of Syracuse's allies marks XIII. 88. 3-4, referring to Syracusan carelessness. Finally, the relationship of the League to Dionysius' hegemony is imperfectly described; for though Dionysius' relationship with Gela, Dexippus, Italiots, and other allies is mentioned (Diod. Sic. XIII. 93. 1, 5; 96. 1; 108. 5; 109. 1), Dionysius and his φίλοι, rather than representatives of the League or a League assembly, decide to evacuate Gela (Diod. Sic. XIII. 111. 1). Similarly in Book XIV, while Dionysius' reception of Geloan, Camarinaean and Acragantine aid (Diod. Sic. XIV. 47. 6) and notices on Messanian and Acragantine defection (Diod. Sic. XIV. 88. 5) suggest a revival of the old League, its formation and character is never discussed. With respect to the composition of the League, the notice in XIII. 56. 1-2 merely notes the alliance between Acragas and Gela and termination of hostilities with Catana and Naxos. Leontini, Camarina and Himera are ignored as is the stance of Catana and Naxos *vis-à-vis* the League. The notices in XIII. 81. 2 and 86. 4-5, moreover, as well as betraying obscurity on the relationship of the allied contingents to the earlier alliance, fail to delineate precisely the position of the earlier mentioned states — Catana, Naxos, Acragas and Gela as well as of the Selinuntine and Himeraean survivors (Diod. Sic. XIII. 63. 3; Cicero, *Verr.* II. 86).

90. The reference in Diod. Sic. XIII. 86. 3 to Himilcon's recourse to Moloch-worship should not be doubted. See now L.E. Stager, 'The rite of child sacrifice at Carthage', *New light on ancient Carthage* (Michigan,

1980), pp. 1-11.

91. See the remarks of M.I. Rostovtzeff, *Social and economic history of the hellenistic world* (Oxford, 1941), vol. 1, pp. 121-2. Pearson, *Greek historians of the west* (forthcoming), on the parallel basis of F. 50/Athen. XII. 519B, regarding Sybaris' trade relations with Miletus, ascribes this note to Timaeus.

92. See L. Maurin, 'Himilcon le Magonid. Crises et mutations à Carthage au début du IVᵉ siècle avant J.C.', *Semitica*, vol. 12 (1962), pp. 5-43.

93. Missile throwing on the part of women is, of course, a popular motif. Thus at Veii in 396 BC, stones and tiles are thrown by women and slaves (Livy, V. 21. 10). At Chios in 202-201 BC, stones and βέλη are thrown by women and slaves (Plut. *Mul. Virt.* 245c). Most famous of all, we have the case of the woman who killed Pyrrhus with a tile (Plut. *Pyrr.* XXXIV. 1-2).

94. Hejnic, 'Das Geschichtswerk des Philistos von Sizilien als Diodors Quelle', pp. 31-5. Examples from the Sicilian section of the *Bibliotheke* include XI. 91. 2 (451 BC); XIII. 44. 6 (410 BC); 88. 4 (406 BC); 91. 1 (406 BC); 96. 5 (406 BC); 108. 2 (405 BC); XIV. 70. 4 (396 BC); 88. 2 (394 BC); 100. 5 (390 BC); XV. 73. 4 (368 BC). Non-Sicilian examples include XI. 27. 1 (479 BC); XIII. 49. 2 (410 BC); XIV. 35. 7 (400 BC); 79. 3 (396 BC); XV. 12. 1 (385 BC); 41. 4 (374-373 BC); 43. 4 (374-373 BC); 70. 1 (369-368 BC). Since, following Hejnic, we note that the author of the *Hellenica Oxyrhynchia* adopted the 'κατὰ θέρη καὶ χειμῶνας' system of Thucydides, the comment of Dionysius of Halicarnassus (*De Thuc.* IX, p. 337. 18) that no historian emulated Thucydides' chronological system need not be taken literally, to the extent of denying use of such a scheme to Philistus. Cf. however W.K. Pritchett, *Dionysius of Halicarnassus on Thucydides* (California, 1975), p. 61, who follows H. Bloch, 'Studies in historical literature of the fourth century BC', *HSPh*, supp. vol. 1 (1940), p. 312, in arguing that Dionysius of Halicarnassus was ignorant of the existence of the *Hellenica Oxyrhynchia*, whence the statement of Dionysius of Halicarnassus, *De Thuc.* IX. 337. 18.

95. Volquardsen, 'Untersuchungen', p. 107. Cf. Stroheker, *Dionysios I*, p. 78; Meister, 'Die Sizilische Geschichte', p. 94.

96. I follow R. Littman, 'The plague at Syracuse in 396 BC', *Mnemosyne*, vol. 37, nos. 1-2 (1984), pp. 110-16, though I am unable to share Littman's view that Diodorus' description is based ultimately on Thucydides' description of the Athenian plague, possibly via Ephorus.

97. More specifically I suggest that the emphasis by Thucydides (II. 53) upon the licence, atheism and anarchy provoked by the experience of the plague has its counterpart in Diodorus' description of Himilcon's sacrilegious conduct, the Libyan revolt and the overthrow of Himilcon. Cf. the comments of Finley, *Thucydides*, p. 161. Cf. Folcke, 'Dionysius', p. 130, who ascribes the account of the plague directly and originally to Timaeus' refusal to grant Dionysius any credit for his victory over Carthage.

98. Thus we note emphasis upon the bravery of the Siceliots collectively, or of individual cities, fighting for salvation, families and country, to the death (Diod. Sic. XIII. 56. 4; 59. 9; 60. 2, 4, 5, 7; 62. 1; 81. 1; 85. 3; 89.

2; 108. 9); the courage of women and children, fighting against all odds (XIII. 55. 4; 56. 6-7; 57. 2-3; 58. 2; 62. 4; 89. 3; 108. 6, 8); the demise of ancient foundations (XIII. 59. 4; 62. 4); the indignities suffered by the Siceliots illustrated by the gloating of the barbarians (XIII. 57. 1), bloodshed and cruelty (XIII. 57. 3; 58. 2; 62. 3; 90. 2; 111. 3-6), the pity of the Greek mercenaries of Carthage (XIII. 58. 1), barbarian impiety (XIII. 58. 2), the barbaric speech of the aggressor (XIII. 58. 2), Greek lamentations (XIII. 57. 1; 89. 1) and Greek desire for revenge upon the oppressor (XIV. 46. 5; 47. 5).

99. As illustrated by the following: Punic and Campanian guile which defeats Selinuntine potential and superior army (Diod. Sic. XIII. 44. 3); Selinus' neglect of her defences (XIII. 55. 6); disorder of Himeraeans and Syracusan ranks resulting in Punic victory (XIII. 60. 7; 87. 1-2); Acragantines succumbing to Punic bribes or fear creating missed opportunity (XIII. 87. 3-4); accusation of treachery lodged against Dexippus (XIII. 87. 4); Dexippus' fifteen-talent bribe (XIII. 88. 7); Syracusan carelessness leading to Punic victory (XIII. 88. 5); Siceliot indecision manifested by an inability to offer adequate counsel (XIII. 91. 1-3); Syracusan gullibility *vis-à-vis* Dionysius (XIII. 91. 4-92; 94; 95; XIV. 7. 6; 45. 2); similar Geloan gullibility (XIII. 93); ineffectiveness of oligarchs (XIII. 92. 3; 112. 4); Syracusan neglectfulness (XIV. 9. 1); Syracusan division on policy (XIV. 9. 4); Syracusan gullibility *vis-à-vis* Aristus (XIV. 10. 3), Dionysius (XIV. 10. 4) and Pharacidas (XIV. 70. 1); Syracusan politically misdirected pride (XIV. 64. 3); Ennaean gullibility *vis-à-vis* Dionysius (XIV. 14. 7); Messanian political ineptitude and division (XIV. 40. 4-7; 56. 3); Siceliot rashness compared with wisdom of Dionysius (XIV. 61. 1-3; 96. 2); and facile luring of Syracusans to bribery (XIV. 70. 3).

100. As illustrated specifically by the communal zeal directed towards the construction of the Epipolae wall (Diod. Sic. XIV. 18. 7); Dionysius' Punic War of 398-396 BC being with the 'most powerful people in Europe' (XIV. 41. 2); the Pansiceliot nature of this war (XIV. 43. 1; 45. 2) and its aim being to prevent Greek (as opposed to purely Siceliot or Syracusan) slavery to Carthage (XIV. 45. 2, 4; 46. 5; 47. 2). As we have argued above, Theodorus' position as delineated in the speech contrasts strikingly with that of Diodorus' narrative in that it totally eschews the depiction of the populist Dionysius and anti-Punic stand. Theodorus accordingly, we maintain, in Diodorus' eyes, is representative of leadership which cannot unify Siceliots in pursuit of the common ideals to which they aspire.

101. Thus Diod. Sic. X. 4. 3; XIII. 96. 4; 112. 1; XIV. 2. 2; 10. 2; 107. 2; XV. 15. 2; 16. 2; 23. 5; 73. 5; XVI. 16. 3.

102. Philistus: τὰ δὲ πολλὰ κατὰ λόγον τοῖς ἀνθρώποις εὐτυχοῦντο ἀσφαλέστερα (ἤ) παρὰ δόξαν καὶ κακοπραγίαν εἰώθασι γὰρ μάλιστα οἱ παρὰ δόξαν ἀπροσδοκήτως εὖ πράσσοντες εἰς ὕβριν τρέπεσθαι; paraphrase of Thucydides III. 39. 4: εἰώθασιν δὲ οἱ πολλοὶ τῶν ἀνθρώπων, οἷς ἂν μάλιστα καὶ δι'ἐλαχίστου ἀπροσδόκητος εὐπραγία ἔλθῃ εἰς ὕβριν τρέπεσθαι; Thucydides III. 39. 4: εἰῶθε δὲ τῶν πόλεων αἱς ἂν μάλιστα καὶ δι'ἐλαχίστου ἀποροσδόκητος εὐπραγία ἔλθῃ, ἐς ὕβριν τρέπειν.

103. Cf. also Nicias' warnings (Thuc. VI. 9. 3; 13. 1), Alcibiades' vices (Thuc. VI. 15. 3) and Pausanias' 'tragic' career (Thuc. I. 129-34). Pro-

ponents of the tragic and moralistic view of Thucydides include Cornford, *Thucydides mythistoricus*, pp. 82ff; de Romilly, *Thucydides*, pp. 322ff (though oddly not citing Cornford); Lloyd-Jones, *Justice of Zeus*, pp. 143-4, 204 note 65; V. Hunter, *Thucydides the artful reporter* (Toronto, 1973), pp. 123ff; Gomme, *HCT*, vol. 1, pp. 89-90; Gomme, 'The greatest war in Greek history', *Essays*, pp. 116-24; Gomme, 'Thucydides and fourth-century political thought', *More essays*, p. 129; Grene, *Image of man in Thucydides and Plato*, p. 84; Finley, 'Thucydides the Moralist', *Aspects of Antiquity*, pp. 51, 56; L. Edmunds, 'Thucydides' ethics as reflected in the description of *stasis*', *HSPhil*, vol. 79 (1975), pp. 73-92; W. Wallace, 'Thucydides', *Phoenix*, vol. 18 (1964), p. 256; A. Parry, 'Thucydides' historical perspective', *YClS*, vol. 22 (1972), p. 47; W.R. Connor, 'A post-modernist Thucydides', *CJ*, vol. 77, no. 4 (1977), p. 293; M. Grant, *The ancient historians*, pp. 102-3; C. Bruell, 'Thucydides' views of Athenian imperialism', *APSR* (1964), p. 15; Fitzsimmons, 'Thucydides' history, science and power', pp. 377, 387, 393. Though cf. L. Edmunds, *Chance and intelligence in Thucydides* (Cambridge, Mass., 1975) with the opposing arguments of V. Hunter, *Phoenix*, vol. 31, no. 4 (1977), pp. 377-8.

104. Similarly Diodorus failed to substantiate the statement on the Thirty Tyrants contained in the *prooemium*. Thus Drews, 'Historiographical Objectives', p. 86. The same tendency to read Timaeus and not accept his basic thesis is seen in the chapters in Diodorus on Agathocles. See Diod. Sic. XX. 79. 5; 89. 5; XXI. 16. 5/F. 120, 121, 123a. The historian whose work was utilised by Diodorus in Books XIX to XXI to balance Timaeus' history was clearly Duris who wrote four books on that individual (F. 16-21, 56, 59). Thus cf. Diod. Sic. XX. 104. 3 with Duris in Jacoby, *FGH*, vol. 2a, no. 76, F. 18/Athen. XII. 84, p. 605 d-e.

Conclusion

In a recent review of three biographical studies of prominent political figures of the late Roman Republic, A.J. Marshall,[1] sounding a timely and highly appropriate word of caution in the face of a resurgence in popularity of publications in ancient biography, suggested — what indeed to many must have appeared patently obvious — that a far more worthwhile task than the composition of biography for the classicist and ancient historian was the careful examination and evaluation of the credibility of the sources which discussed the characters on whom the attention of such biographical studies was focused. It was only by adopting such an approach, he argued, that scholars would take due cognisance of the various influences and forces determining the approach of the sources which they utilised for their biographies and minimise the risk of their assuming an overtly subjective interpretation of such source material. It is within the context of Marshall's guideline that the present modest study has been conceived. As a preliminary to obtaining even a minimal comprehension of the career and personality of Dionysius, we maintain, a clear understanding of the stance and the forces shaping the attitudes of Philistus, Ephorus, Theopompus, Timaeus and Diodorus is mandatory. By an accurate comprehension, moreover, of these sources' treatment of Dionysius I, we suggest, certain generalisations and oversimplifications which in our view have somewhat marred modern assessments of Dionysius can be minimised and largely avoided.

Certainly the fact that there existed in classical antiquity a powerful hostile anecdotal tradition which castigated mercilessly Dionysius for alleged oppression of members of his own family, the tyrant's fellow citizens and Siceliots and Italiots as a whole cannot be denied. Nor can it be gainsaid that much of the testimony furnished by Diodorus, our only surviving substantial and reasonably continuous source for Dionysius' reign, can be utilised by any modern scholar zealous to provide a negative depiction of the tyrant. Further, given the existence of such a hostile anecdotal tradition, highly damaging to the tyrant's reputation, and the data seemingly hostile to the tyrant which can be gleaned from Diodorus' testimony, we agree with M.I. Finley that it is scarcely adequate simply to declare that 'no man at the same time could have been so great a monster'.[2] In antiquity, as in the present, of course, unscrupulous dictators were hardly conspicuous by their absence. Nor, it should be added, has it been the purpose of the present study to present a total re-evaluation of Dionysius and accord the tyrant what might be termed the recent 'Richard III' treatment, exonerating Dionysius from all unscrupulous political motivation and action. Indeed, we continue to maintain in line with Timaeus and indeed with Philistus, assuming the correctness of our analysis of the political thought of Philistus' Περὶ Διονυσίου, that under Dionysius' auspices Greek cities were undoubtedly sacked; that their populations were either transported or exterminated mercilessly at the tyrant's behest; that temples were very probably plundered; and that slaves, freedmen and mercenaries as well as other undesirables constituted a mainstay of the tyrant's support system.[3]

On the other hand, what we are suggesting is that the vast majority of modern assessments of the tyrant's rule which adopt an essentially negative stance towards the tyrant and emphasise the personal and military character of Dionysius' rule as well as what they perceive as the absence of a liberal and democratic spirit at Syracuse,[4] fail to isolate individually and assess for their reliability and truth or lack thereof the various strands which constitute the Dionysian tradition. For one thing, they fail to acknowledge the considerable degree of unreliability which marks the hostile tradition, based as it was initially upon Athenian rather than Sicilian information which, for political purposes, deliberately distorted the tyrant's propagandist aims. Further, we have demonstrated how we can hardly employ as evidence for Dionysius' severe rule the testimony regarding the tyrant's strained relationship with the literati at his court since Dionysius' harsh actions against these figures becomes perfectly understandable within the context of the very real threat emanating from Athens which they posed for Dionysius' effective control at Syracuse. We have further shown that the subsequent evolution of the hostile tradition is equally suspect, based as it was upon Athenian comic, philosophic and Peripatetic distortion, subjective theorising with neutral data and above all the Athenian-derived, highly subjective, unreliable, powerful and negative testimony of Timaeus of Tauromenium. Apart from Timaeus, moreover, we have noted that no other major historiographical source prior to Diodorus adopted an essentially negative stance towards Dionysius and we have suggested that the three major testimonies of Ephorus, Theopompus and Philistus were more trustworthy than that of Timaeus on three grounds: the greater objectivity towards Dionysius betrayed by Ephorus, Theopompus and Philistus; what we perceive as a not insignificant silence on Theopompus' part towards Dionysius' alleged misdeeds; and confirmatory testimony for Philistus' contention that a liberal democratic spirit prevailed at Syracuse, gleaned from epigraphic and numismatic sources as well as from the testimonies of both Plato and Theopompus and indeed Diodorus. Finally we have sought to reject the view that Diodorus' testimony reproduces essentially the hostile account of Timaeus and argued conversely that it is fundamentally based upon the positive testimony of Philistus which emphasised as well as the imperialistic successes of Dionysius, the popularity, relative liberality and broad-based support enjoyed by Dionysius' regime which underlined these ventures. Ancient historians, accordingly, so heavily dependent upon Diodorus' testimony are well advised to approach Diodorus with considerable caution before utilising the data provided by the historian of Agyrium to prove totally and unequivocally the undemocratic, unpopular and repressive character of Dionysius' rule.[5]

Notes

1. A.J. Marshall, 'Review of J. Leach, *Pompey the Great*, R. Seager, *Pompey: A political biography*, and E.G. Huzar, *Mark Antony: A biography*', *Phoenix*, vol. 35 (1981), pp. 281-7.
2. Finley, *Ancient Sicily*, p. 74.
3. Though even with such data, misinterpretation is possible. We should indeed be cognisant of the facts that Dionysius' hostility was essentially directed against Syracuse's 'traditional' Ionian enemies; that the destruction of Selinus, Himera, Acragas, Gela and Camarina was undertaken by Carthage and not by Dionysius; that the tyrant enjoyed the support of a wide variety of states and peoples including Camarina, Gela, Acragas and Selinus (Diod. Sic. XIV. 47. 5-7), Sicani and Elymians (Diod. Sic. XIV. 48. 4), Halyciaeans (Diod. Sic. XIV. 54. 2), Paros (Diod. Sic. XV. 13. 4), Agyrium (Diod. Sic. XIV. 95. 4), Locri (Diod. Sic. XIV. 44. 6) and the Phoenicians (Diod. Sic. XV. 15. 1); that Syracuse as a functioning democracy in the period preceding the rise of Dionysius also employed mercenaries (Diod. Sic. XIII. 80. 4; 85. 3-4); that financial rapacity can hardly be said to be solely characteristic of totalitarian regimes, either ancient or modern (thus Bullock, 'Dionysius of Syracuse

financier', p. 272); and that less negative testimony regarding Dionysius' attitude to temples and religious practice exists side by side with that pertaining to Dionysius' rifling of temples (thus Plut. *Dion* XIII. 3; Diod. Sic. XV. 13. 5; XVI. 57. 2-3).

4. Thus Grote, *History of Greece*, vol. 10 pp. 328-9; E.T. Arnold, *History of Rome* (London, 1871), pp. 392-5; Meyer, Geschichte des Altertums, vol. 5, p. 174; Freeman, *History of Sicily*, vol. 4, p. 5; Freeman, *Sicily: Phoenician, Greek and Roman* pp. 156, 195; Bury, 'Dionysius I of Syracuse', p. 136; M.L.W. Laistner, *History of the Greek world, 479-323 B.C.*, 3rd edn. (London, 1957), p. 280; Stroheker, *Dionysios I*, p. 178; Finley, *Ancient Sicily*, pp. 86-7; Morrow, *Studies in the Platonic Epistles*, p. 146. More charitable assessments are found in Woodhead *s.v.* 'Dionysius', *OCD*, p. 351 and J.K. Davies, *Democracy in classical Greece* (Glasgow, 1978), pp. 208-9.

5. Finley, *Ancient Sicily*, p. 76, admittedly with extreme reticence, does seem to hint at our assessment when he states: 'Yet it must be recognized that he [Dionysius] could command military service from tens of thousands of citizens *many of whom* (italics mine) (i.e. not all, in our interpretation) he raised to that status by enfranchising aliens and by emancipating slaves in large numbers.' Cf., however, pp. 86-7, 'Whatever spark of popular participation in politics there may have been left in Sicily at the end of the fifth century was extinguished during the reign of Dionysius. Henceforth the citizens were subjects rather than citizens.' Cf. pp. 76-7 on Dionysius' personal and military rule and p. 204 on Stroheker's less hostile evaluation of the tyrant as 'too idealized and psychological'.

Select Bibliography

Aalders, G.J.D. 'The date and intention of Xenophon's *Hiero*', *Mnemosyne*, ser. 6, vol. 4a (1953), pp. 208-15

Adamesteanu, D. 'Osservazione sulla battaglia di Gela del 405 a.C.', *Kokalos*, vol. 2 (1956), pp. 142-57

Andrewes, A. *The Greek tyrants*. London: Hutchinson University Library, 1956

Arias, P.E. *Dionigi il vecchio*, Catania: Crisafulli, 1942

Bachof, E. 'Timaeus als Quelle für Diodor XIV, 54-78', *Neue Jahrbücher für classische Philologie*, Abt. 1, vol. 25 (1879), pp. 161-73

—— 'Timaeus als Quelle Diodors für die Reden des dreizehnten und vierzehnten Buches', *Neue Jahrbücher für classische Philologie*, Abt. 1, vol. 30 (1884), pp. 445-78

Barber, G.L. *The historian Ephorus*, Cambridge: Cambridge University Press, 1935

Bartoletti, P. 'Rileggendo Filisto', *Studi Italiani di Filologia Classica*, vol. 24 (1950), pp. 159-60

Bayet, J. *La Sicile grecque*, Paris: Les Belles Lettres, 1930

Beaumont, R.L. 'Greek influence in the Adriatic Sea before the fourth century', *Journal of Hellenic Studies*, vol. 56 (1936), pp. 159-204

Beloch, K.J. 'Die Ökonomie der Geschichte des Timaios', *Neue Jahrbücher für classische Philologie*, vol. 27 (1881), pp. 697-706

—— 'L'impero Siciliano di Dionisio', *Memorie della Classe di Scienze Morali e Storiche dell'Accademia dei Lincei*, ser. 3, vol. 7 (1881), pp. 211-35.

—— *Griechische Geschichte*, vols 2, 3, Berlin-Leipzig: Walter De Gruyter and Co., 1914-27

Berve, H. *Die Tyrannis bei den Griechen*, 2 vols, Munich: C.H. Beck'sche Verlagsbuchhandlung, 1967

Brown, T.S. 'Timaeus and Diodorus' Eleventh Book', *American Journal of Philology*, vol. 73 (1952), pp. 337-55

—— *Timaeus of Tauromenium*, California: University Press, 1958

—— 'Alexander's book order (Plut. *Alex.* VIII)', *Historia*, vol. 16 (1967), pp. 359-68

Bullock, C.H. 'Dionysius of Syracuse financier', *Classical Journal*, vol. 25 (1930), pp. 260-76

Bury, J.B. *The ancient Greek historians*, London: Macmillan, 1909

—— 'Dionysius I of Syracuse', *Cambridge Ancient History*, vol. 6, pp. 108-37, Cambridge: Cambridge University Press, 1927

Busolt, G. 'Diodors Verhältnis zum Stoizismus', *Neue Jahrbücher für classische Philologie*, Abt. 1, vol. 35 (1889), pp. 297-315

Calabi, I. 'Review of A. Gitti, *Studi su Filisto*', *Paideia*, vol. 40 (1954-5), pp. 55-7

Columba, G.M. 'Filisto storico del IV secolo', *Archivio Storico Siciliano*, vol. 17 (1892), pp. 275-311

Coppola, G. 'Una pagina del Περὶ Σικελίας di Filisto in un papiro Fiorentino', *Rivista di Filologia e di Istruzione Classica*, vol. 58 (1930), pp. 449-66

178

De Sanctis, G. *Ricerche sulla storiografia Siceliota*, Palermo: Flaccovio, 1958

Drews, R.H. 'Historiographical objectives and procedures of Diodorus Siculus', Baltimore: Johns Hopkins Dissertation, 1960

—— 'Diodorus and his sources', *American Journal of Philology*, vol. 83 (1962), pp. 383-92

Edmonds, J.M. *The fragments of Attic comedy*, vols 1, 2, Leiden: E.J. Brill, 1957, 1959

Farrington, B. *Diodorus Siculus, universal historian*, Swansea: University of Wales Press, 1937 (Reprinted in *Head and hand in ancient Greece*, London: Watt & Co., 1947, pp. 55-85)

Field, G.C. *Plato and his contemporaries* (2nd ed.), London: Methuen, 1948

Finley, M.I. *Ancient Sicily to the Arab conquest*, London: Chatto and Windus, 1968

—— *Aspects of antiquity*, London: Chatto and Windus, 1968

Folcke, C.A. 'Dionysius and Philistus', Dissertation, New York University, 1973

Freeman, E.A. *History of Sicily*, vols 3, 4, Oxford: Oxford University Press, 1892, 1894

—— *Sicily: Phoenician, Greek and Roman*, London, New York: Fisher Unwin, Putnam, 1892

Gernet, L. 'Mariages de tyrans', *Hommage à Lucien Febvre. Eventail de l'histoire vivante*, Paris: Libraire Armand Colin (1953), pp. 41-53

Gitti, A. 'Sulla colonizzazione greca nell'alto e medio Adriatico', *La Parola del Passato*, vol. 7 (1952), pp. 161-91

—— 'Ricerche sulla vita di Filisto, Adria e il luogo dell'esilio', *Memorie della Classe di Scienze Morali e Storiche dell'Accademia dei Lincei*, ser. 8a, vol. 4, no. 4 (1952), pp. 225-73

—— *Studi su Filisto*, Bari: Adriatica Editrice, 1953

Graham, A.J. *Colony and mother city in ancient Greece*, 2nd edn, Illinois: Ares Publishers, 1983

Grant, M. *The ancient historians*, London: Weidenfeld and Nicolson, 1970

Griffo, P. 'Note sul tempio di Zeus Olympica di Agrigento', *ΑΠΑΡΧΑΙ: Nuove ricerche e studi sulla Magna Graecia et la Sicilia antica in onore di Paulo Enrico Arias*, Pisa: Giardini (1982), pp. 253-70

Grosso, F. 'Ermokrate di Siracusa', *Kokalos*, vol 12 (1966), pp. 102-43

Grote, G. *History of Greece*, vol. 10, London: John Murray, 1869

Guido, M. *Sicily, an archaeological guide*, London: Faber & Faber, 1977

Hammond, N.G.L. 'The sources of Diodorus Siculus XVI', *Classical Quarterly*, vol. 31 (1937), pp. 79-91; vol. 32 (1938), pp. 137-51

Hatzfield, J. 'Note sur la date et l'objet du *Hieron* de Xenophon', *Revue des Etudes grecques*, vols 49-50 (1946-7), pp. 54-70

Hejnic, S. 'Das Geschichtswerk des Philistos von Sizilien als Diodors Quelle', *Studia antiqua A. Salac septuagenario oblata.* Ceskoslovenska Akademie Prague, Sbornik Filologisky (1955), pp. 31-5

Holland, G.R. 'De Polyphemo et Galatea, Commentatio philologica', *Leipzige Studien*, vol. 7 (1884), pp. 139-211

Holm, A. *Geschichte Siziliens im Altertum*, vol. 2, Leipzig: 1874

Huttle, W. *Verfassungsgeschichte von Syrakus*, Prague: F. Kraus, 1929

Jacoby, F. *Die Fragmente der griechischen Historiker.* Leiden: Brill, vol. 2a, 1961; vol. 2b, 1962; vol. 2c, 1963; vol. 3b, 1964 (Text); vol. 3b, 1969

(Komm.)

Karstedt, U. 'Platons Verkauf in Sklaverei', *Würzburger Jahrbücher für die Altertumswissenschaft,* vol. 2 (1947), pp. 295-300

Koerber, W. 'De Philisto rerum Sicularum scriptore', Dissertation, Breslau, 1874

Kothe, H. 'Zur Ökonomie der Historien des Timaios', *Neue Jahrbücher für classische Philologie,* Abt. 1, vol. 29 (1883), pp. 809-13

Kunz, M. 'Zur Beurteilung der Prooemien in Diodors historischen Bibliothek', Dissertation, Zurich: Lehmann, 1935

Laqueur, R. 'Die Prooemien. Die Disposition', *Hermes,* vol. 46 (1911), pp. 161-206, 321-54

—— *s.v.* 'Timaios', P.W.K. *Real-Encyclopädie.* 2nd ser., Stuttgart: Metzlerische Buchhandlung (1937), vol. 6a, cols. 1076-1203

—— *s.v.* 'Philistos', P.W.K. *Real-Encyclopädie,* Stuttgart: Metzlerische Buchhandlung (1938), vol. 19, cols. 2409-2429

—— 'Diodorea', *Hermes,* vol. 86 (1958), pp. 257-90

Lauritano, R. 'Sileno in Diodoro', *Kokalos,* vol. 2 (1956), pp. 206-16

—— 'Ricerche su Filisto', *Kokalos,* vol. 3 (1957), pp. 98-122

Levi, M.A. 'La critica di Polibio a Timeo', *Miscellanea di studi Alessandrini in memoria di Augusto Rostagni,* Turin: Botega D'Erasmo (1963), pp. 195-202

Littman, R. 'The plague at Syracuse in 396 B.C.' *Mnemosyne,* vol. 37, nos. 1-2 (1984), pp. 110-16

Loicq-Berger, M.P. 'Le Bruxellensis 11281 et l'activité littéraire de Denys L'Ancien', *Revue Belge de Philologie et d'Histoire,* vol. 44 (1966), pp. 12-20

—— *Syracuse, histoire culturelle d'une cité grecque,* Brussels: Latomus Publication, 1967

McDonald, A.H. 'Review of T.S. Brown, *Timaeus of Tauromenium*', *Journal of Hellenic Studies,* vol. 79 (1959), pp. 186-8

McKinlay, A.P. 'The Indulgent Dionysius', *Transactions of the American Philological Association,* vol. 70 (1939), pp. 51-61

Manni, E. 'Da Ippi a Diodoro', *Kokalos,* vol. 3 (1957), pp. 136-55

—— 'Sileno in Diodoro?', *Atti dell'Accademia di Scienze e Lettere e Arti di Palermo,* ser. 4a, vol. 18, no. 2 (1957-8), pp. 81-8

—— 'Recenti studi sulla Sicilia Antica', *Kokalos,* vol. 7 (1961), pp. 216-42

—— 'Ancora a proposito di Sileno-Diodoro', *Kokalos,* vol. 16 (1970), pp. 74-8

Mazzarino, S. 'Tucidide e Filisto sulla prima spedizione ateniese in Sicilia', *Bolletino Storico Catanese,* vol. 17 (1939), pp. 5-72

Meier-Welcker, H. *Dionysios I, Tyrann von Syrakus,* Göttingen, Zurich, Frankfurt: Musterschmidt, 1971

Meiggs, R. and Lewis, D. *A selection of Greek historical inscriptions,* Oxford: Oxford University Press, 1969

Meister, K. 'Die Sizilische Geschichte bei Diodor von den Anfängen bis zum Tod des Agathokles. Quellenuntersuchungen zu Buch IV-XXI', Dissertation, Munich: 1967

—— 'Das Exil des Timaios von Tauromenion', *Kokalos,* vol. 16 (1970); pp. 53-9

Meloni, P. 'Il contributo di Dionisio il vecchio alle operazione di Antalcide del 387 a.C', *Rendiconti della Classe di Scienze Morali, Storiche*

Filologiche dell'Accademia dei Lincei, ser. 8, vol. 4 (1949), pp. 190-203

Meyer, E. *Geschichte des Altertums*, vol. 5, Stuttgart: J.G. Cotta'schen Buchhandlung, 1902

Momigliano, A.D. 'Il nuovo Filisto e Tucidide', *Rivista di Filologia e di Istruzione Classica*, vol. 58 (1930), pp. 467-70

—— *s.v.* 'Diodoros', *Enciclopedia Italiana*, Rome: (1949), pp. 924-5

—— 'Atene nel III secolo A. C. et la scoperta di Roma nelle storie di Timeo di Tauromenio', *Rivista Storica Italiana Napoli*, vol. 71 (1959), pp. 529-56

Morrow, G.R. *Studies in the platonic epistles*, New York: Bobbs Merrill, 1962

Mossé, C. *La Tyrannie dans la Grèce antique*, Paris: Presses Universitaires de France, 1969

Nauck, A. *Tragicorum Graecorum fragmenta*, 2nd edn, Leipzig: Teubner, 1889

Niese, B. *s.v.* 'Dionysios', P. W. K. *Real-Encyclopädie*, Stuttgart: Metzlerische Buchhandlung (1905), vol. 5a, cols. 882-904

—— *s.v.* 'Damokles', P. W. K. *Real-Encyclopädie*, Stuttgart: Metzlerische Buchhandlung (1901), vol. 4b, col. 2068

Oost, S.I. 'The tyrant kings of Syracuse', *Classical Philology*, vol. 71 (1976), pp. 224-36

Pace, B. *Arte et civiltà della Sicilia Antica*, Milan-Genoa-Rome-Naples: Albrighi, Segati and Co., vol. 3 (1945), pp. 30-6

Palm, J. *Über Sprache und Stil des Diodorus von Sizilien*, Lund: Gleerup, 1955

Pavan, M. 'La teoresi storica di Diodoro Siculo', *Rendiconti della Classe di Scienze Morali Storiche e Filologiche dell'Accademia dei Lincei*, vol. 16 (1961), pp. 19-52, 117-51

Pearson, L. 'Some new thoughts about the supposed fragment of Philistus', *Bulletin of the American Society of Papyrologists*, vol. 20, nos. 3-4 (1983), pp. 151-8

—— 'Ephorus and Timaeus: Laqueur's thesis rejected', *Historia*, vol. 33 (1984), pp. 1-20

—— *The Greek historians of the west: Timaeus and his predecessors*, Scholars Press, Atlanta, Georgia (forthcoming)

Perrota, I. 'Il Papiro Florentino di Filisto', *Studi Italiani di Filologia Classica*, vol. 8 (1930), pp. 311-15

Pinto, M. 'Il mimo di Senarco contro i Reggini', *Atene e Roma*, n.s., vol. 8 (1927), pp. 69-80

Porter, W.H. 'The sequel to Plato's first visit to Sicily', *Hermathena*, vol. 61 (1943), pp. 46-55

Sanders, L.J. 'Plato's first visit to Sicily', *Kokalos*, vol. 25 (1979), pp. 207-19

—— 'Diodorus Siculus and Dionysius I of Syracuse', *Historia*, vol. 30, no. 4 (1981), pp. 394-411

—— 'Dionysius of Syracuse and the validity of the hostile tradition', *Scripta Classica Israelica*, vol. 5 (1979-80), pp. 64-84

Sartori, F. 'Review of Stroheker, *Dionysios I*', *Athenaeum*, vol. 38 (1959), pp. 209-12

—— 'Sulla δυναστεία di Dionisio il vecchio nell'opera Diodorea', *Critica Storica*, vol. V (1966), pp. 3-66

Schwartz, E. *s.v.* 'Amyntianos', P.W.K. *Real-Encyclopädie*, Stuttgart. Metzlerische Buchhandlung (1894), vol. 1, col. 2008

—— 'Timaios Geschichtswerk', *Hermes*, vol. 34 (1899), pp. 481-93

—— *s.v.* 'Diodoros', P.W.K. *Real-Encyclopädie*, Stuttgart: Metzlerische Buchhandlung (1905), vol. 5a, cols. 663-703

—— *s.v.* 'Ephoros', P. W. K. *Real-Encyclopädie*, Stuttgart: Metzlerische Buchhandlung (1909), vol. 7, cols. 1-16

Simon, E. 'Dramen des älteren Dionysios auf Italiotischen Vasen', ʾΑΠΑΡΧΑΙ: *Nuove ricerche e studi sulla Magna Graecia e la Sicilia antica in onore di Paulo Enrico Arias*, Pisa: Giardini (1982), pp. 479-82

Sinclair, R.K. 'Diodorus Siculus and the writing of history', *Proceedings of the African Classical Association*, vol. 6 (1963), pp. 36-45

Sordi, M. 'I rapporti fra Dionigi I e Cartagine fra la pace del 405/4 e quello del 392/1', *Aevum*, vol. 54, no. 1 (1980), pp. 22-34

—— 'Lo Ierone di Senofonte, Dionigi e Filisto', *Athenaeum*, vol. 58, nos. 1-2 (1980), pp. 3-13

—— 'Dionigi I e Platone', Φιλίας χάριν. *Miscellanea di studi classici in onore di Eugenio Manni*, Rome: Bretschneider (1980), pp. 2015-22

—— 'Ermokrate di Siracusa, demagogo e tiranno mancato', *Scritti sul mondo antico in memoria di Fulvio Grosso a cura di Fidio*, Gasperini, Rome: 6, Bretschneider (1981), pp. 595-60

—— 'Alessandro Magno e l'eredità di Siracusa', *Aevum*, vol. 57, no. 1 (1983), pp. 19-23

—— 'Il fr. 29 Jacoby di Timeo e la lettura augustea di un passo di Filisto', *Latomus*, vol. 43 (1984), pp. 534-9

Stroheker, K.F. 'Platon und Dionysios', *Historische Zeitschrift*, vol. 179 (1952), pp. 225-59

—— 'Timaios und Philistos', *Satura. Früchte aus der antiken Welt O. Weinreich zum 13 März 1951 dargebrachte*, Baden-Baden: Verlag für Kunst und Wissenschaft (1952), pp. 139-61

—— 'Zu den Anfängen der monarchischen Theorie in der Sophistik', *Historia*, vol. 2 (1953-4): pp. 381-412

—— *Dionysios I. Gestalt und Geschichte des Tyrannen von Syrakus*, Wiesbaden: Franz Steiner Verlag, 1958

Suess, W. 'Der ältere Dionys als Tragiker', *Rheinisches Museum*, vol. 109 (1966), pp. 299-318

Tod, M.N. *A selection of Greek historical inscriptions*. vol. 1 (2nd edn) vol. 2 (1st edn), Oxford: Oxford University Press, 1946, 1948

Uggeri, G. 'La battaglia di Gela del 405 a.C. secondo Diodoro e le resultanze topografiche', *Studi Italiani di Filologia Classica*, vol. 39 (1967), pp. 252-9

—— 'Problemi di topografia geloa', *Mitteilungen des Deutschen Archäologischen Instituts* (Rom. Abt.) vol. 75 (1968), pp. 54-63

Vattuone, R. 'Su Timeo F. 29 Jacoby', *Rivista Storica dell'Antichità*, vol. 11, nos. 1-2 (1981), pp. 139-45

Volquardsen, C. 'Untersuchungen über die Quellen der griechischen und sicilischen Geschichten bei Diodoros, XI-XVI', Dissertation, Kiel, 1868

Wachsmuth, C. *Über das Geschichtswerk des Sikelioten Diodoros* (Progr. Leipzig: 1892) (Reprinted in *Einleitung in das Studium der alten Geschichte*, Leipzig: Hirzel, 1895)

Walbank, F.W. 'The bull of Phalaris', *Classical Review*, vol. 59 (1945), pp. 39-42

—— 'Review of Brown, *Timaeus of Tauromenium*', *English Historical Review*, vol. 74 (1959), pp. 333-4

—— 'Polemic in Polybius', *Journal of Roman Studies*, vol. 52 (1962), pp. 1-12

—— 'Three notes on Polybius XII', *Miscellanea di studi Alessandrini in memoria di Augusto Rostagni*, Turin: Bottega d'Erasmo (1963), pp. 203-13

—— *A historical commentary on Polybius*, vol. 1 (1957), vol. 2 (1967), Oxford: Oxford University Press

—— 'The historians of Greek Sicily', *Kokalos*, vols 14-15 (1968-9), pp. 476-98

—— *Polybius*, Berkeley and Los Angeles: University of California Press, 1972

Wellman, E. *s.v.* 'Damon', P.W.K. *Real-Encyclopädie*, Stuttgart: Metzlerische Buchhandlung (1901), vol. 4b, col. 2074

Wells, C.B. 'Review of Brown, *Timaeus of Tauromenium*', *American Historical Review*, vol. 63 (1957-8), p. 1030

Westlake, H.D. 'The sources of Plutarch's Timoleon', *Classical Quarterly*, vol. 32 (1938), pp. 65-74

—— *Timoleon and his relations with the tyrants*, Manchester: Manchester University Press, 1952

—— 'The Sicilian books of Theopompus' *Philippica*', *Historia*, vol. 2 (1953-4), pp. 288-307

—— 'Hermocrates the Syracusan', *Bulletin of the John Rylands Library*, vol. 41 (1958), pp. 239-68

—— 'Review of Brown, *Timaeus of Tauromenium*', *Classical Review*, vol. 9 (1959), pp. 249-50

—— 'Dion. A study in liberation', *Essays on the Greek historians and Greek history*, Manchester: Manchester University Press, 1969

Weter, W.E. 'Encouragement of Literary Production in Greece from Homer to Alexander', Dissertation, Chicago; 1953

Woodhead, A.G. *The Greeks in the west*, London: Thames and Hudson, 1962

—— 'The Adriatic empire of Dionysius', *Klio*, vol. 52 (1970), pp. 503-12

Zoepffel, R. 'Untersuchungen zum Geschichtswerk des Philistos von Syrakus', Dissertation, Freiburg im Breisgau, 1965

Zuretti, C.O. 'L'Attività letteraria dei due Dionisii di Siracusa', *Rivista di Filologia e di Istruzione Classica*, vol. 25 (1898), pp. 529-57; vol. 26 (1899), pp. 1-23

Index Nominum et Locorum